Find God. Find Jesus —
Trust Him 100%. This book omits God and is useless against what is bothering you.

May God Bless You & Keep You. May He put this (my) message in the hands of someone who truly needs it. — D.

INNER PEACE, OUTER SUCCESS

The Reintegration System:
Spiritual Growth, Healing,
Solving Problems and Achieving Goals with
Cutting-Edge Mind Techniques

Nebo D. Lukovich

Reintegration Publishing

Copyright © 2016 by Nebo D. Lukovich

www.re-integration.com

ISBN: 9781519032294

Cover design and illustrations: Nebo D. Lukovich
Editor: Melaina Wright

Disclaimer & Copyright

Neither the publisher nor the author is engaged in rendering professional advice or services to the individual reader. The ideas, procedures, and suggestions contained in this book are not intended as a substitute for consulting with your physician. All matters regarding your health require medical supervision. Persons with mental health problems must not apply the techniques outlined in the book, unless they receive such instruction from an authorized physician. The author shall not be liable or responsible for any loss or damage allegedly arising from any information or suggestion in this book.

The information and procedures contained in this book have been invented by the author and/or compiled from sources deemed reliable, and are accurate and useful to the best of the author's knowledge and intent; however, the author cannot guarantee their accuracy and validity and cannot be held liable for any errors or omissions. The author has made every effort to provide accurate Internet addresses and other contact information at the time of publication, and shall not assume any responsibility for errors or for changes that occur after publication.

This book is © copyrighted by the author and is protected under the US Copyright Act of 2016 and all other applicable international, federal, state and local laws, with ALL rights reserved. No part of this may be copied, or changed in any format, sold, or used in any way other than what is outlined within this book under any circumstances without express permission from the author.

DEDICATION:

To my wife, son, daughter and dear friends.

ACKNOWLEDGMENTS

I am so grateful to my wife, son and daughter, for their unconditional love and unreserved support for my work from its very beginning.

My deep gratitude goes to Melaina Wright, the editor of this book. She is a great professional and hard worker, with superb language expertise. I certainly recommend her to all authors of books like this.

I am also very grateful to several dear friends without whom the development of this book would have been much harder, in various ways.

Maria Mason has put in a great deal of proofreading effort at the early stages of the book's development and some invaluable advice on how to improve the content of the book.

I would like to thank Geomaria George, whose arduous work and dedication to the development and promotion of the Reintegration ideas and techniques, have been priceless to me.

Sonja Jezdic and Rade Madzgalj have greatly supported my family and this book with their immense love and friendship.

Ivana Knezevic and Miso Joskic have given me valuable ideas and friendly advice on how to improve this book.

Ivan Stojiljkovic has given me wisdom and many ideas related to this book, even long before it was written. He started me on my current path.

Andjelka Vulanovic Lazendic and Bobo Lazendic have given me various spiritual assistance and experience which resulted in some of the concepts shown here.

Mari Macesic has inspired a lot of creativity related to this work. I warmly recommend the workshops and seminars she regularly runs in Montenegro.

Aleksandra Damjanovic has put a lot of precious effort and good will into this book's development.

Filip Mihajlovic gave me some great spiritual guidance in his early workshops which I will never forget. Some of his ideas are also here in this book. I highly recommend the workshops, books and courses he leads in Belgrade and abroad.

Table of Contents

INTRODUCTION **12**

PART I: THE CONCEPT **22**

Structure of Human Experience 25
Dealing with Mind Content 29
    Removing or Transforming the Mind Content 29
    Creating the Mind Content 33
    Transforming the Mind Content with Presence 35
In a Nutshell 38
Main Parts of the Reintegration System 40
    Techniques 40
    Personality Reintegration 41
        Parts of Personality 42
        Chain of Goals 46
        Wholeness 50
    In a Nutshell 52

PART II: TECHNIQUES   55

Basic Techniques—Quick, Simple and Effective 57
    Dissolving the Temporary I 57
    Moving to the Heart 62
    Dissolving the Temporary I Plus 65
    Gentle Touch of Presence 67
    Freshness & Acceptance 70
    In a Nutshell 72
Main Reintegration Techniques—Deeply Transformational **75**
    Inner Triangle Technique 75
        The Procedure 78
        Inner Triangle Chart 84
        Real-Life Example 85
        IT Worksheet: "My Guilt" 103

    Additional Remarks 105
    In a Nutshell 106
  Chain Techniques 107
    Single Chain Technique 107
    Real-Life Example 109
    SC Worksheet: Persecutor 114
    Double Chain Technique 115
    In a Nutshell 119
  Convergence Procedure 120
    In a Nutshell 125

Auxiliary Techniques 126
  Relaxation 126
  Getting Answers from the Subconscious 127
    Manual Muscle Testing 127
  In a Nutshell 131

PART III: PERSONAL TRANSFORMATION   133

Holographic Nature of Reality 134
  In a Nutshell 140

Main Elements of Personality to Work on 141
  General Aspects of Personality 143
    Assessment List of Mutual Coherence of General Aspects (example)
    146
  Habits 147
  Beliefs 153
    Replacing Beliefs 156
    Dismantling Beliefs 160
  Traumatic Memories 160
  Decisions 164
  Rules 166
  Emotions 168
  Aversions and Fears 172
  Accusations and Guilt 174
  Inclinations and Desires 177
  Personal Traits 179

- Example of Integrating Honesty using the Double Chain 180
- In a Nutshell 182

Meditation 188
- Sittings 188
  - Relaxation Phase 190
  - Entering the State of Presence 190
  - Occasional Removal of Distracting Mind Content 191
  - Additional Notes 194
  - In a Nutshell 196
- Mindfulness 197
  - Immediately After Waking Up 200
  - Morning Routines 200
  - Meals and Drinks 201
  - Dressing 202
  - Driving/Commuting 202
  - Walking 203
  - Emotions 204
  - Conversations 205
  - Using Electronic Devices 206
  - Talking on a Phone 206
  - Watching TV 207
  - Daily Errands 208
  - Reading 208
  - Observing Thoughts 209
  - Following the Breath before Sleep 210
  - Mindfulness of Breath 211
  - Triggers 212
  - Distractions 214
  - In a Nutshell 215

Importance of Pacing 216
- In a Nutshell 220

Morphic Fields 221
- In a Nutshell 226

Healing 227
- Prayer 228
- Love 230

Presence 233
    Healing through Reintegration Techniques 234
    In a Nutshell 237
Moral Behavior 239
    In a Nutshell 242

PART IV: ACHIEVING GOALS   244
Types of Goal Structures 246
Comprehensive Goal Achievement Process 249
Finding Your Excellence 253
Defining Your Goals 255
    Goal Harmonization Process 256
Reaching the Goal Procedure 265
    Detailed Target State and Mid-Stages 268
In a Nutshell 271
Real-Life Example 275
    Main List of Goals (example) 278
    Assessment List of Mutual Goal Support (example) 282
    Convergence Procedure 282
    Assessment List of Goals-General Aspects Relations (example) 287
    Assessment List of Goals-Fears Relations (example) 290
    Fear of Responsibility—Double Chain Technique 291
    Assessment List of Goals-Beliefs Relations (example) ... 293
    Dismantling Beliefs Technique 294
    Reaching the Goal Procedure 297
Determination Technique 304
    Real-Life Example 307
    Determination Technique Worksheet 313
    Determination Technique Algorithm 316

PART V: CLARIFICATIONS   318
Additional Areas of Application 318
    Identifications 318

    Clearing Relationships 320
    Lucid Dreaming 322
    Helping Others 324
    Cleansing Space and Things 326
    Time Sublimation 327
    In a Nutshell 329

Questions & Answers — 332
The Whole Picture — 341
Conclusion — 347
About the Author — 351
Bibliography — 352
APPENDIX I: Additional Techniques — 356

Alternative DTI 356
Simplified Inner Triangle 359
    Simplified Inner Triangle Chart 361
    Real-Life Example 361
    SIT Worksheet: Money Polarities 368

Group Polarities—Inner Polygram Technique 370
    Two-Way Communication 371
    One-Way Communication 372

APPENDIX II: Lists — 375
    Most Common Polarities 375
    Money Polarities 377
    Most Common Self-Destructive Habits 378
    Basic Identifications 380
    Most common negative beliefs 383

APPENDIX III: Worksheets — 386
    Assessment List of Goals-Beliefs Relations 386
    Assessment List of Mutual Coherence of General Aspects 387

Assessment List of Mutual Goal Support Worksheet.............. 388
Convergence Procedure Worksheets....................................... 389
Determination technique worksheet...................................... 392
Inner Triangle Worksheet 393
Main List of Goals Worksheet 396
Replacing Beliefs Worksheet... 397
Simplified Inner Triangle (SIT) Worksheet 398
Single Chain (SC) Worksheet... 401

INTRODUCTION

"It is far better to light a single candle than to curse the darkness."
— W. L. Watkinson, *"The Invincible Strategy"* sermon

Many of us are longing for a change. Some want to find a deeper meaning to life, or an ultimate spiritual solution. Others are eager to solve their longer-lasting problems, whether they are related to health, relationships, job, psychological issues or something else. Many people have a burning desire to achieve some important goal or simply to fulfill a dream...

Yes, we can do all of this and we can definitely bring a permanent change to our lives. This lasting change can essentially be achieved in two ways: through suffering or through wisdom. Either we painfully push forward through any obstacle or disappointment, learning our lessons the hard way and emerging from the experience more mature, or we choose a path of love, consciousness and wisdom, which also makes us mature, but in a far more enjoyable and effective manner. This book is all about learning the second, superior way.

This is not a fairy tale or some "New Age" promise. On the contrary, we are lucky to have an undeniable opportunity to truly transform our reality... and the result only depends on us.

What makes me so certain of this? Because life has proven it to me over and over again. Every time I decided to change something about myself in a positive way, my life circumstances improved in a very similar manner. And many times I unwittingly changed my thoughts, emotions or other aspects of myself in a damaging way, and—albeit in a very blurred or warped fashion—my life relentlessly followed suit.

I've also seen the same phenomenon countless times with other people. The only real difference is that it's much easier to see the mistakes and flaws of other people than your own. It's always easier to tell somebody "you're wrong!" than to see that it was actually your own fault.

Now, there were some occasions in which other people were indeed making mistakes, yes. But in the end, my life has definitely shown me that many times those people were only responding to projections of my own hidden personal traits, suppressed emotions, false beliefs, and so on. Those traits and other unseen parts of me had been screaming: "Hey, I'm here; please look at me; I'm part of you!"

Luckily, I've seen some of "them," and they were mine, indeed. I truly believe that every single person, every single event, problem, experience, whether positive or negative, each had its origin within me.

The world around us is a strange but relentless mirror.

Of course, I'm not implying that you or any other person is not real, or that everyone is just a reflection from my mirror. You are as real as me, dear friend, as any other human being around us, as any other animal or thing. But I'm *involved* in your individual, unique universe the same way you are involved in mine. Any person or thing of significance to you unconsciously plays a role in mirroring your own internal universe, just as you do theirs. We are all undeniably interconnected.

Many modern scientific discoveries have shown how deeply interconnected we are, in the fields of neuroscience, psychology, or quantum physics, for example. I don't intend to delve too deep into physics here, of course, but it is worth mentioning that some theories and practical experiments within quantum physics have exemplified just how crucial the role of a conscious observer is within the world of quantum occurrences. The best example is the famous "Double-slit experiment."[1]

In short, the experiment involved shooting quantum particles through a couple of narrow slits, then examining where they hit the wall on the other side. It was revealed that the particles, when not being watched by any human eye, formed an 'interference pattern' on the wall, just like a wave would do. But when scientists watched the process, the particles' trajectory changed and instead formed clumps on the wall, just like a particle would do.

The quantum particles changed their behavior depending on the existence of an observer. We can reformulate this conclusion to its most basic level: consciousness somehow subtly influences matter.

Alternatively, there is the "Quantum Entanglement" phenomenon, said by Albert Einstein to be a kind of "spooky action at a distance,"[2] which marked the first real proof of the inherent interconnected properties of subatomic particles. The experimental data involved separating two photons[3] from one another—both of which came from the same parent group of particles, originally—and stimulating only one of them to watch what reaction came from the other. Surprisingly, the unstimulated photon would mimic the actions of its partner, maintaining an identical quantum state... as though they'd never been separated at all.

For example, if one photon was influenced by a measurement and forced to change its quantum state (i.e. spin), the other photon would simultaneously change its spin the same way, no matter their distance, regardless of speed of light limitations. And that's said to be the case with all other quantum systems.

---

[1] See article at Wikipedia, the free encyclopedia:
https://en.wikipedia.org/wiki/Double-slit_experiment
[2] Sea article at Wikipedia, the free encyclopedia:
https://en.wikipedia.org/wiki/Quantum_entanglement
[3] *Photon* is a subatomic particle—carrier of light and all other forms of electro-magnetic radiation.

So, what does that suggest for all of us, considering that *all* particles in this universe were originally part of the same "one system," starting with the Big Bang? The majority of the particles were separated and may have since lost their mutual entanglement, yes, but the notion still exists that virtually everything may still be profoundly linked. Could that not prove that we all are, too?

Much more on all of this exists on the internet waiting to be read, but whether you are a believer or non-believer in those types of things, I will still present to you this unique, practical material on how to radically improve your life from all sides. I call this tool the "Reintegration System," and it's a set of mind-training techniques that will enable you to find your inner peace and spiritual freedom, completely solve your chronic problems, drastically relieve stress, heal yourself and others, profoundly improve your relationships, and safely and permanently achieve goals.

All this is possible only if you willingly transform your own personality, which is the source of your outer experience.

I, for instance, tried for many years to permanently improve my life with every mind technique or teaching I could get my hands onto. There were some standout classes that helped me, but as a whole my results were short-lived. It seemed like every time some progress had been made, I experienced a strong setback and immediately regressed, in an annoying, recurring pattern.

Several years ago I firmly decided to change that. I decided upon an iron will, committing completely to transforming myself. Thanks to that, I slowly began to develop true positive habits. First, I established an everyday meditative practice and worked it into my routine. Despite some health-related hindrances, I established a daily sitting schedule and decisively continued with the practice, cautiously extending it over time.

Now, after two years of persistent work on meditation and mindfulness,[4] my flow of creativity continues to rise more and more.

---

[4] See Wikipedia, the free encyclopedia; https://en.wikipedia.org/wiki/Mindfulness

Ideas for new techniques and bold approaches have blossomed in my mind. Whereas in the beginning I was focused solely on successfully applying the new ideas to myself, I now have a circle of friends that use them too. They seek to solve their own problems and actively achieve their goals, using the newly formed system and aiding with its more extensive development and testing.

I can really say that all techniques found in this book have been tested many times, successfully. Included are numerous examples from real life. This system is like a living organism, developing and growing, always allowing space for personalized improvements.

Finally, I decided to write a book with the intention of helping people around the globe. My friends and I can attest that this book is a stockpile of invaluable mind techniques, that persistently change people's lives. I hope it will give some notable contribution to human development after all.

This volume is a practical guide, filled with many accounts from life, which is important for better understanding of the system and easier application of presented methods. I try to avoid theorizing unless necessary for better explaining the background of techniques.

When it comes to the descriptions of techniques, exercises or instructions, you'll find a lot of illustrations in this book. From my experience, lack of pictures and illustrations sometimes poses a challenge for people that are more visually inclined to grasp the material. The same implications could stem from lack of other modes of content: auditory, kinesthetic, etc. Please feel free to modify the instructions into whichever learning mode or shape is most natural to you. For example, you could either "look" from your heart or "listen" or "feel" from it, or any other formulation, as long as it suits your natural inclinations and preserves the overall spirit of an instruction.

The book covers all main areas of human psychic and spiritual development.

After explaining the core concepts of the Reintegration System, in the first part of this book you will find descriptions of five simple techniques that are essential for all other elements of the system. The techniques are "Dissolving the Temporary I," "Moving to the Heart," "Dissolving the Temporary I plus," "Gentle Touch of Presence" and "Freshness and Acceptance."

You are free to perform these procedures in your everyday life as many times as you want. They are each invaluable on their own and you will surely achieve many great improvements as you practice them. As far as I know, they are quite unique and I don't think that you would succeed in finding anything similar to them on the internet. Most specifically, "Dissolving the Temporary I," "Moving to the Heart" and "Dissolving the Temporary I plus." They will enable you to quickly and efficiently remove any negative thoughts, emotions or sensations, allowing the creation of your desired, positive state of mind.

The other two basic techniques, "Gentle Touch of Presence" and "Freshness and Acceptance," are a refinement of pre-existing ideas and teachings, but they will be essential for some areas of your practice. They are precious and extremely convenient tools in any situation as well.

After the basic techniques, you will find some auxiliary procedures that will be helpful in your practice, but not as essential as the above mentioned "Relaxation" and "Manual Muscle Testing." The "Relaxation," although a well-known and very common technique in many areas of human inner development, in this book is actually enriched with some applications of basic Reintegration techniques. The "Manual Muscle Testing" is widely practiced in applied kinesiology, a part of alternative medicine. Although its practical results are not scientifically confirmed, I really find it helpful in some areas of life and especially of this system so I deemed it worth including it in this book as well.

If you decide to practice the whole Reintegration System and completely transform your life, you will have to learn some of these main Reintegration techniques: "Inner Triangle," "Simplified Inner Triangle," "Single Chain," "Double Chain" and "Convergence Procedure." They are comprehensive and elegant methods with which you will be smoothly solving any problem in your life, as well as various negative states of mind, like depression, fear, anger, negative beliefs, and so forth.

All of these techniques, I would boldly say, are revolutionary in the field. They are more than simple or basic techniques, and if you learn and practice them, you will surely find them to be extremely effective and comprehensive. After having absorbed the main techniques, you will be ready for the more serious work on your personal transformation, presented in Part III.

The concept of personal transformation presented in this book stems from a holographic point of view of the universe and, within that, of our individual reality. In line with that, the famous phrase "change yourself and your reality changes" certainly applies here.

In the third part you will find not only information on most important elements of human psyche, you will learn concrete ways to overcome, transform, remove or integrate them. In other words, you will learn how to *re-integrate* them, since the idea here is that every part of the human personality did initially have a positive, constructive role in our life.

As a part of personal transformation, meditation is priceless and an irreplaceable part of one's spiritual and personal development. I will provide some well-known guidance on meditation sittings and keeping your awareness sharp in everyday life, like mindfulness in various situations. There are also instructions and practical advice about some new approaches and important insights related to this field.

The section about healing, while not minimizing mainstream medical advice or treatment, will give you additional knowledge, both for you and others, on how to stay healthy or recover from an illness. When paired with existing methods of medical treatment, the practices and procedures presented in this book could initiate real miracles.

Moreover, there is a section dedicated to moral behavior and why it is so important for your own development.

Once you make some advances in reintegration work on your personality, you'll be ready for the techniques presented in the fourth part: fulfilling your dreams. It's an attractive, thrilling, but very delicate issue all at the same time. It isn't so much about the actual process of achieving your goals—there are many methods for that out there already—as it is about how you feel when you get there. The problem I've come across is this: I've met many people who achieved important goals in their lives, but hardly any of them seemed any happier for it. Even worse, some complained that other areas of their lives had suffered along the way. But why? The reason is simple: they didn't change the framework components of their personality—beliefs, decisions, and other subconscious structures that are typically negatively-oriented. Those basic structures had been triggered by the fulfillment of the goal, and were subsequently creating mess in people's lives.

Soon, you'll learn how to deal with all of this successfully. You will be armed with the needed tools to safely achieve your goals, while comprehensively improving all other areas of your life. But, if you insist on a faster method for attaining your objectives, I must caution you to change or remove any negative framework from your inner structures, prior to beginning that sort of speedy work.

After just the basic techniques alone, you will be able to solve problems, improve relationships, enjoy regular meditation, practice mindfulness, properly heal, and even do some reintegration work. Then, when you add the Inner Triangle technique and the Convergence Procedure, you will be able to exploit the full potential of the Reintegration System. With your new skillset, the possibilities are boundless.

Indeed, there is no limit to your life. It depends only on you. You will get the required methods and information, but ultimately, you will be the one who takes the action.

– Nebo D. Lukovich
Podgorica, Montenegro
July 24, 2016

Part I
The Concept

PART I: THE CONCEPT

"You are the sky. Everything else—it's just the weather." — Pema Chödrön

Here you will be introduced to the foundations of the Reintegration System—the very structure of all our experiences, what we can do with them and the basic principles of dealing with them.

Although we may be eager to remove or change an unwanted experience, or to quickly create a desired one, we have to be careful in that process. Perhaps that unpleasant event helped you grow into a more mature person, and it would ultimately be better to accept it as is, as a part of your history. Or, maybe that desired experience would not benefit your spiritual or psychological development, instead dulling or spoiling you in the long run.

Thankfully, the techniques presented in this book will give you the tools to safely transform all types of mind content, eliminating entirely the risk of losing a valuable life lesson or piece of your past, and deepening your understanding of personal development. You will learn how to control your thoughts, emotions, sensations, traumas, goals, and sometimes even illnesses through this robust system.

The biggest strength of the Reintegration System is that it covers so many areas of personal development: spiritual growth, meditation, solving problems, healing, interpersonal relations and comprehensive integration of personality. It was carefully designed to cover all these fields through removing, changing or creating the content of one's mind.

The main pillars of the methodology are the following:

1. *There exists an underlying reality, which is supreme and perfect, independent of time and space, yet subtly present in all phenomena. In turn, that Divine presence[5] can transform every experience in the best possible way.*

2. *Everything is interconnected. The apparent separation of entities is an illusion; the subject and his experience are inseparable.*

3. *Our external world is but a mirror of our inner being. Therefore, everyone is completely responsible for their own life.*

4. *All apparently negative inner structures have a genuinely positive origin and purpose. We must not fight any perceived negativity—we should face it, accept it, transform it and thusly reintegrate it.*

5. *This is a world of polarities; every imperfect state has its own imperfect, opposite state. Every negativity should be dealt with alongside its opposite.*

Some of these assertions may seem a bit implausible. Yet, many are backed by and based on contemporary scientific discoveries.

For example, the first principle has its corresponding approach in quantum physics: the *implicate order* as postulated by David Bohm, one of the most influential American theoretical physicists of all time.[6] He assumed that there was an underlying ground, the implicate order, from which whole reality, the *explicate order*, emerges. Within the explicate order, the closest analogies to the first principle could be found in the notions of *quantum vacuum* and *light*. This postulate will be applied specifically in the "Gentle

---

[5] Divine presence will be referred to in this book as Presence.
[6] See article at Wikipedia, the free encyclopedia:
https://en.wikipedia.org/wiki/David_Bohm

Touch of Presence" procedure, but is also present throughout the techniques for healing, meditation sittings and mindfulness.

Also from quantum physics is the *quantum entanglement effect*, the "spooky action at the distance," the experiments which strongly indicate our interconnectedness at a quantum particle level. This principle will be employed in the basic Reintegration techniques, especially in the "Dissolving the Temporary I" procedure.

Then there is the *holographic principle*, well-known in theoretical physics and increasingly accepted in cosmology, which is described in detail in Part III, Personal Transformation (page 134). From there stems the idea of mirroring one's inner being to external reality.

Similarly, the fourth principle has its roots within contemporary psychological methodologies, which show that the subconscious structures that cause unpleasant emotions must not be suppressed nor fought back. Since they inherently have a positive initial purpose, they must instead be understood and transformed.

The fifth principle about *polarities* can be found in many areas of science and life. In quantum physics, it is stated that for every positively or negatively charged particle there is an opposite particle, equal in all properties, except in electrical charge. In a quantum vacuum, the so-called "virtual particles" are continually leaping into existence in pairs of opposites. Biology teaches us that almost all living species have two sexes. Moreover, in various phenomena in life (colors, shapes, movements, living beings), you will find pairs of opposites or complementary traits. This is focused on in the "Inner Triangle" technique.

When these five principles are applied in life, they have huge transformative power. Consequently, we will use them extensively throughout this entire system.

Structure of Human Experience

"Life will give you whatever experience is most helpful for the evolution of your consciousness. How do you know this is the experience you need? Because this is the experience you are having at the moment." — Eckhart Tolle, A New Earth: Awakening to Your Life's Purpose

When we look deep into ourselves, we can get a sense of the apparent dichotomy between our inner being, "I," and our external reality, "no-I." Although the feeling may be blurry, or indistinct, it follows us throughout the entire life, except during deep sleep. It is symbolically shown in Figure 1 below.

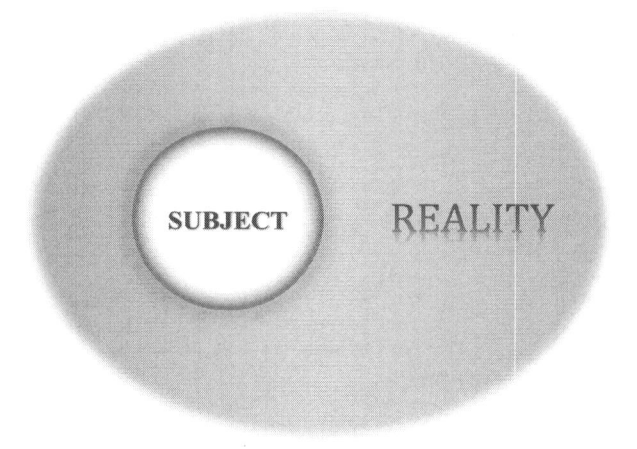

Figure 1: Basic dichotomy

The subject is an apparent center of being, an observer, a conscious "I," who experiences the reality. The key question is: who or what actually is that subject?

It is our source of conscious perception. Although in its true nature it's limitless and indescribable, in this universe of space, time, matter and energy it manifests itself as a kind of condensed energy of being. The physical site of that source of individual reality is fixed within our body, in the chest. It is the Heart, whose nature will be elaborated on later.[7]

Often in this book we will use the term "mind content." It refers to three kinds of mind/body experiences:

- *Thoughts*, including mind pictures and other mind replicas of bodily experiences, which are purely mental entities.

- *Emotions*, which are energy entities stemming mostly from desires and fears.

- *Sensations*, which are experienced through the five senses of the body, such as physical pleasure, pain, itching, eyesight, sounds, taste, smells, etc.

It is important to note that mind content encompasses also all *external events and beings* that one experiences in their individual reality, because all these "externally imposed" experiences are projected into one's mind through the five senses. The individual then *reacts* to the external experience with emotions, or even thoughts of bodily sensations.

Unlike the Heart—the source of our individual reality—there is also a transitory center within our being that *perceives* and *shapes* that reality, even creating many details of it. Thus, as the whole universe is transitory and delusive, a conscious being's center of perception should be considered unsteady too.

We will name the transient subject who perceives the content of mind the "Temporary I." It is an apparent center of the being that perceives the thoughts, emotions or sensations at the particular moment.

---

[7] It seems that the "seat of soul" doesn't always have to be in the Heart. Some people say that their "true center" is in the "hara" (a point just below the navel), or in the "third eye" (a point between the eyebrows), or someplace else. I cannot confirm or deny such claims. However, for the reason of effectiveness, I will stick to the concept of the Heart as the "seat of the soul." Whether it is always the seat of soul or not, the Heart *is* always a very strong and important center within our being.

Accordingly, everyday human experience consists of the "Temporary I" and mind content, as shown in Figure 2.

Figure 2: Structure of Everyday Human Experience

As was pointed out earlier, the Temporary I is not fixed at a single location in human being. Depending on many factors—usually on a state of consciousness—it moves around the body, sometimes even outside of it, although we may rarely be aware of that.

If the idea of "Temporary I" still feels confusing, try finding your sense of I while reading this very text. Where is the center of your being at this moment? What is the I-feeling you get when you experience contents of the mind, in this case the text of this book? The location of that I-feeling may change in relation to the specific nature of the mind content within your reality. Even more precisely, the thoughts, emotions and sensations you're feeling are *created* or *shaped* by this Temporary I.

In many cases, the Temporary I is located on an imaginary line, connecting the brain and the Heart (see Figure 3).

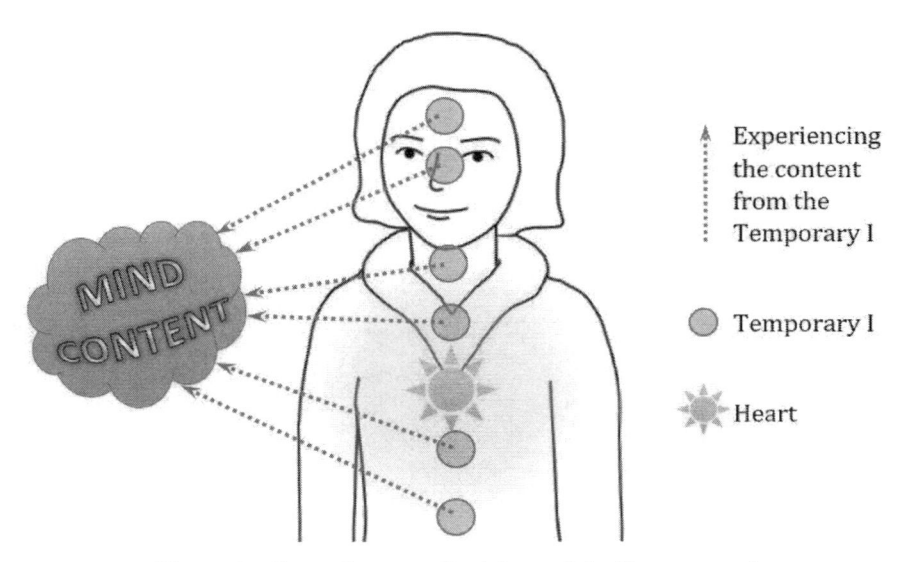

Figure 3: Some Common Positions of the Temporary I

Don't forget that the Temporary I is not technically a *real* center of the being. It is a provisional, false "I" that can move around inside your being or even disappear altogether. The true center of being is considered to be the Heart.

Here is an exercise that will help you to find your current Temporary I:

Look around you. Feel your presence in the room where you are sitting now. Turn your attention inward. Where is the center of your being at this moment? Where do you sense it? Don't think about it, just guess. Maybe it's located inside your head, or neck. Or is it somewhere else? Feel it. Don't try to move it or change it in any way, just accept that your I is there. Do not worry whether the I-feeling is located within the Heart, or not. It can be anywhere, and that's completely natural.

Dealing with Mind Content

"The primary cause of unhappiness is never the situation, but thought about it. Be aware of the thoughts you are thinking. Separate them from the situation, which is always neutral. It is as it is." — Eckhart Tolle

The real power of this system lies in successful mastering all three elementary ways of dealing with mind content (thoughts, emotions and sensations). They are:

- *Removing* a chosen mind content,
- *Transforming* it, or
- *Creating* it.

In dealing with the content, you can also have three approaches:

- To *directly influence it*,
- To *change your relation to it*, or
- To *remove the Temporary I* which is experiencing it.

All three ways are valid, but the last two specifically will be extensively applied within the Reintegration System.

Removing or Transforming the Mind Content

"If you get the inside right, the outside will fall into place. Primary reality is within; secondary reality without."
— Eckhart Tolle, The Power of Now: A Guide to Spiritual Enlightenment

In this section we will tackle not only removing but also transforming the mind content, because they are based on the same principles. In a separate section a unique kind of transforming will be also described—a transformation through the state of Presence.

So, how can we actually remove or transform piece of content of mind? There are many ways of doing this, but let us first re-examine the basic scheme of human experience (Figure 4):

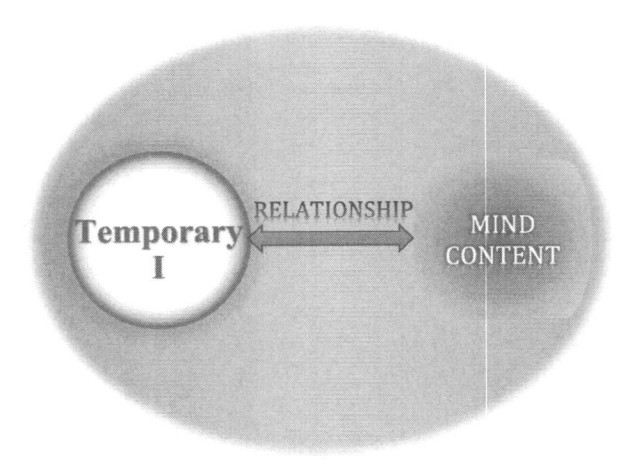

Figure 4: Subject in Relation to the Mind Content

As you can see, we have added some more content to the scheme: the relationship between the Temporary I and the mind content, i.e. whether we like it, dislike it, or any of countless variations of feelings on the subject.

Hence, the subject is experiencing a content of mind in its individual reality. As they have some sort of mutual connection or relationship, we could say that one is influencing the other, and vice versa.

Consequently, the mind content can be transformed or removed from the subject's reality in three ways:

— *By directly influencing the content*; this approach is most common in our human society's way of thinking, because of the widely accepted idea that the contents of mind (including external events) are autonomous and barely, if at all, dependent on the subject who experiences it.

— *By modifying or removing the relationship between the Temporary I and the mind content*; this can be achieved through complete acceptance of or purposeful ignoring of the content, or through changing the attitude toward it e.g. from negative to positive. As a consequence, the content will be transformed or will disappear. The *"Freshness and Acceptance"* technique could be applied to do so.

- *By removing the Temporary I completely*; if the perceiving subject disappears, the mind content will naturally and immediately vanish from one's individual reality. The *"Dissolving the Temporary I"* technique may be effective for this.

Again, you could remove or transform the mind content the old-fashioned way, by influencing it directly, as if it were an external object you could manipulate. You could re-live the experience in your mind completely, as has been done in certain traditional psychological exercises, though that approach demands a lot of energy to complete. Or, you could attempt to make gradual changes to the experience and the environment in which it happens. This usually works, but demands a large time investment.

In the Reintegration System though, we have some very elegant ways to deal with mind contents.

Dealing with simple mind content

If a content of mind is simple, perhaps consisting of only one thought or sensation, then it will often completely disappear if the subject experiencing it (the Temporary I) disappears. So, we can apply the third way of dealing with mind content—removing the subject completely—until it naturally vanishes, weakens or changes.

The key idea of this approach is: **The Temporary I experiences the mind content. If the Temporary I disappears, so does the mind content.**

It's definitely much easier to dissolve the Temporary I only, than to remove the whole experience around it. Plus, even if you were able to dissolve the experience, the Temporary I would still remain within you, ready to resurface and bring a similar experience back into your original reality, sooner or later.

You can also apply another approach—modifying or removing the relationship between the Temporary I and the mind content. In this way the content will be changed or removed in accordance with your relationship to it. This you can achieve by employing the "Freshness & Acceptance" or "Gentle Touch of Presence" procedures.

The key idea of this approach is: **The subject (Temporary I) experiences the mind content. The content will follow the change of the subject's relation to it, either being transformed or dissolved.**

But again, the same limitation arises. If the Temporary I, which created or shaped the mind content, still remains within you, *it could resurface and bring a similar experience back into our individual reality again.*

Fortunately, that rarely happens. When we completely accept the content of mind (as in the "Freshness & Acceptance" and "Gentle Touch of Presence" techniques), we enter a state of Presence and pure consciousness in which our Temporary I often disappears.

Personally, when dealing with unwanted thoughts, emotions or sensations, I prefer the third way—dissolving the subject—because it poses less risk of that same Temporary I returning to the scene. However, the other two techniques are equally valuable for key segments of life and spiritual practice, and all three will be covered in detail in later parts of this book for you to choose between yourself.

Dealing with complex mind content

It's quite a different story to attempt removal or transformation of an experience which is intricate or repetitive. The application of *basic* techniques is often not enough. Even after the removal of the Temporary I, the mind content may not disappear permanently.

In those cases, you would need to employ some of the *main* Reintegration techniques described in Part II of the book, instead. One example would be the section on "Transforming the Mind Content with Presence," which utilizes Presence and pure consciousness.

There are, of course, many other strategies for solving these types of situations. You could try to re-experience the mind content as a whole, thus releasing its hold on you, or you might prefer to make small, gradual changes to the content until it is transformed. This is a popular recommendation in behavioral psychology.

For instance, if a person has trouble with public speaking, a gradual approach may be best. First you would try speaking in a protected and simple environment, then slowly expand the audience until the client can speak in front of a large group of strangers. This strategy has proven to be effective. However, it takes a lot of time and effort to complete the whole process.

In this book we will be oriented toward solving the real roots of problems as effectively and rapidly as possible.

Creating the Mind Content
"The best and most beautiful things in the world cannot be seen nor touched, but are felt in the heart." — Helen Keller

There's plenty of positive mind content that people wish to have. Confident thoughts, fruitful beliefs, correct decisions, sublime emotions... but even after a successful removal of negative mind content, there is sometimes a gap left over to be filled.

The usual approaches to this are auto-suggestions or visualizations. However, the solution in the Reintegration System is neither a standard auto-suggestion nor a common visualization. It's a different way of plunging into a wanted content. It's grabbing the Temporary I that is experiencing the desired mind content and moving it straight to the Heart.

But what is the Heart exactly? Is it the physical heart, or something else? And why the Heart at all?

For the purposes of this book, we will attribute the word "Heart" *not* to the physical heart itself, nor to the left-of-chest physical location of the heart, but to the "I-point" area, where people usually point at with their forefinger when speaking about themselves in the first-person singular. That area is like an invisible circle, two or three inches wide, touching the skin from the inside (see Figure 5). This Heart is extremely important in our lives—it is considered the true center of our being, the seat of the soul, and the source of love and energy.[8]

Figure 5: Position of the Heart

The Heart sends into reality one's specific vibration frequency, which is the sum of one's beliefs, emotions and other patterns. The Heart is the source of our individual reality, and it's crucial to comprehend and appreciate its importance in our lives.

---

[8] The HeartMath Institute (www.heartmath.org) is being conducted extensive research on the Heart and its effects. For example, they discovered that there is a donut-shape electro-magnetic field which surrounds the Heart with a diameter of roughly two meters. "The heart generates the largest electromagnetic field in the body. The electrical field as measured in an electrocardiogram (ECG) is about 60 times greater in amplitude than the brain waves recorded in an electroencephalogram (EEG)." Source:
https://www.heartmath.org/articles-of-the-heart/science-of-the-heart/the-energetic-heart-is-unfolding/

It is also vital to have harmony between the Heart and the Mind. Whenever practicing the basic techniques from this chapter, especially the "Moving to the Heart" procedure, try to focus on truly strengthening the connection and congruence between the two.

Effectively beginning the creation process of your desired mind content is simple: you must feel it. You could visualize it, or engage the other inner equivalents of the five senses (hear it, touch it, and so on) to become aware of which Temporary I is experiencing the content. Make sure to feel for the location of the Temporary I. Then, gently move it to the Heart. After that, we again experience the same mind content from the Heart, but this time we adopt the *identity* which is correspondent to our desired content. Stay with that identity for five to ten seconds; the more the better.

Every early disturbance to this state of experiencing the desired content represents an inner obstacle. Luckily, we have an effective tool to dissolve these obstacles: "Dissolving the Temporary I."

Transforming the Mind Content with Presence
"Yesterday I was clever, so I wanted to change the world. Today I am wise, so I am changing myself." — Rumi

Often we experience mind content that we wouldn't like to remove completely, but only to improve or transform. Although we could do that by removing it first, then creating a better version, the best way is to experience it from the state of Presence (or Pure Consciousness). A corresponding technique, called the "Gentle Touch of Presence," will be explained in detail later, in Part II.

Presence is the deepest state of consciousness, where you simply *are*, as a sentient being. You determinedly exist. You are aware of yourself and your environment, without any thought or emotion. You are just present, here and now, in the moment. It's the state of "I am"-ness, and that "I" is not a Temporary I, it's your true I, your consciousness. Essentially, your Temporary I in this state doesn't exist at all. What's left is Pure Consciousness. [9]

The main point here is to get into the state of Presence. There are many ways to do that, and one of them is certainly the Reintegration technique "Dissolving the Temporary I."

Once firmly rooted in the Presence, you gently re-experience the content in your mind. You are aware of your Presence and at the same time you are experiencing the content.

After a while, you may notice that your content has been sublimely transformed into something else; something softer or more positive. Sometimes it will entirely disappear (see Figure 6).

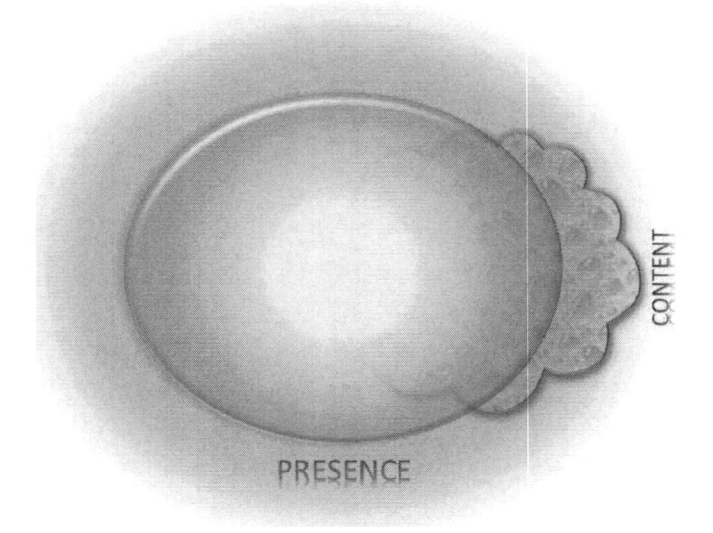

Figure 6: Presence and Mind Content

Whatever the way we choose to get into the state of Presence, "treating" a mind content with Presence will be very effective in transforming it.

---

[9] In his remarkable books "The Power of Now" and "A New Earth," the German author Eckhart Tolle beautifully explains the concept of Presence, so I warmly recommend his work if you want to get more details on this concept.

While in Presence, you will not only observe yourself and your environment, but will also take any necessary action. It is possible that you will have some thoughts needed for executing that action. Nevertheless, if your state of Presence is, that action will be perfect.

But once again, if you want to solve a complex problem, treating it with Presence only may not be enough, so you would need to consult the main Reintegration techniques described in Part II.

In a Nutshell

The main pillars of the Reintegration System are:

1. *There is an underlying reality, which is supreme and perfect, independent of time and space, yet subtly present in all phenomena.*

Practical implication: *Divine presence can transform every experience in a best possible way.*

2. *Everything is interconnected. The apparent separation of entities is an illusion.*

Practical implication: *The subject and their experience are inseparable.*

3. *Our external world is but a mirror of our inner being.*

Practical implication: *Everyone is completely responsible for their own life.*

4. *All apparently negative structures have a genuinely positive origin and purpose.*

Practical implication: *We must not fight any perceived negativity—we should face it, accept it, transform it and thusly reintegrate it.*

5. *This is a world of polarities. Every imperfect state has its own, also imperfect opposite state.*

Practical implication: *Every negativity should be dealt with alongside its opposite.*

<u>Structure of human experience</u>:

There are three categories of human experience:

1. *Thoughts,*
2. *Emotions,*
3. *Sensations.*

Everyday human experience consists of a transitory subject and mind contents. The part of you that experiences the contents of mind is called the "Temporary I." It is not fixed at a single position and can move around the body, sometimes even outside of it.

In dealing with the content, there are three approaches:

- *Directly influencing it,*
- *Changing the subject's relation to it,*
- *Removing the Temporary I which experiences it.*

Heart:

The Heart is the "I-point" area, where we point at with our forefinger when speaking about ourselves in the first-person singular. It is like an invisible circle, two or three inches wide, touching the skin from the inside. The Heart is the true center of our being, the seat of the soul, and the source of love and energy.

Ways of dealing with mind content:

- Remove it,
- Create it,
- Transform it.

Removing the mind content:

Since the Temporary I experiences the mind content, if the Temporary I dissolves, the mind content disappears too.

Creating the content:

A desired mind content can be sustainably created by feeling or visualizing it, while being aware of where the Temporary I is that is experiencing the content. Next, we move the Temporary I to the Heart. Then we again experience the same mind content from the Heart.

Transforming the mind content with Presence:

Experience the content in your mind while firmly rooted in the Presence. It will be transformed in the best possible way.

Main Parts of the Reintegration System

"Your vision will become clear only when you look into your heart. Who looks outside, dreams. Who looks inside, awakens." — Carl Jung

Our intention in the Reintegration System is to make our lives happier and more accomplished. To do that, we'll need to not only address all the above-mentioned ways of changing the mind content, but will need to apply them cautiously, comprehensively and systematically. We will have to transform many aspects of our personality, of our conscious and subconscious mind, sustainably.

In order to attain that target, the Reintegration System has been divided into three main parts:

- Techniques
- Personal transformation
- Achieving goals

Since achieving goals is such a natural part of personal transformation, I won't be covering it too particularly in Part I of this book. However, the entirety of Part IV is dedicated to extensive goal-fulfillment techniques.

Techniques

Naturally, this is the basis of the whole system. There are basic, auxiliary and main techniques, all of which were designed specifically for use in Reintegration.

The *basic techniques* are like building blocks, used to address essential ways of dealing with the content of mind—how to remove, transform or create a mind content. There is "Dissolving the Temporary I" (for removing mind content) and "Moving to the Heart" (for creating content). Other basic techniques are either a combination of these two ("Dissolving the Temporary I plus"), or have another purpose—refining or transmuting the mind content ("Gentle Touch of Presence" and "Freshness & Acceptance").

Auxiliary techniques are here only to improve the effectiveness of basic or main techniques. Their use is recommended, but not required. They are particularly helpful during situations when you are confused or indecisive after performing other Reintegration techniques. When this issue shows up, you could quickly ask your subconscious mind for an answer by using, for example, the "Manual Muscle Testing" method.

The *main techniques* are the pillars of the system. The "Inner Triangle" (shortened: IT) is the central and most comprehensive technique, while the "Single Chain" and "Double Chain" are alternative, simplified versions which may be more useful under some circumstances.

All these IT variations are designed for solving problems via transforming parts of the personality, leading them to their highest state of existence or even merging them.

Among the main techniques is also the "Convergence Procedure," which is somewhat different in nature than the IT and its versions. It also deals with the parts of personality, but unlike the IT, its purpose is primarily to harmonize them.

Personality Reintegration

After learning both the basic and main Reintegration techniques, we will be ready for the most important step: the re-integration of our personality.

Why do I call it re-integration, and not simply integration? First, it's connected to the fourth postulate of this system: *all apparently negative structures have a genuinely positive origin and purpose.* Every seemingly challenging part of our personality was initially part of the highest intention for our being. It is over time that it degraded and became a lower state of delusion. Our aim is to target such parts, and work them *back* into the wholeness of our being.

The name also stems from my personal opinions regarding past lives,[10] and the assumption that one must continue re-integrating parts of their self in future lives as well. I believe that at the very beginning of our existence we were unified entities; complete and nearly perfect beings; but we have transformed over many, many years of experiences and suffering, slowly but radically changing into today's shape. Personalities are now filled with many fears, obsessions, misconceptions, self-defeating beliefs, and more. Now, the time has come to become united once again; to fuse all our parts back into one unified, impeccable character.

That being said, of course, you do not need to subscribe to that ideology in order to successfully utilize the system… the first two conceptions of which are: *parts of personality* and *chain of goals*.

Parts of Personality

The concept of "parts of a personality" is well-known in modern psychology. Our personalities are a complicated aggregate of elements, some of which are, themselves, multifaceted in nature. There are subpersonalities, complexes, traits, and other mental and emotional patterns in our psyche.

"A 'part of personality' is our mental representation of an aspect of personality that we recognize repetitively in ourselves and in other

---

[10] In fact, it is more complicated than just saying "previous lives." In accordance with the theory of relativity, time is interchangeable with space within the space-time continuum and, in a way, time is only the fourth (or first!) space dimension in that continuum. Our consciousness is moving steadily along that fourth axis of the space-time chart. This is actually giving us the impression that everything is changing. We are moving along that time axis and everything else around us seem to be moving as well. Nevertheless, the whole fourth-dimensional existence is fully stable in the space-time continuum.

Therefore, our lives in the "past," from the perspective "outside" of the space-time continuum, are actually simultaneous existences. It's just a matter of point of view—from which coordinate of the space-time you are observing an event. You could even have some lives in the future that are your "previous" lives, meaning the roots of some events in this life stem from those lives.

people. It is a pattern within personality that may be expressed in how a person thinks or feels, or in the individual's behavior."[11]

"A subpersonality is, in transpersonal psychology, a personality mode that kicks in (appears on a temporary basis) to allow a person to cope with certain types of psychosocial situations. Similar to a complex, the mode may include thoughts, feelings, actions, physiology, and other elements of human behavior to self-present a particular mode that works to negate particular psychosocial situations. The average person has about a dozen subpersonalities."[12]

"A complex is a core pattern of emotions, memories, perceptions, and wishes in the personal unconscious organized around a common theme, such as power or status."[13]

In all main Reintegration techniques, the problem or unwanted state is "shaped" into a distinct part of our personality. For example, within the Inner Triangle's specific approach, an unpleasant pattern of behavior is considered as a part of our personality, together with its opposite part, all the time actively involving the sense of I, here and now. Through the merging of the opposite parts and their parallel integration with the I, the problem is solved in an effective and often permanent way.

This method is actually based on the "subject plus polarities" scheme (Figure 7):

---

[11] Source: https://www.psychologytoday.com/blog/the-personality-analyst/201402/finding-new-parts-personality, John D Mayer Ph.D., The Personality Analyst, posted: Feb 10, 2014

[12] Source: https://en.wikipedia.org/wiki/Subpersonality

[13] Source: Shultz, D. and Shultz, S. (2009). Theories of Personality. (9th Ed.). Belmont, CA: Wadsworth, Cengage Learning.

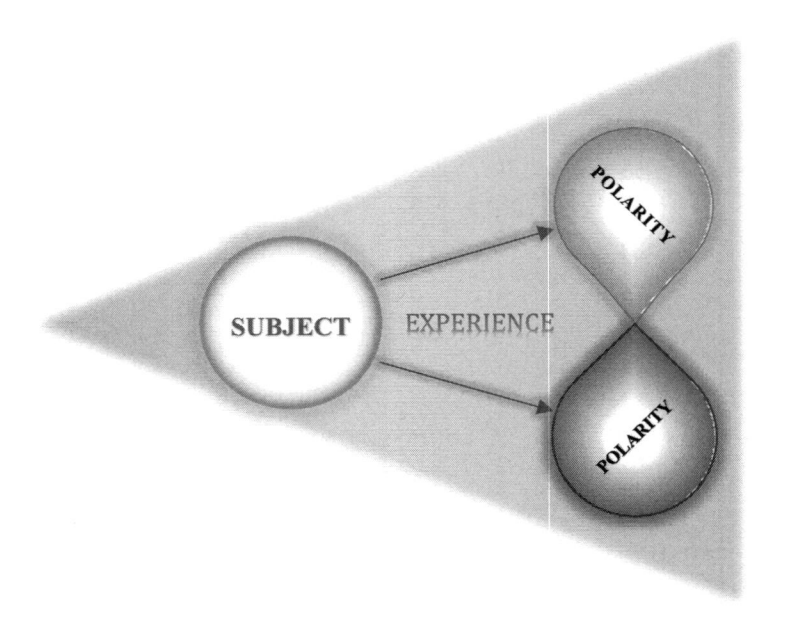

Figure 7: Subject and Polarities

Almost every experience or mind content, whether "positive" or "negative," is based on this triangle. There is the Subject (Observer), the 1st polarity (entity) and the 2nd polarity (entity).

Sometimes both polarities are obvious to the subject, but often one is invisible, "hidden" in the subconscious. Like particles in quantum physics, the polarities actually spring out of an "empty space" of energy, as from the quantum vacuum. In order to exist for a while, quantum particles appear in pairs of two oppositely charged particles, "living" for some period of time before merging and annihilating one another.

Practically the same happens in the Inner Triangle. You will find that the polarities of the experience or mind content will gradually get closer to you (the subject), and to each other. While doing so, they become brighter and lighter until it looks something like Figure 8:

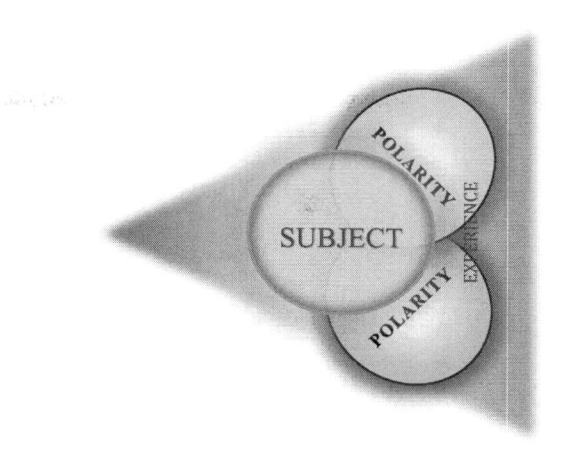

Figure 8: Subject and Experience—the next stage

This occurs through a "chain of goals," which will be described in the next section.

In the end, the polarities may spontaneously merge with one another and the subject, leaving a single entity at the highest state of being. We may call it Being, Emptiness, Fullness, Love, Light, Sunyata… it is beyond any word. Through this, the mentioned entities can finally conclude their separate existence and be at peace.

To achieve this end-state, we would use the basic technique "Dissolving the Temporary I." Or, for techniques oriented toward mindfulness or achieving goals, we would use "Dissolving the Temporary I Plus," "Moving to the Heart," "Gentle Touch of Presence" or "Freshness & Acceptance," together with some of the auxiliary techniques.

In fact, there may be times that there are two or more pairs of polarities in the process, a *polygram*, for which there are contingencies you will be able to find in the Appendix.

Chain of Goals

"The road to hell is paved with good intentions ... but so is the road to heaven. Good intentions aren't the problem. It's their execution that isn't working out well. There needs to be a better way." — Michael Watson[14]

Every challenge in life, every unpleasant or painful experience, every personal trait has a divine root.

How is that possible? Let me explain.

The supposed original state of every living being is Happiness, which manifests as either Peace, Love or Joy. But when that being is confronted with a dynamic and non-perfect environment, it develops ways to acclimate to the newly changed surroundings, through a process we'll call the "Chain of Goals." It may form beliefs or predispositions which actually limit the being's perception of the world around it. In this way, the being is no longer in a state of complete or absolute Peace. Consequently, it creates its first goal: to get back the lost Peace. An example of the Chain of Goals is symbolically shown in Figure 9 below.

---

[14] Michael Watson, International Trainer of NLP and Ericksonian Hypnosis, source: http://www.phoenix-services.org/blog/

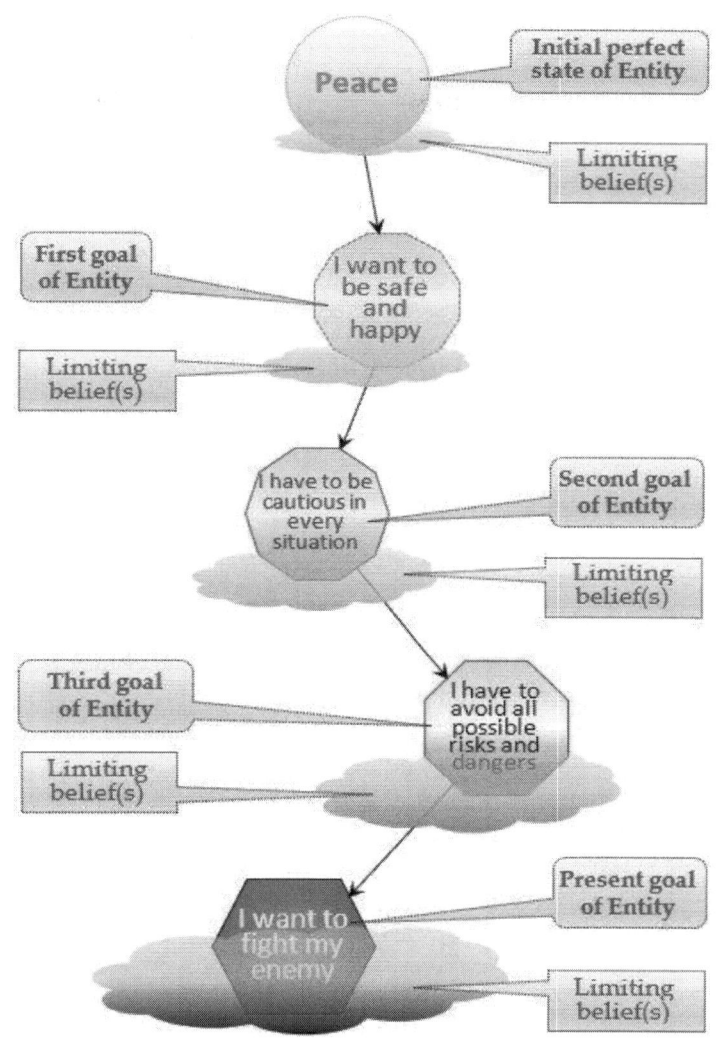

Figure 9: Example of a Chain of Goals

In the example shown above, the individual experiences the new environment as not completely satisfying. Perhaps they think, "I'm not totally safe," or "my Peace is not complete." Thus, a goal for getting back that original state of Peace spontaneously emerges: "I want to be safe and happy (again)." It seems like a logical reaction, but in reality, these preconceptions pile on top of each other, burying the original goal deeper and deeper.

Usually, there is a passage of time between the emergences of each goal. Then, the new environment, which may feel puzzling or challenging due to their skewed perception or belief, induces new, even more limiting beliefs. Those could be "I am not safe," "this is a dangerous environment," or similar. Now, the next goal naturally forms within the conscious being: "I have to be cautious in every situation." That limits them furthermore, putting strict boundaries around the perceived interior and external dangerous surroundings. The individual contracts and becomes more "dense."

As a result, even more challenging circumstances develop around the individual.

This process goes on and on. Finally, in our example, the individual finds him or herself apparently locked inside a harsh and hostile environment, forced to fight against enemies. At this stage, one becomes extremely heavy, contracted and sealed, confined within firm self-induced borders between inner and outer world.

Of course, there is a way out of this.

From a higher point of view, as the whole chain of goals has been revealed, it becomes obvious that this process of descending from Peace to the current harsh circumstances is actually a big misunderstanding. Despite its best effort and good intentions, the individual has trapped themselves in a cycle of descent. This happens unintentionally, due to error, delusion or misinterpretation of the environment and him or herself.

Let's elaborate on a few more views on common states of being, which could help to give a clearer picture of the Chain of Goals process in general.

The highest Basic state is the Supreme Happiness of Being, and it is threefold: *Love*, *Peace* and *Joy*.

But, as we can learn from many life examples of the Chain of Goals, these three states might be *spoiled* or *degraded*. In fact, people very often try to find these higher states through their degraded forms.

Love in its degraded form is *infatuation* or *obsession*. People try to find Love through romantic obsession toward another human being, which ends up in anguish in most of cases.

Peace in its degraded form is *drugs* and *alcohol*. Unfortunately, so many individuals try to find inner peace by suppressing their unpleasant feelings. They do so by dulling their consciousness any way they can, often by abusing addictive substances.

Joy in its degraded forms are *sensual bodily pleasures*. One's own body is an understandable place to start the search for joy, as the chain of goals causes one to look inward, and seek immediate allayment within the realm they know best.

The lowest basic states are *anger*, *fear* and *pain*. In their original state, all of them were actually positive in nature. Yet, once passed through dense filters of false beliefs, negative rules and other elements of personality which I will elaborate upon later, they become anger or rage, aversion or fear and sorrow or pain.

Anger was originally *determination* or *firmness*.

Fear was originally *caution* or *thoughtfulness*.

Pain was originally *seriousness* or *diligence*.

Every human experience or mind content has elements of at least some of these basic states.

In dealing with emotional difficulties it could also be helpful to know the following:

- *Love* dissolves *anger*.
- *Peace* dissolves *fear*.
- *Joy* dissolves *pain*.

This will be useful in many situations when we have to choose which higher state is to be reached in order to dissolve some particular lower state of mind.

I have to emphasize that the streak of descending goals and perceptions is not endless. Every single conscious (or temporary unconscious) being will begin the process of *ascending* at some point in their existence. Initially, that process is very unstable and volatile, with some aspects of life still descending and other ones beginning ascending, but as time goes by, the individual becomes more and more firm and determined in their orientation toward the original Happiness or Source.

Wholeness

"You are not separate from the whole. You are one with the sun, the earth, the air. You don't have a life. You are life." — Eckhart Tolle

"My mathematics is simple: one plus one = one." — Dejan Stojanovic, The Shape

Though up to this point we've focused on the parts of personality, chain of goals, and polarities, stay assured that the main idea in this book is *not* splitting issues into fragments, although it may seem so. It is about how to achieve a state of wholeness, unity or ultimate freedom.

Apparent fragmentation of problematic states or mind content is only a temporary way of extracting them from the background "noise" of unconsciousness and integrating them into the wholeness of our personality, one-by-one or even many-at-once.

The catch in this self-development work is that every negative state of mind resembles more a spider web than an individual knot. Yes, you will definitely be able to unravel many of these "knots" with the basic or main Reintegration techniques, but after that you will have to deal with the much wider web of similar experiences that support each other. This "web" is even capable of healing itself, so any holes made from the successful removal of a problem, that might otherwise have been "filled" with a new problem, can instead be filled or repaired by a high state of mind. That way, you can tirelessly continue with your work of self-betterment, so as to avoid any further reemergence of negative content.

The web is a kind of half-conscious entity, as is the case with parts of personality. It's an entity made of pure energy—a conglomerate of mutually similar emotions, thoughts and sensations. It strives for its own survival and growth. It can find some crafty ways to embitter our lives by reviving the problems we thought we'd successfully overcome earlier. I will also refer to these webs as "morphic fields," a subject that will be covered more in Part III.

How does one deal with these webs, or morphic fields?

First, we identify the key mind content that is supporting the web. There is always some root content that, if removed, would crumble the entire foundation of the problem. We do this with Reintegration techniques (or other spiritual or psychological methods).

Once we've removed the root components, we must approach the web as a whole. There are some interesting approaches for this in contemporary psychology, one of the most influential being "Gestalt Therapy." I highly recommend it, though its techniques and methods are pretty different from the content in this book.

Nevertheless, the Reintegration System, including meditation sittings and mindfulness, will deal with psychological webs and morphic fields efficiently, too.

Don't worry, you will learn the whole system, step by step.

In a Nutshell

The Reintegration System has three main components:
- Techniques
- Personal transformation
- Achieving goals

Techniques:
There are basic, auxiliary and main techniques.

Basic techniques address the essential ways of dealing with the content of the mind—how to remove, transform or create a mind content. They are: "Dissolving the Temporary I" (for removing mind content), "Moving to the Heart" (for creating content), "Dissolving the Temporary I plus" (for both removing and creating content), and for refining or transforming mind content there are "Gentle Touch of Presence" and "Freshness & Acceptance."

Auxiliary techniques are here only to improve the effectiveness of basic and main techniques. Their use is not required. The main auxiliary techniques are *Relaxation* and *"Manual Muscle Testing" method*.

Main techniques are in place for solving complex problems, dealing with repetitive mind content and reintegrating all parts of one's personality. They are: *The Inner Triangle Technique, Simplified Inner Triangle Technique, Single Chain Technique, Double Chain Technique* and *The Convergence Procedure*.

Parts of Personality:

A pattern within one's personality that may be expressed in how a person thinks or feels, or in the individual's behavior. In the Reintegration System, a problem or unwanted state of mind is viewed as a distinct part of the personality and reintegrated as such into the unity of one's being.

Chain of Goals:

The original state of every being is a kind of Supreme Happiness, expressed through states of peace, love or joy. Due to a challenging environment, one gradually develops self-limiting beliefs or perceptions of reality, which in turn negatively influences their surroundings. That begins a slow, steady process of worsening, which spurs the formation of a temporary Chain of Goals, striving at each step to achieve a better state of being one rank improved from the current state.

Wholeness:

The ultimate goal of our work is to achieve a state of Supreme Happiness, Wholeness and Freedom. Apparent fragmentation of unwanted states of mind is a temporary way of extracting them from the background "noise" of unconsciousness and integrating them into the unity of our being.

Part II
Techniques

PART II: TECHNIQUES

"To become really good at anything, you have to practice and repeat, practice and repeat, until the technique becomes intuitive"
— Paulo Coelho, Aleph

Do we really need the use of techniques at all to improve our happiness in life? Some people don't. Indeed, there are individuals whose souls radiate pure peace and love to everyone around them, and whose personalities are already cohesive. To those people, it's relatively easy to employ spiritual practices without any apparent technique involved; they simply continue radiating their Presence around them more and more intensely.

Unfortunately, most of us are not yet at that "level." At one point in my life, I was so frustrated with the fact that none of the spiritual methods I was using were working (I hadn't yet realized that I was the problem, not the procedures), that I completely switched over to a path called 'Neo-Advaita Vedanta.' That approach, or at least the one I was introduced to, offers no techniques and absolutely no practices. Instead, it asks you to question everything you know: all beliefs, assumptions and perceptions. It even questions the very nature of Self and existence itself.

For some time, I convinced myself that it was working. I tried to be persistent with the 'practice without any practices,' sure that I was approaching a revelation on the true nature of my existence. But, as more and more time passed, it became clear that there had been no real advancement. In fact, I was getting more and more anxious and had more problems in my life. I even entered a phase in which I forgot to do any self-inquiry at all, for days.

My unconscious parts, suppressed long ago, began to rear their ugly heads and roar straight into my face. The Neo-Advaita approach completely crumbled away for me. I simply wasn't mature enough for that type of 'practice.' While the path was great by itself, it demanded an already spiritually evolved and mature person. It's just not designed for us, ordinary people. I still appreciate the path, however, and don't want to discourage anyone already on it. Go ahead; maybe it's for you, who knows.

After such a completely defeating experience, I realized that I needed a structured approach, after all. But this time my determination was significantly boosted. I started regular meditation sessions, including mindfulness practice, and after a time began doing psychological and spiritual techniques that would become the precursors of later Reintegration procedures.

This structured approach works for me and for many, if not the majority, of seekers for inner wisdom and happiness. We only must remain consistent in our work, to "practice and repeat, practice and repeat," until it becomes intuitive and habitual.

If conscientiously and persistently practiced, the techniques in this book will surely change your life in the most beautiful and surprising ways. You will notice a change, at least temporarily, even after finishing only one procedure. In that sense, it is advisable to add a supplementary element to all these procedures, especially to the main techniques: *an assessment*. Although I won't mention it much throughout the book, the assessment of your target condition, done before and after the process, could bring about great benefits to your practice. So, before each process, assign a value (e.g. from 0 to 10) to your unwanted or desired state, and do the same evaluation immediately after the process. Put it on a paper. You will be amazed by the difference, especially after gaining some experience in this work. These regular assessments will turbo-charge your overall practice by giving you confidence and proof of the results.

Basic Techniques—Quick, Simple and Effective
"Don't tell me about your effort. Show me your results." — Tim Fargo

The basic techniques of the Reintegration System are incredibly effective. Once they become habitual, they require very little conscious effort and can be completed extremely fast.

You could, in fact, choose to learn only the basic techniques alongside persistent meditation practice, and that alone may be sufficient for you to achieve great advancements in all areas of your life. They will be at your disposal in every situation, in all circumstances, whenever and wherever you want.

These are the 5 basic techniques:

- Dissolving the Temporary I (DTI)
- Moving to the Heart (MH)
- Dissolving the Temporary I Plus (DTI+)
- Gentle Touch of Presence (GTP)
- Freshness & Acceptance (FA)

While learning these procedures, I recommend that you perform them at least 20 times each, in a slow and concentrated manner. Doing this will ensure that they begin to settle within your subconscious mind as new routines.

After this initial training, you can start using them either as standalone techniques or as parts of more complex methods, which will be described thoroughly in follow-up chapters.

Dissolving the Temporary I
"This, too, will pass." — Eckhart Tolle

"Dissolving the Temporary I," or DTI, is an incredibly simple technique used throughout the Reintegration System for removing unwanted content of the mind. It may also be referred to as the "Dissolving technique" in some places in this book.

Note that you probably won't find the DTI or a similar technique anywhere else. As far as I know, it's a completely unique procedure.

With "Dissolving the Temporary I" you are removing the foundation of your transitory experience, of the actual content of the mind. That foundation is your own ephemeral 'I,' which we will call in this system the "Temporary I" (Figure 10).

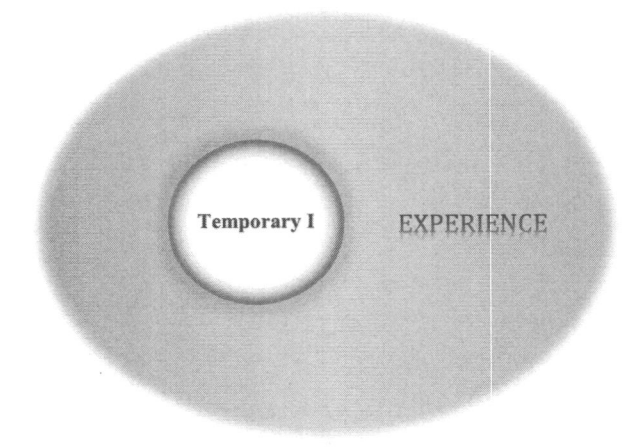

Figure 10: Temporary I and its Experience

Temporary I is your subtle feeling of self, your I-feeling within your body at the moment, while you are experiencing some mind content. It is typically located in your head, neck or upper chest, although it could be positioned in another area of your body, depending on the experience itself.

Through the act of pure observation, the Temporary I can shape the temporary experience, usually by dividing your unity of Self into two or more pairs of polarities.

If the foundation of the experience is eliminated, then the experience itself will vanish. Therefore, if the Temporary I disappears, so will the experience that it produces.

Again, the Temporary I is *not* the Heart. Unlike the Temporary I, which shapes our reality, the Heart creates our individual reality.

More precisely, through the Heart, our consciousness is continually *choosing* only one specific layer out of many possible unmanifested alternate layers and, as a result, creating our individual reality. The Temporary I then models it, more or less.

We will use this axiom for our first basic technique, the DTI. One method of dissolving the Temporary I is via expanding, as symbolically shown in Figure 11.

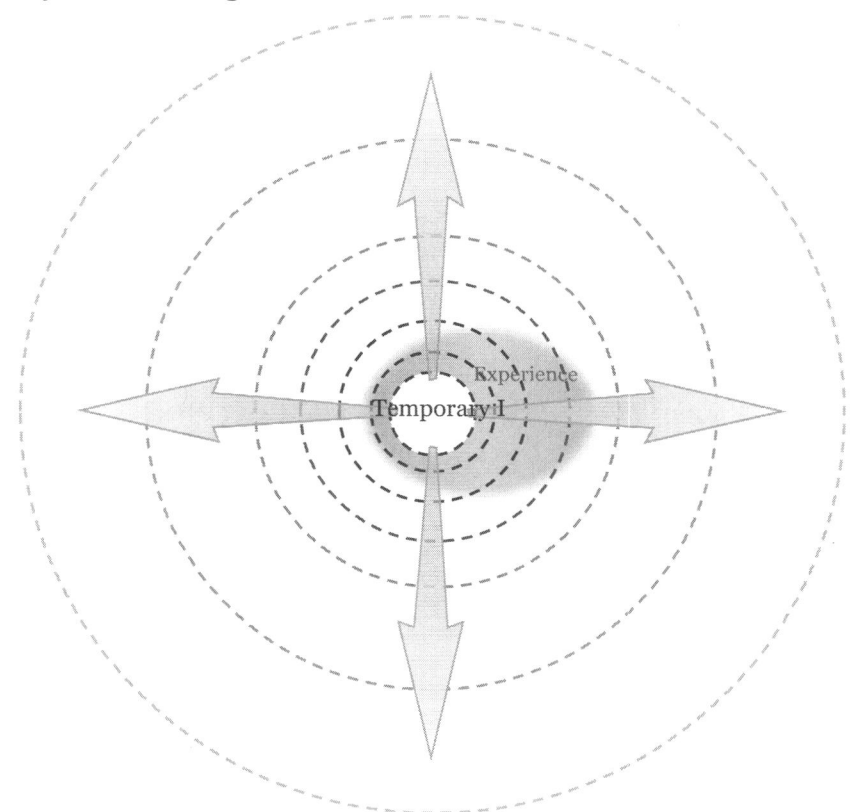

Figure 11: Dissolving the Temporary I

There are also other methods for dissolving this ephemeral I. One alternative is through acceptance, which is described in the Appendix. However, I strongly recommend you first learn the basic techniques described in this section, and only explore alternative DTI protocol once you have enough experience, if needed.

In the main approach, the Temporary I is forced to disappear through a swift and extreme expansion, up to the moment when it outgrows its own existence and ceases to exist. After that point, our being enters a state of pure consciousness that lasts around 5 to 10 seconds, in which there is no experience. We are just an observer, a pure Being. Once that fades, we may continue onto another main technique or simply resume anything else we were doing at that time.

The procedure is short and simple:

1. Notice, slightly, the content of your experience.
2. Feel from which vantage point your Temporary I is experiencing the content.
3. Rapidly increase the feeling of your Temporary I while breathing in deeply, up to the point where your I-feeling outgrows its own existence and enters pure consciousness.
4. While breathing out, imagine the whole existence shrinks down and disappears inside that pure consciousness.
5. Stay a while within that pure consciousness. There is no "I" and no existence anymore.

For example, during the third step, I usually imagine my I-feeling as an inflating balloon, expanding extremely quickly, encompassing and outgrowing our planet, solar system, galaxy, the whole universe and multiverse. In the fourth step, I feel the balloon deflating and shrinking down to such a small size inside of me (of my pure consciousness) that it simply ceases to exist. There is a subtle notion that my I disappears, as well as everything else.

To make this process as easy as possible, I recommend that you first do this exercise at least ten to fifteen times:

1. Notice your body and its position in the room or environment around it.

2. Notice your subtle I-feeling within your body at that moment. It is usually in your head, neck or upper chest, but it could also be located in another part of your body. In order to easily find that I-feeling, ask yourself: "From which point am I experiencing the world now? Where is the center of my being at this moment?"
3. Imagine that you, as that I-feeling (not the body), are suddenly growing bigger, pushing outside the boundaries of your body, room, city, of the planet, the solar system, the galaxy. Imagine your I-feeling encompassing the cosmos and all of everything. Meanwhile, the whole experience is but a small ball within you, becoming smaller and smaller. Eventually, it disappears.
4. You are now the void, nothingness. You don't exist anymore. Nothing exists anymore. There is only the void. It has always been and it will always be.

Do this exercise repeatedly, until that whole process becomes brief, habitual and automatic to you. Then you are ready to do the DTI.

You could imagine the disappearance of your Temporary I differently, though. The important thing is that the expansion goes on and on until the Temporary I is gone. The only criterion you could use for examining the success of the process is whether you find your consciousness pure, empty of content and diffused afterward, or not.

So, there is no need to relive or identify the experience (as is the case with several psychological or therapeutic techniques), or to expand the entire mind content (as in many other techniques). We are only doing an expansion of the Temporary I, which is simpler, faster and more effective in the end.

Apart from its application within the more complex techniques of the Reintegration System, you can also DTI in countless common situations. For example, if you become aware that you are overwhelmed with thoughts, you can dissolve the vantage point from which you are experiencing them. Or, if you find yourself flooded with emotions, note the location of your Temporary I and start the technique. Of course, if these thoughts, emotions or any other mind content or experience on which you were doing the DTI arises again, just repeat the technique until it vanishes. Similarly, if you're in the company of an unfriendly or annoying person, you may quietly do this technique on the Temporary I from which you are feeling the annoyance.

There is no limit to the practical implementation of the DTI, as it requires only seconds of mild, conscious effort to profoundly detach from the unpleasant situation.

Moving to the Heart
"The way is not in the sky... The way is in the heart." — The Buddha

Moving to the Heart (MH) is a simple protocol for creating a desired content of the mind. This technique is mostly suitable for methods aiming at achieving goals.

Once again, the Heart is the source of our individual reality. Therefore, if we move our Temporary I into the Heart and merge with it (as shown in Figure 12), a content of mind which we had been experiencing through the Temporary I will now gain true strength and foundation—because we will be experiencing it from the Heart. That's why we can consider the MH process as the true creation of mind content.

The MH consists of five steps:

1. Visualize and feel the desired content of your experience.
2. Find the vantage point of the Temporary I from which you are experiencing the content.
3. Move that Temporary I to the Heart. Let it sink naturally, deeply into your Heart. Leave it there.
4. Notice this same content from its new point of view, with an emphasis on your *identity* as a person who now perceives the

content. Tell yourself: "I am the one who is experiencing this mind content," and feel from your Heart this new persona.

5. Stay in this state of experiencing the desired identity and mind content from the Heart for at least 10 to 20 seconds. If you can't retain yourself in this state due to appearance of another content of mind, do the DTI on that content, then repeat steps from 1 to 4.

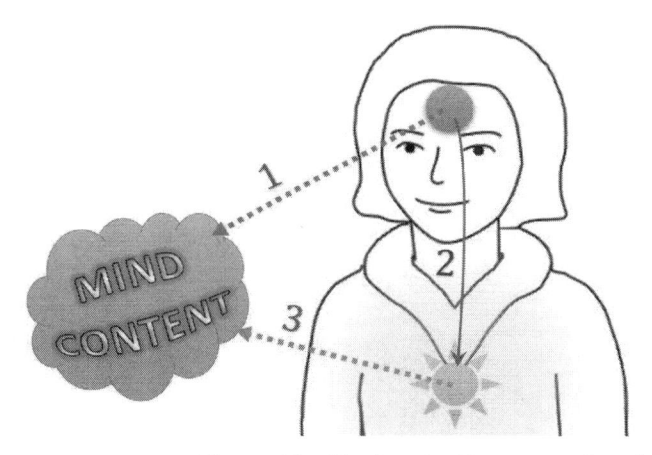

1. Experiencing the content from the Temporary I

2. Moving the Temporary I to the Heart

3. Experiencing the content from the Heart

Figure 12: Moving the Temporary I to the Heart

The *first step* is similar to the well-known process of visualization, backed with corresponding emotions, although here we have no need to maintain prolonged visualization. It is sufficient to keep the content only long enough to proceed to step two.

Let's say your desired content is to pass an exam. You could create a concrete picture in your mind where you are reading the results. They are very good for you and you feel happiness. This corresponding emotional background is very important for every successful visualization process.

The *second step* is quite straightforward, since you are already familiar with noticing the Temporary I from the previous subsection on "Dissolving the Temporary I."

So, while you are experiencing this scene of successfully passing the exam, just try to feel where your "I-feeling" is at this moment.

It may be in your head, neck, upper chest, somewhere between or someplace else.

The *third step* is moving the Temporary I to the Heart. Now, if possible, keep your attention on your mind content and move your Temporary I at the same time. If you can't do that, just focus on your Temporary I unless it's in the Heart.

Don't think too much about how to do this, just allow the ephemeral center of your being to crawl naturally to the Heart area. For those of you that are visual learners, you might imagine that you (your center—the Temporary I) are moving on an elevator from your present position (say, from your head) to the Heart. But the most important thing in this process is that you really *feel it*.

The *fourth step* is a really essential part of the whole protocol. Now, your Temporary I and your Heart have merged. You are experiencing the desired mind content again, but this time from the Heart. The emphasis here is on feeling the *identity* of the being who is experiencing the content. You are such-and-such person who has that-and-that experience and you *feel* this straight from your Heart.

In our given example, you will announce to yourself (or your partner): "I am the one who has passed the exam very successfully." Or, even better, "I am an excellent student who has passed this exam very successfully." *And you feel this identity whole-heartedly, from this new point of view—the Heart.* So, your new identity is corresponding to your desired content: "I am an excellent student."

It is advisable to formulate this MH statement before the MH procedure, so you do not have to pause before embodying it.

If this "identity" formulation is not applicable to your particular situation, you can use a statement which begins with "I feel that..." or whatever works for you. The main idea is to feel your new "I" identity from the Heart.

The *fifth step* is just as important as all the others. In fact, one of the strongest indicators of your impending achievement of the goal is the stability of the appropriate desired content within you. If the content vanishes quickly, or some distracting mind content appears, that indicates you are far from the accomplishment. If you can stay for longer periods and without much effort in the state of the imagined goal being already achieved, you are very near to the actual attainment.

With this technique you may, for example, put yourself right into a desired pleasant emotion, mental picture or state of mind... the precondition being that your mind is not overwhelmed with other content, so you can focus for several seconds on the desired experience. Because of this, it is better to complete any needed DTI before starting the MH, as that will ease the whole MH process.

Dissolving the Temporary I Plus
"Rise above the storm and you will find the sunshine." — Mario Fernandez

This variant of the DTI will be important in some of the techniques dealing with opposite structures, beliefs and goals. With it we are removing an unwanted mind content and *adding a new desired mind content* (we can also call it the *"target content"*), all in a single, unified process.

Essentially, this procedure is a combination of the Dissolving the Temporary I (DTI) and Moving to the Heart (MH), so it can be considered as a *derived technique*. It is an act of unification of mind and heart.

With the first part of the technique (the "DTI part") you are dissolving the unwanted content within your mind. Then, from that state of pure consciousness, you are introducing a new content and merging it with the Heart's will, as symbolically shown in Figure 13.

The "Dissolving the Temporary I Plus" (or, shortened, DTI+) in its first five steps is the same as normal DTI. The difference is that we are adding the target (desired) content with a sixth step, as part of

Moving to the Heart procedure, which in this way becomes an integral element of the DTI+.

The procedure consists of these six steps:

1. Notice slightly the content of your experience.
2. Feel the Temporary I from whose vantage point you are experiencing the content.
3. Expand your Temporary I to the point where your I-feeling outgrows its own existence, and enter a state of pure consciousness, while inhaling deeply.
4. While exhaling, imagine that the whole existence is shrinking down and disappearing inside that pure consciousness.
5. Stay a while within the pure consciousness. There is no "I" and no existence.

   (With these first five steps, the DTI part, we have removed your unwanted content of mind. Now comes the MH part, with which we will create the wanted, target content.)

6. After 5-10 seconds spent in pure consciousness, feel the target content from the Heart, with an emphasis on your new identity as the person perceiving the content. Tell yourself: *"I am the one who is experiencing this mind content,"* and feel from your Heart this new identity. Optionally, you can state again from the Heart's vantage point: *"I choose to be the person who experiences... (the target content)."* [15]

---

[15] I will refer to this statement in many locations in this book as the "MH Statement."

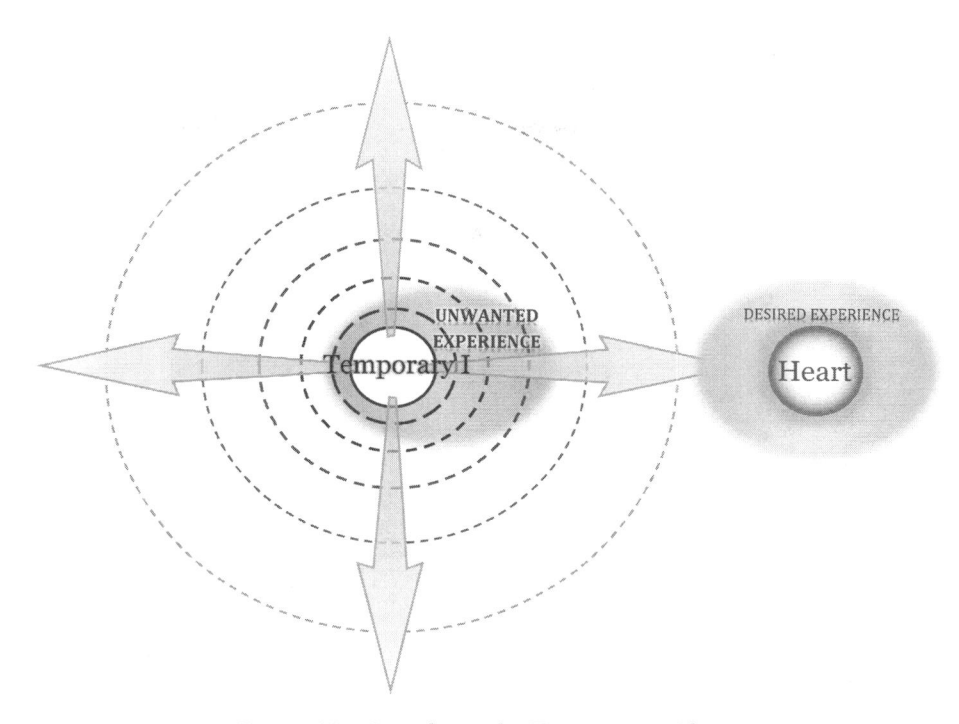

Figure 13: Dissolving the Temporary I Plus

This DTI+ technique can be applied to various unpleasant experiences in everyday life, just like the original DTI. The difference is that, with DTI+, you are immediately adding a desired experience to replace the previous, unpleasant one with. So, instead of simply staying in a state of Presence or Pure Consciousness at the end of the exercise, you are deliberately moving into another experience at your will.

Gentle Touch of Presence

"All true artists, whether they know it or not, create from a place of no-mind, from inner stillness." — Eckhart Tolle

The first point in the Gentle Touch of Presence (GTP) is to enter a state of Pure Consciousness or Presence. From there, we are able to transform, refine or transmute an unwanted content of mind into another, better one. By simultaneously remaining aware of the state of Presence in which we are at the moment, and of the unwanted mind content, we will get a new, much better or "softer" content or the content will disappear (see Figure 14). In fact, we may not know what the resulting content will be whatsoever.

If you are already in that state, you can, of course, skip the first step. Here is the procedure:

1. Feel from which Temporary I vantage point you are experiencing the present moment. Do the DTI. You will find yourself in a state of pure consciousness, the Presence. Stay in that state for roughly ten to fifteen seconds.

2. Now, softly bring the issue you are dealing with into that Presence. Be that Presence, while gently experiencing the issue. Envelop that issue with your Presence. It is important to have them both together, the Presence and the issue, simultaneously. Keep that "togetherness" as long as possible, until the issue completely disappears, or at least your unpleasant "gut feeling" related to the issue, vanishes.

Figure 14: "Touching" the Content with Presence

The concept of being conscious in the present moment, which brings one into the state of Presence, had been developed and nurtured in ancient times, especially in religious teachings of Buddhism and Hinduism. Today's spiritual teachers, like Eckhart Tolle, and even many new approaches in psychology, often emphasize the importance of living in 'the now.'

Once you are in the Presence, you can deal with any type of experience, *both wanted and unwanted*. The GTP will ease and diminish the unwanted mind contents, and enrich or improve the pleasant experiences. Pure consciousness is the ultimate intelligence, the perfect benevolence. Through the GTP technique it will "do" what is best for you. Hence, with this method you can solve or reintegrate complex issues or parts of your personality.

Freshness & Acceptance
"Sell your cleverness and buy bewilderment." — Rumi
"The only true wisdom is in knowing you know nothing." — Socrates
"Whatever you fight, you strengthen, and what you resist, persists." — Eckhart Tolle

In this technique, we don't deal with the Temporary I at all; instead we are oriented toward the external mind content.

This basic technique can be done whenever and wherever you want. By nature, the Freshness & Acceptance (FA) is most suited to everyday, not-too-heavy contents of mind. It is ideal for mindfulness: being here and now as much as possible.

It is very simple:

1. *Freshness*—perceive the content as though it is completely new to you.
2. *Acceptance*—fully accept the content with all of your heart. You will know you've done so when you have neither adherence nor aversion toward it. *(In this way you are freeing yourself of searching for possible explanations of the content.)*

In other words, when you notice some unwanted content, which can be either inside or outside of your mind, put yourself in the position of an innocent child. Feel the awe of a kid seeing something entirely new. Accept wholeheartedly the content. Be fine with it. Be indifferent to it.

The FA concept is very similar to the concept of *Not-knowing*. As the concepts of living in the now, freshness and acceptance, the *Not-knowing* approach was developed and nurtured in ancient times, especially in Buddhism.

"'Not-knowing' is emphasized in Zen practice, where it is sometimes called 'beginner's mind.' An expert may know a subject deeply, yet be

blinded to new possibilities by his or her preconceived ideas. In contrast, a beginner may see with fresh, unbiased eyes. The practice of beginner's mind is to cultivate an ability to meet life without preconceived ideas, interpretations, or judgments.[16]

Try to place yourself into a state of pure *Not-knowing* toward some experience. Just feel that you know nothing about that and be fine with that. That state doesn't even have to be related to any content at all, whether internal or external. Just feel at the moment that you know literally nothing and be absolutely OK with that. You will enter a state of pure consciousness for a while.

For example, you feel offended by a rude colleague and your anger is mounting. Quickly imagine that you've heard these words for the first time in your life. You don't even know what their meaning is. Tell yourself something like: "What did he say? I just don't understand. I have no clue what that was and, after all, I don't care. I am fine with it all, anyway." In the first part of the statement you *pretend* that you encounter the situation for the first time in your life and you don't know what it is. With the second part, you accept it. In this way, you are free from further investigation into the meaning of the situation. This is *not* suppressing of an experience. It's simply shifting your point of view into genuine, innocent state of mind.

The *Not-knowing* state includes both steps from FA technique. If you are in the state of knowing nothing about something, you can also sense a feeling of freshness or even awe toward the content. When you are content with the absence of any knowledge about the content, it is practically the same as the second step in FA: acceptance.

Although there are still some slight differences between *Freshness & Acceptance* and *Not-knowing*, the latter is interchangeable with the FA wherever you are supposed to do it.

---

[16] Source:
http://www.insightmeditationcenter.org/books-articles/articles/not-knowing/

In a Nutshell
Dissolving the Temporary I (DTI)

The purpose of this technique is to remove unwanted mind content.

The procedure:
1. Notice slightly the content of your experience.
2. Feel your Temporary I from which vantage point you are experiencing the content.
3. Breathe in deeply. While doing that, expand your Temporary I up to the point where your I-feeling outgrows the whole existence (whatever that means to you) and enters pure consciousness.
4. While breathing out, imagine the whole existence is shrinking down and disappearing inside that pure consciousness.
5. Stay a while within pure consciousness. Notice that there is no "I" and no existence anymore. There is only the original, pure Being, the "is-ness."

Moving to the Heart (MH)

The main purpose of this technique is to create desired mind content.

The procedure:
1. Visualize and feel the desired content of mind.
2. Find the Temporary I from whose vantage point you are experiencing the content.
3. Move that Temporary I to the Heart. Let it sink naturally into your Heart. Leave it there.
4. Notice the same content from its new point of view within the Heart, with an emphasis on your identity as a person who perceives the content. Tell yourself: "I am the one who is experiencing this mind content," and feel from your Heart this new identity.
5. Stay in this state of experiencing the desired content from the Heart for at least 10 to 20 seconds. If you can't retain yourself in this state due to appearance of another content of mind, do the DTI on that content, then repeat steps from 1 to 4 (by doing this, you will eliminate some subconscious obstacles to having the actual experience represented by your desired mind content).

Dissolving the Temporary I Plus (DTI+)

The purpose of this technique is to remove an unwanted mind content, and immediately create a new desired mind content in its place.

The procedure:

1. Notice slightly the content of your experience.
2. Feel your Temporary I from which vantage point you are experiencing the content.
3. Breathe in deeply. While doing that, expand swiftly your Temporary I up to the point where your I-feeling outgrows the whole existence (whatever that means to you) and enter pure consciousness.
4. While breathing out, imagine the whole existence shrinking down and disappearing inside that pure consciousness.
5. Stay a while within the pure consciousness. There is no "I" and no existence.

(With these first five steps of the DTI part of the protocol, we have removed an unwanted content of mind. Now is the MH part, with which we are creating a wanted, target mind content.)

6. After 5-10 seconds spent in the pure consciousness, feel the target content from the Heart, with an emphasis on your identity as a person who perceives the content. Tell yourself: *"I am the one who is experiencing this mind content,"* and feel from your Heart this new identity. Optionally, you can state again from the Heart's vantage point: *"I choose to be the person who experiences... (the target content)."*

Gentle Touch of Presence (GTP)

The aim of this technique is to transform, refine or transmute a content of mind into another, better one.

The technique:

1. Feel your Temporary I from which vantage point you are experiencing the present moment. Do the DTI. You will find yourself in a state of pure consciousness, or Presence. Stay in that state for roughly ten to fifteen seconds.

2. Bring the issue you are dealing with into the Presence. Be that Presence, while gently experiencing the issue. Envelope that issue with your Presence. Bring both the Presence and the issue together, experiencing them simultaneously. Keep that "togetherness" as long as possible, until the issue completely disappears, or your unpleasant "gut feeling" related to the issue vanishes.

Freshness & Acceptance (FA)

The purpose of this technique is similar to the GTP's aim—to transform or remove a mind content. It is more oriented toward dealing with lighter thoughts and emotions, especially as a part of mindfulness.

1. *Freshness*—perceive the content you are dealing with as completely fresh and new for you.
2. *Acceptance*—fully accept the content with your whole heart. You will know that you've fully accepted it once you neither have adherence nor aversion toward it. *(In this way you are freeing yourself of any search for possible explanations of the content.)*

Main Reintegration Techniques—Deeply Transformational

"Even those things we like least about ourselves have some positive purpose." — Connirae Andreas, Tamara Andreas, Core Transformation: Reaching the Wellspring Within

First, I must give credit to Connirae and Tamara Andreas for their great book "Core Transformation," in which they thoroughly describe their elegant and highly beneficial system of the same name. In developing the main Reintegration techniques 'the Inner Triangle,' 'Single-' or 'Double-Chain Techniques' and 'Convergence Procedure,' I was hugely inspired by their approach.

As is the case with Core Transformation, the main Reintegration techniques are based on dealing with the Chain of Goals, as described in the previous chapter. Of them, the Inner Triangle is the most comprehensive procedure, but it also demands more time and effort on the user.

Inner Triangle Technique

"One does not become enlightened by imagining figures of light, but by making the darkness conscious. The latter procedure, however, is disagreeable and therefore not popular." — C.G. Jung

The Inner Triangle (IT) is an apparently complex procedure, but once you get familiar with it, you will see how simple and efficient it is.

It is designed primarily for solving chronic problems, although its area of application could be much wider, depending on one's creativity.

The Inner Triangle is based on the concepts of Parts of Personality and Chain of Goals. To begin, you must take the problem you are dealing with and consider it a separate part of your character, like a half-conscious entity. By defining it as a unique and distinct being (either within your own psyche or outside of it), you are pulling it out of the "sea of the unconscious." Then, you are able to start a sort of communication with it, in order to get some important information related to the problem. Finally, you find the opposite part in your mind and treat it in the same way as the first.

During the IT process, by going up the chain of goals of the parts, you are not erasing any of the entities: you are reintegrating them. They may merge together and thus end the process, or remain separate, but have been brought up to their highest states of being, either way having been reintegrated into the unity of your being.

First, you become aware of your sense of I, the Temporary I, right there in the moment.

Then, consider your problem as the first polarity. Its opposite would be the second polarity (see Figure 15).

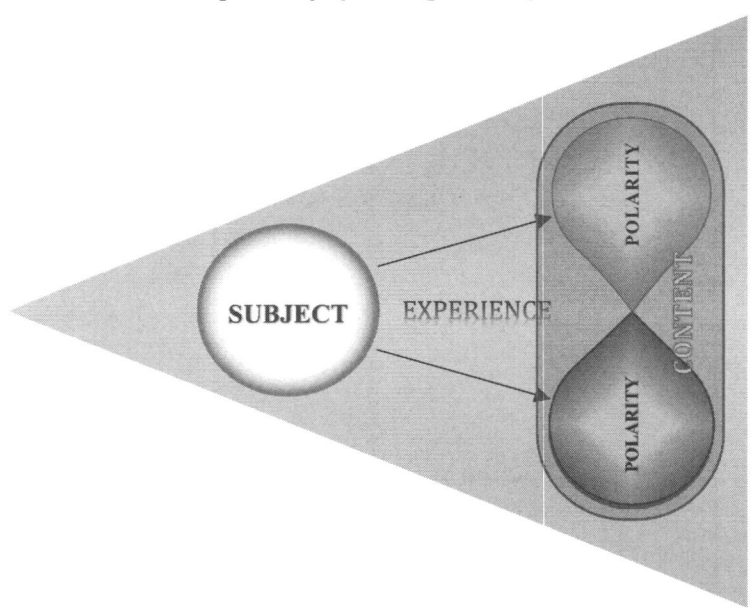

Figure 15: Subject (or Temporary I) and Polarities

Treat these polarities as conscious, or half-conscious entities. You will need to communicate with them in order to find out their goals and aversions, step-by-step. You will "persuade" them that those goals have been fulfilled and that they are safe from their aversions, or that the aversions will never manifest. Goals and aversions are in this way fulfilled and secured.

After that, in order to completely dissolve the goals and aversions of the polarities, you identify with them and do the Dissolving technique (DTI) on them. In this way, one layer of the problem has been solved and space for the next circle of entities' goals and aversions has been released.

By asking the polarities for their next goal or aversion and releasing them in the same way, you will gradually cleanse both polarities. After each circle of questions and answers (as shown symbolically at Figure 16) they will get closer to each other, bringing them to their highest (initial) state and often "forcing" them to merge completely in the end.

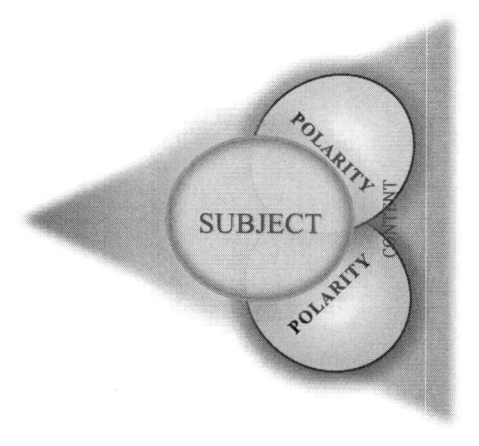

Figure 16: Subject (or Temporary I) and Polarities Getting Closer to each other

Now, before dealing with the polarities in each circle, you must bring your attention to your I here and now, apart from the polarities, and cleanse it using the DTI. The process will bring your I here and now to its highest state of being, while merging with the above-mentioned polarities.

The Procedure

Here we will delve into a more detailed explanation of the Inner Triangle technique (as symbolically shown in Figure 17 later on). You can find a blank worksheet that will make your practice a lot easier in the Appendix III. Also, here is the full address of all downloadable material in this book:

https://www.dropbox.com/sh/vc7t7808gr50g30/AABvA-OdcN9vrJUjQJc4onepwa?dl=0

Preparation:

1. **Sit up straight, eyes closed or half-open** (whatever is more suitable for you). **Relax.**

2. **Determine the location of your I** at this moment. Determine where exactly this Temporary I is located; write down the answer.

3. **Define the first polarity**—*usually your unwanted, unpleasant state:*

   a) Name it and write that down.

   b) *It is a part of you, no matter how it looks or where it is located—inside or outside of you. You will communicate with it.* Tell your subconscious to make this part of your personality distinct and mature for the purposes of clear communication.

   c) Ask yourself: If that polarity had distinct qualities, how would it be represented? Determine its qualities, such as shape, size, color, brightness, texture, perhaps even age, sound, or symbol. Anything you see or feel. Determine also where it is located. Write everything down.

   d) Greet it, as you would greet any person you respect.

4. **Define your second polarity**—*a state opposite to the first polarity (usually a desired or pleasant one):*

- a) Ask yourself: "Is there a part of me that is opposite to the (first polarity)?"[17] Name that polarity; write down the name.
- b) Tell your subconscious to make this part of your personality distinct and mature for the purposes of clear communication with it.
- c) Determine its qualities—how it looks like (shape, size, color, brightness, etc.), perhaps its age and anything else you see or feel. Determine where it is located. Write everything down.
- d) Greet it, as you would greet any person you respect.

Execution:

(First circle)

5. **Return to your I, here and now, from step 2.** Do you have any thought, emotion or sensation? Write down the answer. If you do, feel again your Temporary I from which vantage point you are experiencing that content. If you do not, the Temporary I will probably be somewhere inside your being.

    Do the Dissolving technique (DTI), either way.

6. **Now focus on your first polarity.**

    a) *(Communication with polarity)* Look at it from here and now. Ask it two questions:

    (1) **"What do you want at this moment?"** Write down the answer. Tell the polarity: **"Your goal has just been fulfilled!"** Feel your statement as true.

---

[17] This is not particularly something to search a lot for. Just try to find what you feel is the opposite to the current part. If it is an emotion, use the Plutchik's wheel, described in Part III, section "Emotions." You can even get a simple label for that part, for example "The calm part of me." However, if you still feel unable to find the opposite polarity or right label for it, you can use Manual Muscle Testing (MMT, also described in part II of this book) for clarifying that.

- (2) **"What would you like to avoid at this moment?"** Write down the answer. Tell the polarity: **"You have been completely secured and freed from this aversion, from now on!"** Feel your statement as true.

  b) *(Identification with polarity)* Enter the polarity. Identify with it. Feel its being.

- (1) From its point of view, feel its goal (the answer to first question). As that entity, do the Dissolving technique on the goal (answer).

- (2) From its point of view, feel its aversion (the answer to second question). As that entity, do the Dissolving technique on the aversion (answer).

7. **Now focus on your second polarity.**

    a) *(Communication with polarity)* Look at it from here and now. Ask it two questions:

- (1) **"What do you want at this moment?"** Write down the answer. Tell the polarity: **"Your goal has just been fulfilled!"** Feel your statement as true.

- (2) **"What would you like to avoid at this moment?"** Write down the answer. Tell the polarity: **"You have been completely secured and freed from this aversion, from now on!"** Feel your statement as true.

  b) *(Identification with polarity)* Enter the polarity. Identify with it. Feel its being.

- (1) From its point of view, feel its goal (the answer to first question). As that entity, do the Dissolving technique on the goal (answer).

- (2) From its point of view, feel its aversion (the answer to second question). As that entity, do the Dissolving technique on the aversion (answer).

(Next circle)

8. **Return again to your I, here and now, from step 2.** Check if you have any thought, emotion or sensation and write down the answer.

    Do the Dissolving technique.

9. **Focus on your first polarity.**

    a) *(Communication with polarity)* Look at it from here and now. Ask it two questions:

    (1) **"Now that you have fulfilled your previous goal, what do you want at this moment, which is even more valuable?"** Write down the answer as its second goal. Tell the polarity: **"This goal has also been fulfilled!"** Feel your statement as true.

    (2) **"Now, since you have been secured and freed from your previous aversion, forever on, is there something which is even more important that you would like to avoid at this moment?"** Write down the answer. Tell the polarity: **"You are completely secure and free from this aversion too, from now on!"** Feel your statement as true.

    b) *(Identification with polarity)* Enter the polarity. Identify with it. Feel its being.

    (1) From its point of view, feel its second goal. As that entity, do the Dissolving technique on that goal.

    (2) From its point of view, feel its second aversion. As that entity, do the Dissolving technique on that aversion.

10. **Focus on your second polarity.**

    a) *(Communication with polarity)* Look at it from the here and now. Ask it two questions:

(1) **"Now that you have fulfilled your previous goal, what do you want at this moment, which is even more valuable?"** Write down the answer as its second goal. Tell the polarity: "This goal has also been fulfilled!" Feel your statement as true.

(2) **"Now, since you have been secured and freed from your previous aversion, forever on, is there something more that you would like to avoid at this moment?"** Write down the answer. Tell the polarity: "You are completely secure and free from this aversion too, from now on!" Feel your statement as true.

b) *(Identification with polarity)* Enter the polarity. Identify with it. Feel its being.

(1) From its point of view, feel its second goal. As that entity, do the Dissolving technique on that goal.

(2) From its point of view, feel its second aversion. As that entity, do the Dissolving technique on that aversion.

11. Repeat the whole circle (one or more times).

You will have to repeat the whole circle, again and again, as long as you have any content (thoughts, emotions, sensations) at *any* step.

After each step, the answers from both polarities will be getting more and more positive. Also, you will probably notice that the polarities are apparently getting closer to each other, closer to your heart, more and more transparent and/or brighter.

12. Merge/integrate the polarities.

At the end of the procedure, when you have no more answers for the polarities and find yourself in one of the highest states (Love, Peace, Joy, Nothingness), the polarities could spontaneously merge. If that doesn't happen, ask both polarities to merge.

If nothing happens again, it simply means that these entities are not mutual polarities at all. They were not connected in that way, however, you did succeed in guiding them to their highest state and integrating them into your personality.

Whether they merged or not, ask them to fill up and overwhelm your body and your whole being with their divine energy.

Note: There is also an alternative approach if you are having issues with establishing effective communication with your polarities during the IT work.

In that case, you just skip the communication part and enter both polarities at the very beginning of the process. You identify (become) the first polarity and then the second, rather than posing the questions to them. You won't get the answers through dialog with the polarities, you do it on your own, from the points of view of these polarities. Instead of posing a question to that entity "outside of you," you just ask yourself as that entity questions like this: "What is my goal at this moment?" and do the Dissolving technique (DTI) on the answer that you subsequently become aware of.

Everything else is pretty much the same. We could call this variation "Alternative Inner Triangle (AIT) Technique."

Inner Triangle Chart

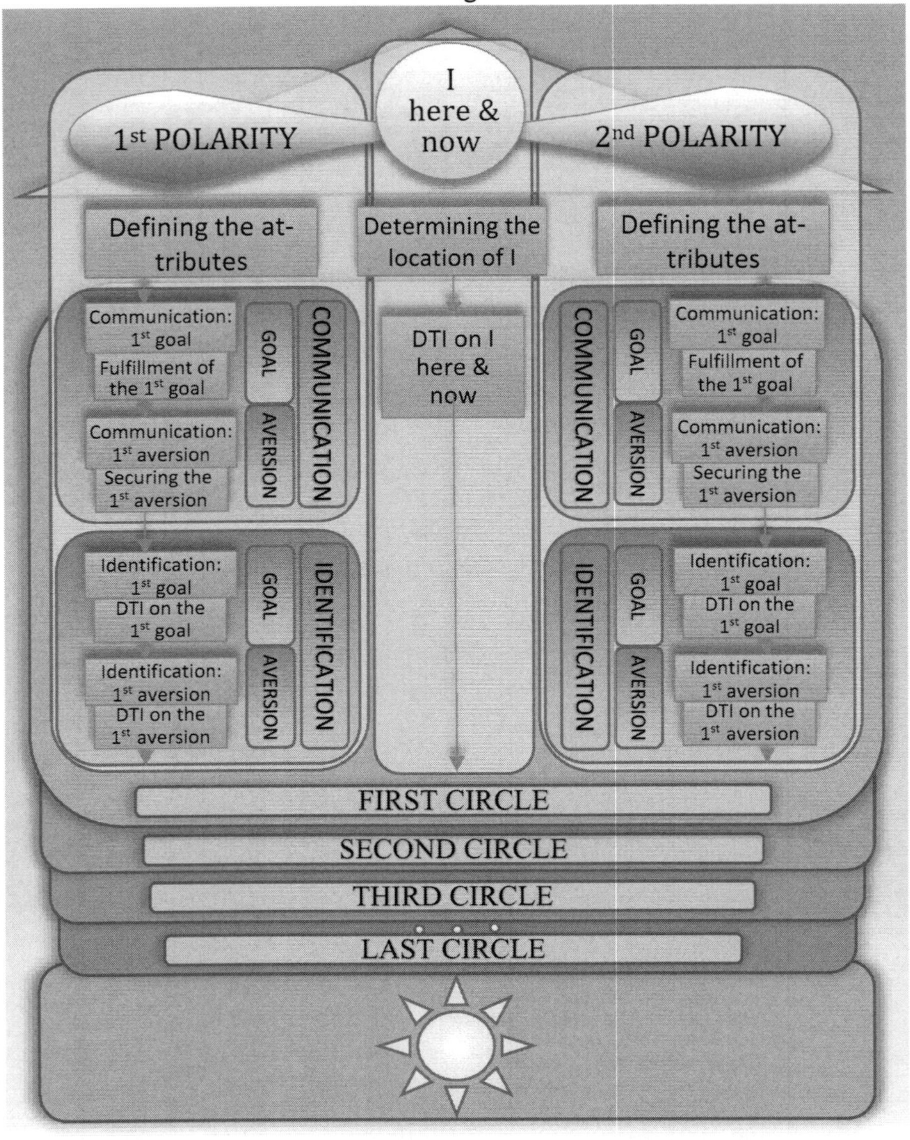

Figure 17: Inner Triangle Procedure

Real-Life Example

"William" had a problem with a strong sense of guilt for almost every bad thing in his life. We did the IT process on his problem. You will see all basic information extracted from this process in the subsection "IT Worksheet: My Guilt," in Figures 18, 19 and 20.

Here is the IT procedure in practice, with every question or instruction passed to William, and, of course, his responses.

1. *(William sits up straight and relaxes).*

2. *Instructor:* Determine the location of your I at this moment.

   William: It is somewhere here *(pointing with his index finger)*, inside my neck.

3. *(Defining the first polarity)*

   Instructor: Define your unpleasant state as the first polarity in our process. Name it.

   William: That would be my guilt for the many things I've done in my life, especially to some of my friends, although I had good intentions. Well, I have to define it in a few words, right? Simply, it's **my guilt**. *(Bolded by the author for the sake of clarity, as in the rest of this text.)*

   Instructor: OK. Your guilt. It is a part of you, no matter what it looks like or where it is located—inside or outside of you. You will communicate with it. In order to make that communication easier and more effective, tell your subconscious to make this part of your personality distinct and mature for the purpose of clear communication with it.

   William: (nodding, after a while) OK.

   Instructor: Determine its qualities. How does it look? What is its shape, size, color, brightness, texture, or perhaps its age and anything else you see or feel. Determine where it is located.

William: It's a dark red mass, inside and around my head and torso... It doesn't have any particular shape, it's just a big messy thing... And it's pretty old, don't know how much...

Instructor: OK, there it is. Greet it, as you would greet any person you respect.

William: (nodding)

(Defining the second polarity)

Instructor: Define your second polarity—that could be a state which you feel is opposite to the unwanted polarity; name it.

William: (after some time) It's guilt of other people. My accusations toward them. Other's guilt.

Instructor: OK. The **other's guilt.** Keep in mind that it is also a part of your personality. So tell your subconscious to make this part mature enough to be able to communicate.

William: OK.

Instructor: Determine its qualities. How does it look? What is its shape, size, color, brightness, texture, or perhaps its age and anything else you see or feel. Determine where it is located.

William: It's a ball; a big, brown ball encompassing my head and part of my chest. It's also old.

Instructor: Greet it, as you would greet any person you respect.

William: OK.

(Execution)

4. *Instructor:* Now return to your I, here and now, in this room. Do you have any thoughts, emotions or sensation?

   William: Yes, actually, **I was thinking about the effectiveness of this process. I'm not quite sure that we'll do something with any of this...**

Instructor: OK. Feel your Temporary I from which vantage point you are experiencing that content. Where is it located?

William: **It's in the upper part of my neck.**

Instructor: Good. Do the Dissolving technique.

William: (after some time, nodding) OK, I've done it.

5. *(Dealing with the **first polarity** through communication and identification with it)*

   a) *(Communication part)*

   Instructor: Now focus on your **first polarity—your guilt**. Look at it from the here and now. I'll remind you that it was a dark red mass, inside and around your head and torso; it didn't have any particular shape, it was just a big messy thing, pretty old. Tell me about its qualities and location *now*.

   William: **It's somewhat brighter...**

   Instructor: Very good. Ask it: "What do you want at this moment?" Wait for its response, which could be in any form—words, sounds, pictures or something else. Tell me what its response is.

   William: There is a thought in my head, it's like that guilt is telling me: **"I'm guilty! I want to avoid punishment!"**

   Instructor: Yes, that's it. Now tell it decisively: "Your goal has just been fulfilled!" Feel your statement as true.

   William: OK.

   Instructor: Now pose a question to the polarity: "What would you like to avoid at this moment?"

   William: Another thought... It tells me: **"I don't want anybody to look at me. They'll see my guilt."**

Instructor: Good. Tell the polarity: "You have been completely freed and secured from this aversion, from now on!" Feel your statement as true.

William: OK.

b) *(Identification part)*

Instructor: Now enter the polarity. Identify with it. Feel its being.

William: OK, I'm in it.

Instructor: From its point of view, feel its goal ("I'm guilty! I want to avoid a punishment!").

William: OK.

Instructor: Feel the Temporary I from which vantage point you, as that entity, are experiencing the goal (quoting: "I'm guilty! I want to avoid a punishment!"). Do the Dissolving technique.

William: (After some time) OK, I did it. I feel emptiness...

Instructor: That's good. Stay in it for a while. Enjoy it... Now we are going on. From its point of view, feel its aversion ("I don't want anybody to look at me. They'll see my guilt.").

William: OK.

Instructor: All right. Feel the Temporary I from which point of view you, as that entity, are experiencing that aversion ("I don't want anybody to look at me. They'll see my guilt."). Do the Dissolving technique.

William: (with a relief) Great.

6. *(Dealing with the **second polarity** through communication and identification)*

   a) *(Communication with polarity)*

   Instructor: Indeed. Rest for a few seconds... Now we are dealing with the second polarity—it's the **other's guilt**. Look at it from here and now. It was a ball, a big brown ball encompassing your head and part of your chest. It also was old. Tell me about its qualities and location at this moment.

   William: OK. **The ball looks the same.**

   Instructor: Ask it: "What do you want at this moment?"

   William: **I just want to hide my own guilt and accuse other people...**

   Instructor: Good. Tell the polarity: "Your goal has just been fulfilled!" Feel your statement as true.

   William: (nodding)

   Instructor: Ask it: "What would you like to avoid at this moment?"

   William: **I have to avoid others thinking that I'm the culprit.**

   Instructor: Very good. Now tell the polarity: "You are completely free and secure from this aversion, from now on!" Feel your statement as true.

   William: (nodding)

   b) *(Identification with polarity)*

   Instructor: Now enter the polarity. Identify with it. Feel its being.

   William: OK.

   Instructor: From its point of view, feel its goal ("I just want to hide my own guilt and accuse other people...").

William: (nodding)

Instructor: As that entity, do the Dissolving technique on the goal (answer). Do the Dissolving technique.

William: (nodding)

Instructor: From its point of view, feel its aversion ("I have to avoid others to thinking that I'm the culprit.").

William: OK.

Instructor: Now, feel the Temporary I from which vantage point you, as that entity, are experiencing that aversion. Do the Dissolving technique.

William: Done.

(Second circle)

7. *Instructor:* Great! *(After a while)* Now return to your **I, here and now**. Check if you have any thoughts, emotions or sensation.

   William: **I feel quite strange; I can't explain, but it's a nice feeling.**

   Instructor: OK. Feel your Temporary I from which vantage point you are experiencing that strange feeling. Where is it located?

   William: It's in my head now.

   Instructor: Good. Do the Dissolving technique.

   William: (after some time, nodding) Wow... What bliss...

8. *(Dealing again with the **first polarity** through communication and identification)*

   a) *(Communication with polarity)*

   Instructor: OK. Now come back to this process. Focus again on your first polarity. It's **your guilt**. Look at it from here and now. If you remember—it was a dark red mass, inside and around your head and torso; it didn't have any particular shape, it was just a big messy thing, pretty old, somewhat brighter last time. Tell me, did its qualities and location change now?

William: Well... **Again, it's brighter somehow, and it's smaller... It encompasses my neck and chest now...**

Instructor: Yes. Good. You are doing great. However, pose a question to it: "Now that you have fulfilled your previous goal, what do you want at this moment, which is even more valuable?"

William: **I don't want to hurt anyone; I'll accept my guilt.**

Instructor: This is the second goal. Tell the polarity: "This goal has also been fulfilled!" Feel your statement as true.

William: OK.

Instructor: "Now, since you have been secured and freed from your previous aversion, forever on, is there anything more that you would like to avoid at this moment?"

William: **I want to hide from other's attention. They'll see my guilt.**

Instructor: Tell the polarity: "You are completely secure and free from this aversion too, from now on!" Feel your statement as true.

William: (nodding) OK.

b) *(Identification with polarity)*

Instructor: Enter the polarity. Identify with it. Feel its being.

William: (nodding)

Instructor: From its point of view, feel its second goal: "I don't want to hurt anybody, I will accept my guilt."

William: (nodding)

Instructor: Feel the Temporary I from which vantage point you, as that entity, are experiencing the goal. Do the Dissolving technique.

William: Done.

Instructor: From its point of view, feel its second aversion: "I want to hide from other's attention. They'll see my guilt."

William: OK.

Instructor: Feel the Temporary I from which vantage point you, as that entity, are experiencing the aversion. Do the Dissolving technique.

William: OK.

9. *(Dealing again with the **second polarity** through communication and identification)*

   a) *(Communication with polarity)*

   Instructor: Good. Now, focus on your second polarity: **the other's guilt**. Look at it from here and now. It was a big brown ball encompassing your head and part of your chest. It also was old. Tell me about its qualities and location at this moment.

   William: **The ball is much brighter now. It's moved toward the chest; its center is in my neck.**

   Instructor: Good! Ask it: "Now, having your previous goal fulfilled, what do you want at this moment, which is even more valuable?"

   William: **I want to punish the others for their mistakes.**

   Instructor: OK. This is the second goal of this polarity. Tell it now: "This goal has also been fulfilled!" Feel your statement as true.

   William: OK.

Instructor: "Now that you have been secured and freed from your previous aversion, forever on, is there anything more that you would like to avoid at this moment, which is even more important?"

William: **I don't want injustice! I don't want others to pass without punishment.**

Instructor: Tell the polarity: "You are completely secure and free from this aversion too, from now on!" Feel your statement as true.

William: OK.

b) *(Identification with polarity)*

Instructor: Enter the polarity. Identify with it. Feel its being.

William: (nodding)

Instructor: From its point of view, feel its second goal: "I want to punish the others for their mistakes."

William: (nodding)

Instructor: Feel the Temporary I from which vantage point you, as that entity, are experiencing the goal. Do the Dissolving technique.

William: OK. Done.

Instructor: From its point of view, feel its second aversion: "I don't want injustice! I don't want others to pass without punishment."

Instructor: Feel the Temporary I from which vantage point you, as that entity, are experiencing the aversion. Do the Dissolving technique.

William: Done.

(Third circle)

10. *Instructor:* Very good. Now, return again to your I, here and now. Check if you have any thought, emotion or sensation.

    William: **Nothing...**

    Instructor: Anyway, feel your Temporary I. Where is it located?

    William: **It's in my neck again.**

    Instructor: Good. Do the Dissolving technique.

    William: (after some time, nodding) OK.

11. (Dealing again with the **first polarity** through communication and identification)

    a) *(Communication with polarity)*

    Instructor: Now focus again on your first polarity. Look at it from here and now. It was a dark red mass, but somehow brighter and smaller last time. Tell me about its qualities and location at *this* moment.

    William: **It's a yellow ball now, in the upper part of my chest.**

    Instructor: Ask it: "Now, having your previous goals fulfilled, what do you want at this moment, which is even more valuable?"

    William: Hmmm... Yes... **I want to show to my parents that I'm a good boy.**

    Instructor: Great; this is the third goal. Tell the polarity: "This goal has also been fulfilled!" Feel your statement as true.

    William: OK.

    Instructor: Now, tell the entity: "Since you have been secured and freed from your previous aversions, forever on, is there anything more that you would like to avoid at this moment?"

William: **I don't want to betray my parents' expectations.**

Instructor: This is the third aversion. Tell the polarity: "You are completely secure and free from this aversion too, from now on!" Feel your statement as true.

William: (nodding)

b) *(Identification with polarity)*

Instructor: Enter the polarity. Identify with it. Feel its being.

William: (nodding)

Instructor: From its point of view, feel its third goal: "I want to show to my parents that I'm a good boy."

William: OK.

Instructor: Feel the Temporary I from which vantage point you, as that entity, are experiencing the goal. Do the Dissolving technique.

William: OK... I've done it.

Instructor: From its point of view, feel its third aversion: "I don't want to betray my parents' expectations."

William: OK.

Instructor: Feel the Temporary I from which vantage point you, as that entity, are experiencing the aversion. Do the Dissolving technique.

William: Done...

12. *(Dealing again with the **second polarity** through communication and identification)*

   a) *(Communication with polarity)*

   Instructor: Focus again on your second polarity, **the other's guilt**. Look at it from here and now. Remember, it was a big brown ball, but much brighter last time. So, what are its qualities and location at *this* moment?

   William: **The ball is yellowish now. It's smaller and it's in the upper part of my chest.**

   Instructor: Great. Ask it: "Now, having your previous goals fulfilled, what do you want at this moment, which is even more valuable?"

   William: **I want relief.**

   Instructor: Nice. We have the third goal of this polarity. Tell it: "This goal has also been fulfilled!" Feel your statement as true.

   William: (nodding)

   Instructor: Good. Ask it: "Now that you have been secured and freed from your previous aversions, forever on, is there anything more that you would like to avoid at this moment, which is even more important?"

   William: **I'm not the culprit. I want my parents to accept that I'm not guilty.**

   Instructor: OK. That's the third aversion. Tell the polarity: "You are completely secure and free from this aversion too, from now on!" Feel your statement as true.

   William: (nodding)

   b) *(Identification with polarity)*

   Instructor: Enter the polarity. Identify with it. Feel its being.

   William: (nodding)

Instructor: From its point of view, feel its third goal: "I want relief."

William: (nodding)

Instructor: Feel the Temporary I from which vantage point you, as that entity, are experiencing that goal. Do the Dissolving technique.

William: Done.

Instructor: From its point of view, feel its third aversion: "I'm not the culprit. I want my parents to accept that I'm not guilty."

Instructor: Feel the Temporary I from which vantage point you, as that entity, are experiencing the aversion. Do the Dissolving technique.

William: OK.

(Fourth circle)

13. *Instructor:* Very good. Now, return again to your I, here and now. Check if you have any thought, emotion or sensation.

    William: **Nothing.**

    Instructor: Anyway, feel your "temporary I." Where is your I located?

    William: **It's in the upper part of the chest.**

    Instructor: OK. Do the Dissolving technique.

    William: (after some time, nodding)

14. *(Dealing again with the **first polarity** through communication and identification)*

    a) *(Communication with polarity)*

       Instructor: Now focus again on your first polarity. Look at it from here and now. Tell me about its qualities and location at this moment.

William: **It's a yellow ball still, and center of the ball is in my heart now.**

Instructor: OK. Ask it: "Now, having your previous goals fulfilled, what do you want at this moment, which is even more valuable?"

William: **I need love and attention from my parents...**

Instructor: This is the fourth goal. Tell the polarity: "This goal has also been fulfilled!" Feel your statement as true.

William: (nodding)

Instructor: OK. Ask it: "Now, since you have been secured and freed from all your previous aversions, forever on, is there anything more that you would like to avoid at this moment and which is even more important?"

William: (after a while) **Actually, I can't find anything.**

Instructor: OK, it's not a problem, don't force too much. If there is no content, we are skipping this step.

William: (nodding)

b) *(Identification with polarity)*

Instructor: Now, enter the polarity again. Identify with it. Feel its being.

William: (nodding)

Instructor: From its point of view, feel its fourth goal: "I need love and attention from my parents."

William: (nodding)

Instructor: Feel the Temporary I from which vantage point you, as that entity, are experiencing the goal. Do the Dissolving technique.

William: Done it.

15. *(Dealing again with the **second polarity** through communication and identification)*

    a) *(Communication with polarity)*

        Instructor: Focus again on your second polarity, **the other's guilt**. Look at it from here and now. Tell me about its qualities and location at this moment.

        William: **Now, the ball is yellow and it's in the center of my chest.**

        Instructor: Ask it: "Now, having all your previous goals fulfilled, what do you want at this moment, which is even more valuable?"

        William: **I just want my parents to love me.**

        Instructor: Great. This is the fourth goal of this polarity. Tell the polarity: "This goal has also been fulfilled!" Feel your statement as true.

        William: (nodding)

        Instructor: Ask it: "Now, since you have been secured and freed from all your previous aversions, forever on, is there anything more that you would like to avoid at this moment, which is even more important?"

        William: **There is no aversion anymore.**

        Instructor: That's OK. Good.

        William: (nodding)

    b) *(Identification with polarity)*

        Instructor: So, again, enter the polarity. Identify with it. Feel its being.

        William: (nodding)

        Instructor: From its point of view, feel its fourth goal: "I just want my parents to love me."

William: (nodding)

Instructor: Feel the Temporary I from which vantage point you, as that entity, are experiencing that goal. Do the Dissolving technique.

William: OK, I'm done.

(Fifth circle)

16. *Instructor:* Great. Return again to your I, here and now. Check if you have any thought, emotion or sensation.

    William: **Nothing again.**

    Instructor: However, feel your "temporary I." Where is your I located?

    William: **I'm centered right in my heart.**

    Instructor: Great. Do the Dissolving technique.

    William: (nodding)

17. *(Dealing again with the **first polarity** through communication and identification)*

    a) *(Communication with polarity)*

    Instructor: Now focus again on your first polarity. Look at it from here and now. Tell me about its qualities and location at this moment.

    William: **It's shiny white. It's in my heart.**

    Instructor: OK. Ask it: "Now, having your previous goals fulfilled, what do you want at this moment, which is even more valuable?"

    William: **Nothing. There is only a deep sense of peace.**

    Instructor: Are you sure?

    William: Absolutely.

Instructor: OK, ask it: "Now, since you have been secured and freed from all your previous aversions, forever on, is there anything more that you would like to avoid at this moment and which is even more important?"

William: **No, nothing. Only peace.**

Instructor: Great. You have integrated the first polarity.

William: Yes.

18. *(Dealing again with the **second polarity** through communication and identification)*

   a) *(Communication with polarity)*

   Instructor: Now, return your attention again to your second polarity, **the other's guilt**. Look at it from here and now. Tell me about its qualities and location at this moment.

   William: **The ball is white and shiny. It's also in the heart.**

   Instructor: Ask it: "Now, having your previous goals fulfilled, what do you want at this moment, which is even more valuable?"

   William: **Nothing but peace.**

   Instructor: Good. Are you sure that there are no more goals of this polarity?

   William: (*nodding*) Yes I am.

   Instructor: Let us check aversions. Ask it: "Now that you have been secured and freed from all your previous aversions, forever on, is there anything more that you would like to avoid at this moment, which is even more important?"

   William: **No aversions. Just peace.**

   Instructor: OK. Good. You have integrated the second polarity too.

William: This is great…

19. (**Merging/integrating** *the polarities.*)

Instructor: Yes, great. Now, invite both polarities to merge.

William: (nodding) They've merged. They are one.

Instructor: Invite that merged, unified entity to completely fill your body and your whole being with its delightful energy.

William: (nodding, after a while) Yes… I feel great. It's a serene feeling.

Instructor: Wonderful. Thank you. We did the whole process.

William: Thank you.

IT Worksheet: "My Guilt"

Circle #	Temporary I		Done?
	Location	Content	
1.	Somewhere inside my neck.	I was thinking about the effectiveness of this process. I'm not quite sure that we'll do something with any of this…	✓
2.	In my head.	I feel quite strange; I can't explain, but it's a nice feeling.	✓
3.	In my neck again.	N/A	✓
4.	In the upper part of the chest.	N/A	✓
5.	I'm centered right in my heart.	N/A	✓
6.	Merged!	N/A	✓

Figure 18: "Here and Now" Position

Circle #	First polarity					Done?
	Name	Qualities	Location	Goal	Aversion	
1.	My guilt	Dark red mass, doesn't have any particular shape, it's just a big messy thing… It's pretty old.	Inside and around my head and torso…	I'm guilty! I want to avoid a punishment!	I don't want to be punished.	✓
2.		It's brighter somehow, and it's smaller.	Encompasses my neck and chest.	I don't want to hurt anyone; I'll accept my guilt.	I want to hide from others' attention. They'll see my guilt.	✓
3.		Yellow ball.	Upper part of my chest.	I want to show to my parents that I'm a good boy.	I don't want to betray my parents' expectations.	✓
4.		Yellow ball.	The center of the ball is in my heart.	I need love and attention from my parents…	N/A	✓
5.		It's shiny white.	In my heart.	Nothing. There is only a deep sense of peace.	N/A	✓
6.	Merged!	N/A	N/A	N/A	N/A	✓

Figure 19: "First polarity" Position

Cir-cle #	Second polarity					
	Name	Qualities	Location	Goal	Aversion	Done?
1.	Other's guilt	A big brown ball, also old.	Encompasses my head and part of my chest.	I just want to hide my own guilt and accuse other people…	I have to avoid others to think that I'm the culprit.	✓
2.		The ball is much brighter.	The ball has moved toward the chest; its center is in my neck.	I want to punish the others for their mistakes.	I don't want injustice! I don't want others to pass without punishment.	✓
3.		The ball is yellowish now.	It's smaller and it's in the upper part of my chest.	I want relief.	I'm not the culprit. I want my parents to accept that I'm not guilty.	✓
4.		The ball is yellow.	It's in the center of my chest.	I just want my parents to love me.	N/A	✓
5.		The ball is white and shiny.	It's in the heart.	Nothing but peace.	N/A	✓
6.	Merged!	N/A	N/A	N/A	N/A	✓

Figure 20: "Second polarity" Position

Additional Remarks

After gaining some experience in this technique, it is a good idea to collect all your notes and worksheets from each process, scan through the goals and aversions that have been done and find if any of these were recurrent. Those are your *individual goals and aversions*, characteristic of your personality. Make a list of them and periodically pass through it using the Dissolving technique (DTI).

By doing this, you can more effectively cut through even the most rigid structures in your psyche, which will be reflected as a withdrawal from the most problematic people and situations in your life. You will also ease and accelerate the process of clearing up inner obstacles and fears.

It's worth noting that our personality is not simply a collection of many chains of goals. It is a network. All these goals and aversions are interconnected on many levels, and often in unexpected ways. So, by going frequently through your list of individual goals and aversions, you will be reducing and transforming that network of typically unpleasant experiences.

In a Nutshell

The Inner Triangle Technique

This technique is designed for solving complex and lasting problems, but its application is not limited to that.

The Inner Triangle is based on the concepts of Parts of Personality and Chain of Goals. You have to consider a problem that you are dealing with as a separate part of your being, while being aware that the part is an entity with a certain level of consciousness.

The technique consists of these steps:

1. Sit up straight, eyes closed or half-open, and relax.
2. Determine the location of your I, here and now.
3. Define the first polarity.
4. Define the second polarity.
5. Do the DTI on your I here and now.
6. Focus on your first polarity; ask it for its goal and aversion and imagine that the goal and aversion have been fulfilled. Do the DTI both for the goal and aversion.
7. Focus on your second polarity and do the same as in step 6.
8. Repeat steps 5 to 7 as long as you have any content at any step and until the polarities merge with each other and with you.

Chain Techniques

Although all the main techniques in the Reintegration System are based on the "Chain of Goals" concept, only the "Chain Techniques" are named after that concept. It's because the principle of moving down the symbolic chain is pronounced the most in these protocols. There is no inner triangle; you are focused only on the problem and its inner representation as a separate part of personality.

There are two approaches to choose between for releasing the goals—either through direct communication or identification with the parts and doing the DTI.

Depending on the complexity of the problem, the Single Chain or even Double Chain process could be significantly quicker than the Inner Triangle. Yet, if you have enough time for your work, I certainly recommend doing the complete Inner Triangle process.

Single Chain Technique

If you are short on time or having problems with the apparent complexity of the IT process at the beginning of your practice, you can do the simplest procedure focused on a single chain of goals. We can call it the *Single Chain* (SC) technique.

The procedure is simple—we are going up through the chain, focusing only on higher and higher goals:

1. Sit up straight, eyes closed or half-open, and relax.
2. Define the entity which is representing your problem.
3. Find the first goal of that entity and release it either through communication or identification.
4. Find higher and higher goals of the entity and release them subsequently, until the entity reaches its highest state.

On Figure 21 below you can see the symbolic illustration of the Single Chain process.

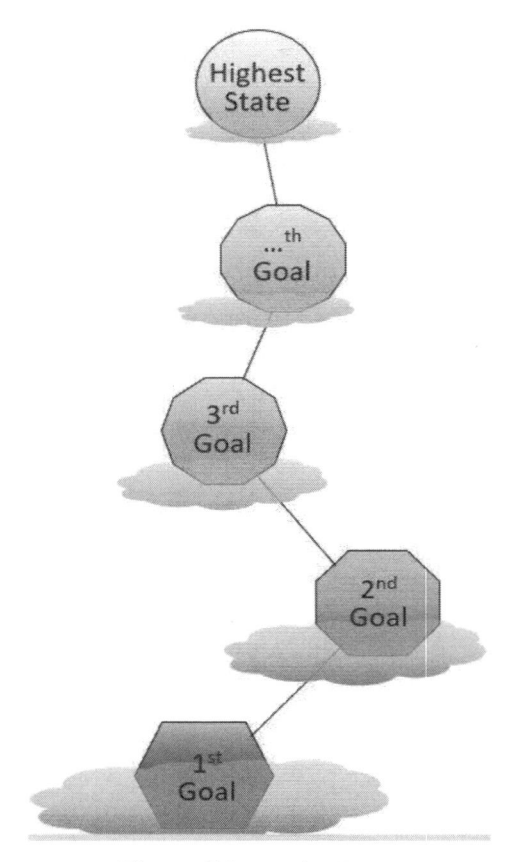

Figure 21: Single Chain

Here is a more detailed description of the procedure:

1. **Define the entity which is representing your problem:**
   Ask yourself: If that problem or state had distinct qualities, how would it be represented? Determine those qualities, such as color, shape, brightness, texture, sound, perhaps symbol and anything else you see or feel. Determine where it is located.

2. **Find the goal of that entity:**
   Either:

- Ask the entity: "What is the goal that you want to fulfill with this behavior?" Wait for an answer. When an answer comes, thank the entity and tell it: "Your goal has just been fulfilled!" Feel your statement as true.

Or, if you prefer:
- Identify with the entity, see through its "eyes." Ask yourself: "What is my goal at this moment?" Do the DTI on that goal.

3. **Find the next goal of the entity:**
   Either:
   - Ask the entity: "Now that the previous goal(s) is/are fulfilled, what is your next most valuable goal that you want to fulfill?" Wait for an answer. When the answer comes, thank the entity and tell it: "This goal has also been fulfilled!" Feel your statement as true.

   Or, if you prefer:
   - Identify with the entity; see through its "eyes." Ask yourself: "Having realized my previous goal(s), what is my next goal at this moment, which is even more valuable?" Do the DTI on that goal.

4. **Find higher and higher goals of the entity and release them subsequently, until the entity reaches its highest state.**

It is advisable to write down every answer.

Note that through expressing its goals within the Single Chain procedure, the entity can actually express both desires (inclinations) and fears (aversions).

The empty worksheet for the Single Chain technique you can find in the Appendix III.

Real-Life Example

After a few years of developing and practicing Reintegration techniques, I shared them via email with one of my friends who needed some help, but didn't have money for any qualified assistance at that time. For our purposes, we will call him Dario. He had a problem with the repetitive appearance of a person (actually a different person in different periods) who was causing him trouble, pressing or even persecuting him in some way. The person would usually bully, threaten and ridicule him in high school, after that at university and, when he graduated, also at work. Whenever one such person disappeared, another would appear very soon, acting similarly to the previous one. It seemed to him that it was a never-ending circle.

Dario was not in a position to ask for assistance from a trained instructor, so he decided to deal with this problem alone, at home. In his letter, he described the process which was extremely successful in the end. (The Worksheet from this process is shown in Figure 22.)

"...I became acutely aware of this problem fairly recently, a year ago, although the very problem had existed for almost fifteen years. I dealt with it using many techniques, but to no avail.

When I finished reading your working material, I assumed that the Single Chain technique would be the best option for me, especially due to limitations in my closest environment—I have a job with many commitments and a family with really demanding children (and wife☺). I succeeded in isolating myself from all of this for a half an hour, did the SC procedure and the result was astonishing to me—the Persecutor has never, never again returned to my life! I know that the problem has been definitely solved because I feel it. It's such a relief!

It was a very emotional and even dramatic process. I relaxed and recalled a few pretty traumatic characteristic situations in which one of the persecutors was involved. I asked myself: "How would the Persecutor in my life generally be represented? How would he look and what would be his characteristics?"

I got the picture of a demon in front of me. It (or he) was pretty scary! The red-blackish being with long ears and horns was ominously staring at me. At that moment, I decided to just communicate with him, feeling that I wouldn't be brave enough to identify every time with that being and do the DTI for each goal. I greeted him with respect which didn't please him though.

After asking the question of what was his goal he answered very clearly:

— I want blood, revenge!

It was a harsh answer, but I wasn't surprised, since I knew that it's very common to get really menacing or offending responses at the beginning of the process. I thanked him and informed him that his goal had been fulfilled. I even imagined blood in my mind and felt that he had his revenge for everything. Then I continued calmly with the next question, seeking for his higher goal. It was immediate and striking:

— I want you to finally realize through pain that you must release love from your heart!

Emotions were flooding me. Some pictures had appeared in my mind with my not-so-good behavior to others. Maybe that influenced the next answer:

— I want you to realize how the others feel when you are retaliating, when you are cold, when you are tormenting them somehow!

I felt that. Maybe for the first time, I deeply regretted some things I'd done that I never thought I should regret for. Then it continued with sobering responses to my continued questions.

— I want you to be happy through love. I want you to forgive others. When you are not forgiving someone, you are suffocating him.

— I am that which has been unforgiven.

I was stunned. I would always remember this statement. I had never forgiven some people before and here was the result, in front of me. Still staring at me, although somehow softer now. Then he continued with unforgettable advice, after each question.

— Don't expect too much from others.

- I want you to realize that you are not better than others, not above others; I want you to ground yourself to earth.
- There is no need to fear others. They are the same as you. Don't oppose them, don't compete. Open your heart to them.
- I am actually a spirit—an angel who is helping you in your life.

In front of my "inner eyes," the creature transformed into a beautiful white angel with wings! I was completely overwhelmed by energy; my body was engulfed by shimmering light. A wonderful, astonishing experience. Eventually, I continued to ask questions to this transformed being.

- I want love and freedom. Love will liberate you. I want you to return to God.

He wants the best possible ending for me...

- I want you to return to God.

... And he wants the same outcome for himself as well.

- Peace.

This was the end of the process, without any doubt. Nothing was left except deep, blissful peace.

Since then, my life has really changed. Not only have I never again met any person with that role of persecutor toward me, but I also have learned so many things in this unforgettable interaction with that angel. Of course, there are still people or situations in my life that seem to me unpleasant in some way, but I look at them completely differently—they are my best teachers, they are always precisely pointing at me as the source of every unpleasant (and pleasant) experience. Now I definitely know that I am the creator of my own reality!

I keep using these techniques at home. The processes done after this one were, more or less, softer, lighter, and even faster. Maybe because I now often use the complete IT procedure, always with DTI *basic technique which relieves a lot of emotional charge immediately. Maybe the new layers of my personality now are not so acute and charged with emotions, so it's becoming easier and easier. I don't know. But surely this first process was a kind of real breakthrough. (...)"*

SC Worksheet: Persecutor

Circle #	Name	Qualities & Location	Goal	Done?
1.	Perse-cutor	A demon in front of me - the red-blackish being with long ears and horns	I want blood, revenge!	✓
2.			I want you to finally realize through pain that you must release love from your heart!	✓
3.			I want you to realize how the others feel when you are retaliating, when you are cold, when you are tormenting them somehow!	✓
4.			I want you to be happy through love. I want you to forgive others. When you don't forgive someone, you are suffocating him.	✓
5.			I am that which has been unforgiven.	✓
6.			Don't expect too much from others.	✓
7.			I want you to realize that you are not better than others, not above others; I want you to ground yourself to earth.	✓
8.			There is no need to fear others. They are the same with you. Don't oppose them, don't compete. Open your heart to them.	✓
9.		A beautiful white angel with wings	I am actually a spirit – an angel who is helping you in your life.	✓
10.			I want love and freedom. Love will liberate you. I want you to return to God.	✓
11.			I want you to return to God.	✓
12.			Peace.	✓

Figure 22: Single Chain Worksheet (Real-Life Example)

Double Chain Technique

There is also another form of Chain Technique, a form in which we are asking the part both for its inclinations (desires) and aversions (fears). In this way, we are getting a double chain of corresponding inclinations and aversions in each step.

The procedure is simple: we will go up through the chain, focusing only on higher and higher goals:

1. Sit up straight, eyes closed or half-open, and relax.
2. Define the entity which is representing your problem.
3. Find the first inclination (preference or desire) of that entity and release it either through communication or identification.
4. Find its first aversion (or fear) and release it either through communication or identification.
5. Find higher and higher inclinations and aversions of the entity and release them subsequently, until the entity reaches its highest state.

You could use the detailed description of the Single Chain procedure for this technique as well, replacing the word "goal" with "inclination" and adding one more similar step related to aversions and it looks like this:

1. Define the entity which is representing your problem:

Ask yourself: If that problem or state had distinct qualities how would it be represented? Determine those qualities, such as shape, color, brightness, texture, sound, perhaps symbol and anything else you see or feel. Determine where it is located.

2. Find an inclination of that entity:

Either:
- Ask the entity: "What do you want at this moment?" Wait for an answer. When the answer comes, thank the entity

and tell it: "Your goal has just been fulfilled!" Feel your statement as true.

Or, if you prefer:
- Identify with the entity; see through its "eyes." Ask yourself: "What do I want at this moment?" Do the DTI on that goal.

3. **Find an aversion of that entity:**

   Either:
   - Ask the entity: "What would you like to avoid at this moment?" Wait for an answer. When the answer comes, thank the entity and tell it: "You have been completely secured and freed from this aversion, from now on!" Feel your statement as true.

   Or, if you prefer:
   - Identify with the entity; see through its "eyes." Ask yourself: "What would I like to avoid at this moment?" Do the DTI on that aversion.

4. **Find the next inclination of the entity:**

   Either:
   - Ask the entity: "Now that the previous goal(s) is/are fulfilled, what do you want at this moment, which is even more valuable?" Wait for an answer. When the answer comes, thank the entity and tell it: "This goal has also been fulfilled!" Feel your statement as true.

   Or, if you prefer:
   - Identify with the entity; see through its "eyes." Ask yourself: "Having fulfilled my previous goal(s), what is my next goal at this moment, which is even more valuable?" Do the DTI on that goal.

5. **Find the next aversion of that entity:**

   Either:

- Ask the entity: "Now that you have been secured and freed from your previous aversion(s), forever on, is there anything which is even more important that you would like to avoid at this moment?" Wait for an answer. When the answer comes, thank the entity and tell it: "You are completely secure and free from this aversion too, from now on!" Feel your statement as true.

Or, if you prefer:
- Identify with the entity; see through its "eyes." Ask yourself: "Now that I've been secured and freed from my previous aversion(s), forever on, what else would I like to avoid at this moment, which is even more important?" Do the DTI on that aversion.

6. **Find higher and higher inclinations and aversions of the entity and release them subsequently, until the entity reaches its highest state.**

It is strongly recommended to write down every answer, since it is very difficult to remember all previous steps.

On Figure 23 below you can see the symbolic illustration of the Double Chain process.

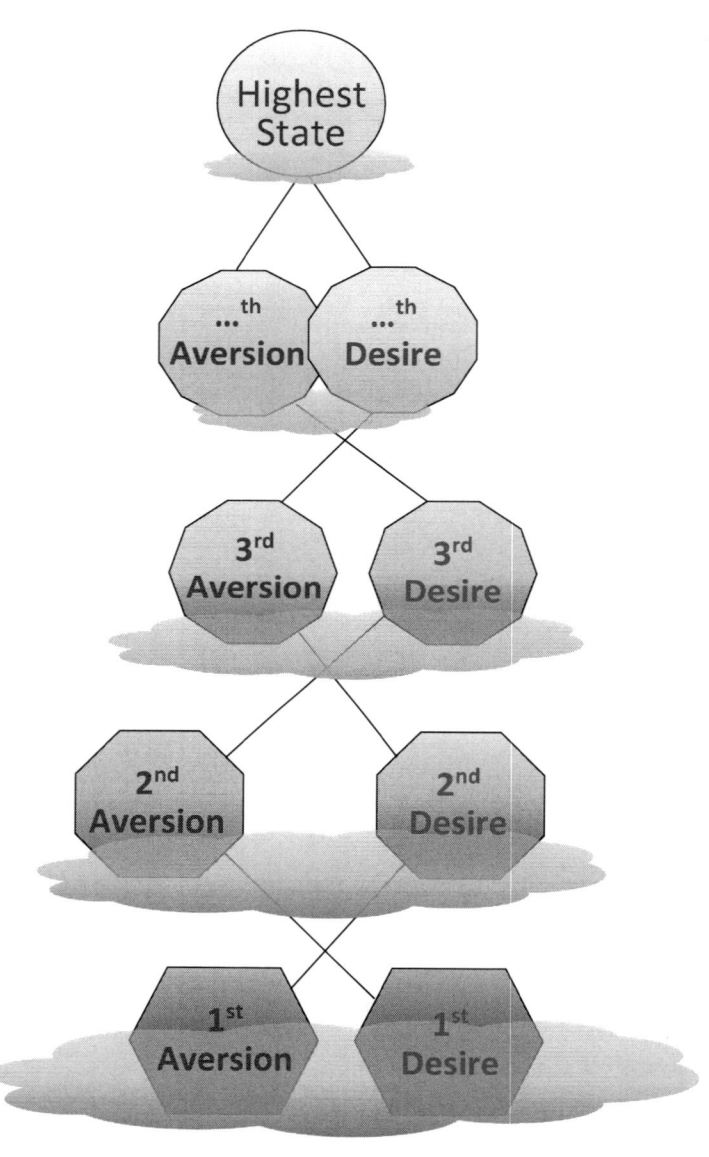

Figure 23: Double Chain

In a Nutshell
The Single Chain technique (SC)

This technique is also designed for solving complex and enduring difficulties, but its application is preferable only if one has limited time to work. Otherwise, the Inner Triangle is recommended. Depending on the problem and many other factors, the SC process might take somewhere between 15 and 30 minutes.

The technique consists of the following steps:

1. Sit up straight, eyes closed or half-open, and relax.
2. Define the entity which represents your problem.
3. Find the first goal of that entity and release it either through communication or identification.
4. Find higher and higher goals of the entity and release them subsequently, until the entity reaches its highest state.

The Double Chain technique (DC)

This technique is also designed for solving complex and enduring difficulties, but its application is preferable only if one has limited time to work. Otherwise, the Inner Triangle is recommended. Depending on the problem and many other factors, the DC process might take somewhere between 15 and 30 minutes.

The technique consists of the following steps:

1. Sit up straight, eyes closed or half-open, and relax.
2. Define the entity which represents your problem.
3. Find the first inclination (preference or desire) of the entity and release it either through communication or identification.
4. Find its first aversion (or fear) of the entity and release it either through communication or identification.
5. Find higher and higher inclinations and aversions of the entity and release them subsequently, until the entity reaches its highest state.

Convergence Procedure

It's reasonable to assume that one would only have to take care of the "negative" elements of their personality. However, in some cases we will inevitably have to deal with our "positive" parts as well. I put both words in quotation marks because sometimes something which seems "negative" to us actually turns out to be positive, and vice versa, so you can almost never definitively denote something as completely bad or good.

The elements of our personality which we consider to be "good" or "positive" are usually just the traits that we are most proud of (honesty, reliability, efficacy, decisiveness, perfectionism). Or, they could be other elements like beliefs ("People are inherently good," "God is just," "Life is good"), habits, decisions, desires, and so on.

These parts are indeed pushing us ahead in our lives (usually), yet it may happen that they are mutually incompatible or misaligned. That's the scenario when we have to harmonize them in order to solve or avoid problems.

One of the most effective approaches for that is the Convergence Procedure (CP), with which we harmonize our parts and converge them toward some mutual benefit.

In short, within this procedure you are using the "inner triangle" methodology again, but this time you are not trying to find the goals or aversions of both parts. Instead, you are basically asking each part why its purpose is being opposed by the other part. Then you are mutually harmonizing them by utilizing the DTI, MH and DTI+ protocols.

The first part in the Convergence Procedure is usually a trait, state, thing or anything we would like to accomplish or get. For instance, we have a goal to achieve wealth, but we haven't been successful in that yet. Meanwhile, we have concluded that its achievement is obstructed by one of our *positive* traits that we would certainly like to keep (for example, spiritual devotion). Our goal (wealth) would be the first part/polarity. The second part would be the spiritual devotion.

During the process, we will be mainly focused on the first part's purpose, and to change the second part in a way that it supports the first part's purpose. However, it often happens that the first part also has to be transformed to some extent, in order to get both of them aligned.

So, don't use the CP if you want to get rid of some problem, or to reintegrate some negative part of your personality. You have the Inner Triangle or Chain techniques for that purpose.

One more thing: it is common during the Convergence Procedure for some negative goals or aspects of your positive traits to appear. If that happens, you can pause the Convergence Procedure and do the Single Chain protocol on that part's negative aspect, starting from its concrete answer from which it expressed that "negativity" and proceeding normally with SC questions/answers format, until you lead that part to its highest state. Then you can continue with the CP protocol again.

Here is the detailed procedure:

1. Sit up straight, eyes closed or half-open, and relax.
2. Determine the location of **your Temporary I at this moment**. Do the DTI procedure on it.
3. Define clearly the part with which you intend to harmonize another part. It will be your **first part** (name, location, qualities).
4. Define clearly the part which apparently opposes your first part. It will be your **second part** (name, location, qualities).
5. **Work with the first part**:
    Either:
    i) Ask it: *"Why is the second part (state its name) obstructing the achievement of your purpose?"* Wait for an answer. Do the DTI on the answer.

Or, if you prefer:
ii) Identify with the part, see through its "eyes." Ask yourself: *"Why is the second part (state its name) obstructing the achievement of my purpose?"* Do the DTI on the answer.

6. **Work with the second part:**

    Either:
    i) *"Are you objecting to the purpose of the first part (state its name)?"* Wait for an answer.

    If the answer to this question is "yes," ask *"Why?"* Do the DTI on the answer. Then proceed to step 7.

    If the answer is *"no"* (i.e. no objections to the purpose of the first part), just proceed to step 7.

    Or, if you prefer:
    ii) Identify with the part, see through its "eyes." Ask yourself: *"Do I feel any objection to the purpose of the first part (state its name)?"* Wait for an answer emerging in your mind.

    If the answer to this question is *"yes,"* ask "Why?" When you get an answer, do the DTI and proceed to step 7.

    If the answer is *"no,"* just proceed to step 7.

(Next circle:)

7. Determine again the location of **your Temporary I at this moment**. Do the DTI.

8. **Work with the first part:**

    Either:
    i) *"Does the second part (state its name) fully support the achievement of your purpose?"* Wait for an answer.

    If the answer to this question is *"no,"* ask *"Why?"* and do the DTI on the answer that has emerged. Proceed to step 9.

If the answer is *"yes,"* just proceed to step 9.

Or, if you prefer:
ii) Identify with the first part, see through its "eyes." Ask yourself: *"Does the second part (state its name) fully support the achievement of my purpose?"* Wait for an answer to appear within your mind.

If the answer to this question is *"no,"* ask yourself *"Why?"* When you get an answer, do the DTI and proceed to step 9.

If the answer is *"yes,"* just proceed to step 9.

9. **Work with the second part**:

Either:
i) *"Do you fully support the purpose of the first part (state its name)?"* Wait for an answer.

If the answer to this question is *"no,"* ask *"Why?"* and do the DTI on the answer that has emerged. Proceed to step 10.

If the answer is *"yes,"* just proceed to step 10.

Or, if you prefer:
ii) Identify with the part, see through its "eyes." Ask yourself: *"Do I fully support the purpose of the first part (state its name)?"* Wait for an answer to appear within your mind.

If the answer to this question is *"no,"* ask yourself *"Why?"* When you get an answer, do the DTI and proceed to step 10.

If the answer is *"yes,"* just proceed to step 10.

10. **Repeat steps 7 to 9 until you find no inconsistencies between the parts.** Finally, determine once more the location of **your Temporary I at that moment.** Do the **DTI+ procedure** with this MH statement: *"I feel that all my parts fully*

support the purpose of the first part (state its name) and contribute to it."

Don't forget to write down all the answers and to thank the parts each time they give you an answer to your questions.

You can find a real-life example of this technique in the Part IV, page 282.

Additionally, you can find the empty form for doing the Convergence Procedure in the Appendix III.

In a Nutshell

Convergence Procedure

1. Sit up straight, eyes closed or half-open, and relax.
2. Do the DTI on your **Temporary I at this moment**.
3. Define the **first polarity**—a part of you which you want to harmonize another part with.
4. Define the **second polarity**—a part which you want to harmonize with the first one.
5. Get an answer from the **first part** on why the second part is obstructing the achievement of its purpose. Do the DTI on the answer.
6. Get an answer from the **second part** on whether it is objecting to the purpose of the first part. If the answer is affirmative, do the DTI on it.
7. Do the DTI on your **Temporary I at this moment**.
8. Get an answer from the **first part** on whether the second part fully supports the achievement of its purpose. If the answer is negative, do the DTI on it.
9. Get an answer from the **second part** on whether it fully supports the first part's purpose, or not. If the answer is negative, do the DTI on it.
10. **Repeat steps 7 to 9** until there is no inconsistency between parts. Then, find your Temporary I at that moment and do the **DTI+ procedure**, with this MH statement: *"I feel that all my parts fully support the purpose of the first part and contribute to it."*

Write down all the answers. Thank the parts each time they give you an answer to your questions.

Auxiliary Techniques

As with the basic techniques, I would strongly recommend that you learn and exercise these "auxiliary techniques," which could be of utmost importance to you during many parts of the Reintegration processes. You will be able to use them in your everyday life, with convenience.

Relaxation

For every main Reintegration procedure described in this book, the precondition is to completely relax the mind and body.

As long as you are using a relaxation technique which is effective for you and not overly complicated or time-consuming, it is fine for our purposes. However, as a preparation for various Reintegration techniques, my recommendation would be the following approach:

1. Sit up straight, eyes closed. If you are lying on a bed, open your eyes in order to not fall asleep. Focus on your breath. Slowly and deeply inhale through your nose, feeling the breath as it moves down to your abdomen. Reverse the process as you exhale through your mouth. Do this for 1 or 2 minutes.

2. Mentally scan your body. Notice how your body feels, starting at your toes and going up to your head, including face. Become aware of all places and body parts in which you feel tension, together with accompanying sensations. For every tense place pay close attention to your I-feeling (or Temporary I) which is experiencing that sensation and do the Dissolving the Temporary I (DTI) technique described previously.

This will be enough to get into a state of relaxation which will allow you to do more complex techniques.

Getting Answers from the Subconscious

You will probably encounter situations during your Reintegration work in which you will be confused or indecisive about what to do next. Perhaps you want additional information related to the process or mind content that you are dealing with. Perhaps you just need to be pointed in the right direction.

What can one do in that case? First, you should carefully contemplate the situation. If it doesn't take a lot of time, that's fine. But if you find yourself stuck in thinking, that's not promising for the whole process. Involving too much logical mind when you are actually facing your subconscious is not beneficial and will only block the natural flow of Reintegration.

The best way is to ask your subconscious. I personally use the ancient Chinese book "I Ching" (Book of Changes) for getting wise pieces of advice in the form of "hexagrams." But it requires a lot of time and effort to learn how to use that system and that's definitely beyond the scope of this book.

There are also ways to get quick answers from your subconscious, or more precisely, from your body as a kind of "conductor" for the answers. For that, I would recommend a technique called "Manual Muscle Testing."

However, I must warn you that these techniques for "asking the subconscious," including the Manual Muscle Testing, are *not* scientifically approved and they are *not* fully reliable. I only suggest them to you as an optional direction.

Manual Muscle Testing

Manual Muscle Testing (MMT) became popular relatively recently, when chiropractors and massage therapists discovered it. It is being used mostly in Applied Kinesiology (AK), as *"a technique in alternative medicine claimed to be able to diagnose illness or choose treatment by testing muscles for strength and weakness."*[18]

"A manual muscle test in AK is conducted by having the patient resist using the target muscle or muscle group while the practitioner applies a force. A smooth response is sometimes referred to as a "strong muscle" and a response that was not appropriate is sometimes called a "weak response." (...) These differences in muscle response are claimed to be indicative of various stresses and imbalances in the body."[19]

I will not go into an evaluation of the medical usefulness of Muscle Testing. In the Reintegration System we will use it only for the purpose of alleviating the decision-making process within some of the procedures presented here.

There are many varieties of MMT. I will describe two that I assume might be the easiest for a beginner, but you can certainly search the Internet and find the most appropriate method for you.

Method 1:

Relax. Do the Moving to the Heart (MH) technique. Once centered in the Heart, you will be able to access your vast subconscious information more easily. Then, focus your mind on an issue and ask your subconscious a simple question. For example: *"Is my liver healthy?"*

Use your fingers to form an 'OK' sign on both hands. Intertwine the loops formed by your index finger and thumb on each hand (see Figure 24). Try to sustain the loop of your non-dominant hand, while trying to break it with your dominant hand. All the while think of the question.

---

[18] Source: https://en.wikipedia.org/wiki/Applied_kinesiology
[19] Source: Ibid.

If you succeed in sustaining the connection of index finger and thumb in your non-dominant hand, then the answer is "yes." If you can't maintain the connection, then the answer is "no."

Don't hold your fingers too firmly. Find your individual "middle" force which is enough to sustain the OK sign in your non-dominant hand. Then, ask yourself some question for which the answer is obviously "yes," or state a true sentence aloud, like: "My name is ..." or "I was born on ..." Then, ask yourself a question with an obviously negative answer, for example "Was I born on Mars?" In this way, you will eventually get a sense of how strong the connection between the fingers should be in order to get reliable results. And then don't think about the firmness of the connection anymore, think only about the issue.

You have to practice a little bit if you want to master this technique enough to use it successfully.

Figure 24: Manual Muscle Testing, method 1

Method 2:

Relax. Do the MH technique. Focus on an issue and ask your subconscious to give you an answer that you are interested in.

Use the index finger of your dominant hand to test the strength of the index finger and thumb connection forming an okay sign on the non-dominant hand. Insert the index finger of your dominant hand into the okay sign (see Figure 25). Try to break the okay sign with the finger of your dominant hand, while you think of the issue.

If the okay sign doesn't break, then the answer is "yes." If it breaks, then the answer is "no."

Figure 25: Manual Muscle Testing, method 2

Some people might have a problem with determining which one is their dominant or non-dominant hand. If you are one of those, do some experiments, play with both combinations, while thinking both about "certainly positive" and "certainly negative" questions. If you are still uncertain, don't overthink it, just choose a dominant hand and keep practicing.

In a Nutshell
Relaxation

1. Focus on your breath. Slowly and deeply inhale through your nose, feeling the breath as it moves from down to your abdomen. As you exhale, feel the breath as it moves in opposite direction. Do this 1 to 2 minutes.
2. Mentally scan your body, starting from toes, going all the way up to your head. Become aware of places and body parts in which you feel tension. For every tense place pay close attention to your Temporary I which is experiencing that sensation and do the DTI.

Manual Muscle Testing

Method 1:

Focus your mind on a question. Intertwine the loops formed by your index finger and thumb on each hand. Try to sustain the loop of your non-dominant hand, while trying to break it with your dominant hand. All the while think of the question.

If you sustain the OK sign of your non-dominant hand, then the answer is "yes." If you can't maintain the connection, then the answer is "no."

Method 2:

Focus your mind on a question. Use the index finger of your dominant hand to test the strength of the index finger and thumb connection forming an OK sign on the non-dominant hand. Insert the index finger of your dominant hand into the OK sign. Try to break the OK sign with the finger of your dominant hand, while you think of the issue.

If the OK sign doesn't break, then the answer is "yes." If it breaks, then the answer is "no."

Part III
Personal Transformation

PART III: PERSONAL TRANSFORMATION

"Reality is that which when you stop believing in it, it doesn't go away." —
Philip K. Dick, Valis

What is reality? Does the out-there exist at all? What is the nature of our individual universe... and how do we transform it in a way that we want?

It's hard to give a definitive answer to these questions. We just don't know for certain. But there are some clues from modern physics, psychology and a few spiritual traditions we can follow in that quest.

Physics has gone through a huge paradigm transformation in the last one hundred years, starting from Einstein's Theory of Relativity, through the Quantum Theory, up to the recent groundbreaking advancements in the fields of String Theory and Cosmology.

Quantum Theory tells us that, at the microscopic level, everything becomes blurred and uncertain. Everything is possible, and given enough time, everything could and *will* happen. Thanks to the amazing Double Slit experiment, we have learned without any doubt that properties of an elementary particle will completely change depending on a conscious observer. There are fully valid interpretations of this theory which also predict that everything we don't see or feel by our senses just doesn't exist in a concrete form. It exists only as a potential reality full of infinite number of different possibilities. But when one pays attention to a part of that potential reality, the "wave function" of all these particles immediately collapses and only *one* of that infinite number of possibilities becomes true.

So, what we can learn from these mind-boggling advancements in science? It is this: we can change our individual universe and it depends on us *only*. While everything is possible, that possibility depends, again, on the conscious individual. The *holographic principle* teaches us what the real connection is between inner and outer reality; it is expressed in the 3rd postulate of the Reintegration System: *our external world is but a mirror of our inner being.* The very practical consequence is: *Everyone is completely responsible for their own life.*

Holographic Nature of Reality
"Reality is merely an illusion, albeit a very persistent one." — Albert Einstein

Holography is a photographic process which records, onto photographic film, the phases and amplitudes of light waves reflected from the object being captured. This photographic film is called *holographic*. Each point on the hologram receives light reflected from every part of the illuminated object and contains the complete visual record of the object as a whole.

The hologram itself is not an image and is apparently meaningless when observed by a human eye. But, thanks to interference patterns in it, when the hologram is suitably lit, it diffracts the light and in that way produces a virtual image. The resulting image appears in a complete three-dimensional form with highly realistic perspective effects (see Figure 26 below).

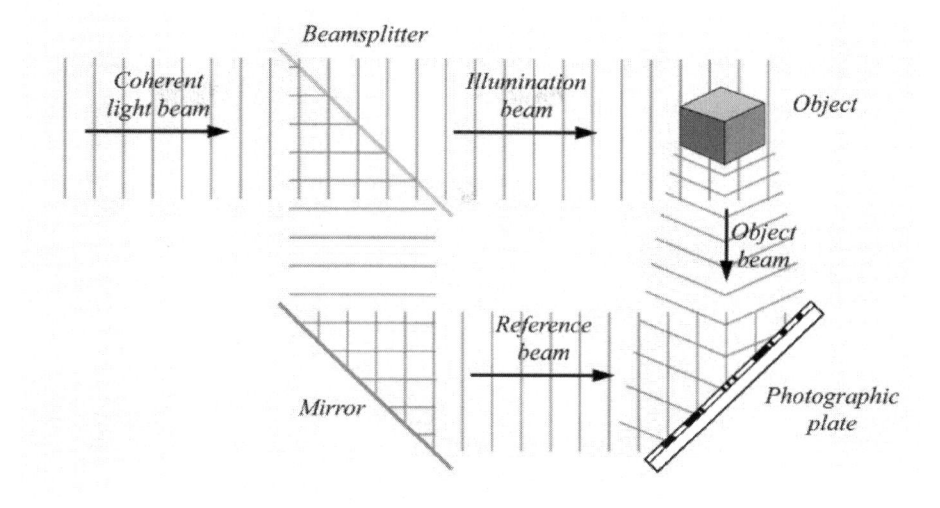

Figure 26: Recording a Hologram [20]

Each part of the hologram contains all the information about the complete whole. If the hologram is broken into several parts, and is again exposed to the laser beam, it does not give the parts of the object, but again, the same whole. If we continue with breaking these parts, they will still give the whole 3D picture.

For the purpose of clarifying ideas presented in this book, we will consider the hologram as an object whose elements have all the characteristics of the whole object, or all information about the object.

There is a theory in modern physics on the holographic nature of our universe. It has been derived directly from string theory and it proposes that the 3D universe we live in is but a holographic projection of a 2D surface at the periphery of the cosmos. Also, a very thorough and systematic picture of the holographic nature of our universe and practically everything in it, is shown in "The Holographic Universe," a book written by Michael Talbot. He lucidly expounds many details about the emerging holographic paradigm in

---

[20] Credit: Bob Mellish; source:
https://commons.wikimedia.org/wiki/File:Holograph-record.svg

quantum physics, neuroscience and several other realms of human experience.

If we consider the entire universe as a hologram, it means that every part of it has information about the entire whole: the cosmos. Consequently, every human being is a holographic component. Every piece of our reality, every unit which nature is rooted in space, time, matter and energy—that means every event, particle, atom, complex structure, life being, star, galaxy, anything—is part of the universal hologram and is itself a hologram.

Speaking this way, it is easy to conclude that, for example, each hexagram of the ancient Chinese "Book of Changes" (I Ching) is actually a holographic element in which the information on our individual universe is contained, at the moment of getting answers. Therefore, we could extract information about everything from any piece of it, if only we knew how to find it.

Usual understanding of space and time implies causal chain of events, something like the trajectory of balls on a pool table—if we know the path of the first ball, we know exactly the trajectory of another ball that was hit. However, science, which is itself mostly based on this understanding, came to the undeniable view that the causal links are not the only type of connection between events. Moreover, there is a much deeper, essential linkage between the elements of the universe. This interconnectedness of everything is based on the holographic principle, expressed through *synchronicity*.

Synchronicity is mostly revealed in *simultaneous* events which are in some way connected within our consciousness. It is a non-causal connection between two or more events. Let's say, somewhere far away from us something has happened to our relative, which we simply could not know about. At the same time, we have just noticed someone who reminded us of the relative, and we perceived that person in a way that we could connect with our relative, and also anticipate what has happened to her.

The meaning of the term "synchronicity" is mainly limited to a meaningful connection between events happening at the same or approximate point in time. I think that the notion of synchronicity should be viewed in a much broader context which is not bound by the simultaneity of events. There are many events whose meanings somehow predict other events, and from considerable time distance; two events that are not and cannot be each other's cause and effect. For example, it happens that in the dream we see an event in its symbolic form, and a few days later that very event happened. That is a kind of coincidence as well.

So, what is synchronicity? In short: a meaningful coincidence. There definitely are some events, non-causally linked, which for some observers still have in common some important traits and are similar or even identical.

The holographic principle is also expressed in the previously mentioned "Quantum entanglement" phenomenon, which shows that the two photons simultaneously change their spins, although they cannot physically "communicate."

The hologram is one of the keys to understanding not only the universe, but also our own spiritual growth. What is within us is around us, and vice versa. Change yourself and your individual reality will change as well. Everything that is characteristic of our lives—friends, foes, relationships, work, family—is in fact a projection of our inner, mostly unconscious, reality. If you have an external enemy, it means that you have some unintegrated part of your personality that you need to become aware of.

Thus the premise here for all our work is the principle of mirroring, i.e. our internal reality is mirrored in external reality (see Figure 27, that shows mirroring of beliefs and traits mostly).

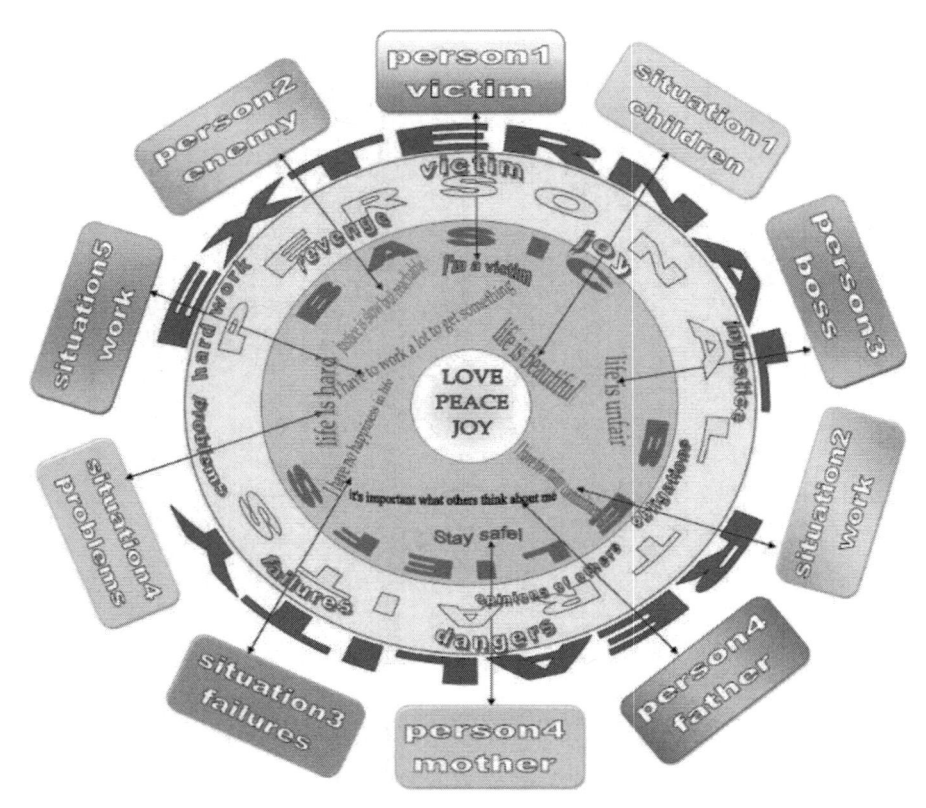

Figure 27: Symbolic and Simplified Display of an Example of Personal Reality

For example, there is a process of suppressing personality traits that happens to most all human beings during childhood, without exception. It takes place as part of our upbringing, learning the basics of unselfish and socially acceptable behavior. As toddlers, we behave inconsiderately on many occasions, in accordance with our basic needs—food, parental love, possessions, pain avoidance, playing, and so on. When a little child, for instance, sees an interesting toy in the hands of their brother or sister, they will try to grab the toy forcefully, with no consideration on other's needs. The parents then criticize the toddler for this unacceptable behavior, demanding the child stops doing anything like that.

Over time, the child will remember that this behavior is unfavorable to their basic need for parental love. They deliberately suppress the impulse for doing such a thing and thus, finally stop. But, the selfish impulse is not released. It is only moved into the subconscious level, from where it tries to continue its expressing.

The suppressed need always finds its way to express itself, because it's a question of its very existence as a distinct energetic entity. In this particular example, the need for taking desired things from others to fulfill one's own needs, first tries to emerge again as the child's concrete act. As the child has learned its lesson and deliberately suppresses the need all over again, this entity now tries to find a different path. It expresses itself through another person which acts exactly in accordance with the suppressed behavior, but this time toward the child. When the child grows up, the suppressed entity will continue expressing itself during the whole life of that individual. It will bring into his life people that act selfishly toward him, again and again. Doing this way, it just feeds itself up, trying only to survive.

All the suppressed needs, desires, fears, emotions and other parts of our personality, whether inhibited during one's childhood or any time later, express themselves either through various inner problems—psychic difficulties, bodily disabilities, illnesses, or through external people or circumstances.

Although meditation, by its nature, is the strongest propellant of one's personal or spiritual development, there are many other structured ways for working on one's personality. That work, of course, inevitably influences individual reality, so we could say that personal development within the Reintegration System covers both internal and external life.

Therefore, if we work on elements of our inner life, our external life will follow that, and this is the premise of this whole book. In the next section, we will see what the inner parts we should deal with are.

In a Nutshell
Holographic Nature of Reality

One of the basic axioms in the Reintegration System is the Holographic Principle, which essentially asserts: every piece of an entity contains all information on the entire entity. The totality mirrors in all of its parts and the parts are smaller versions of the totality itself.

Every human being perceives her or himself along with the external world, and that world is his or her individual universe. Every living being has its own specific individual universe.

In our everyday life, what we perceive as the external reality is our individual universe. Since we are part of it, we inherently have all information about it, in accordance with the Holographic Principle. Not only that, we are the source of it. Our individual universe is but a projection of ourselves. The outer world mirrors our inner realms. All our suppressed desires, fears, beliefs, decisions, dreams, thoughts, emotions, memories, hopes and everything else within us is being continuously externalized or projected onto the 3D reality show in which we are immersed our whole lives.

Our ultimate goal is to reach a state of lasting happiness. Buddhists would say that Nirvana, or freedom from suffering, is indeed possible. I also believe it is, but in order to achieve that we have to completely harmonize all our inner parts and reintegrate them into the whole, unified being. The outer world will reflect our inner harmony and the suffering will be gone forever.

There's only one catch: it's not an easy task at all. Yet, we have all the needed tools at our disposal, such as the Reintegration System, to help us along the way.

Main Elements of Personality to Work on

"One does not become enlightened by imagining figures of light, but by making the darkness conscious. The latter procedure, however, is disagreeable and therefore not popular." — C.G. Jung

Our areas of interest in this work depend primarily on the specific individual traits and the particular personality's structure, but generally speaking, it is advisable to cover these main elements of our personality:

- General aspects
- Habits
- Beliefs
- Decisions
- Traumas
- Emotions
- Fears
- Guilt
- Desires
- Traits

They are symbolically represented in Figure 28.

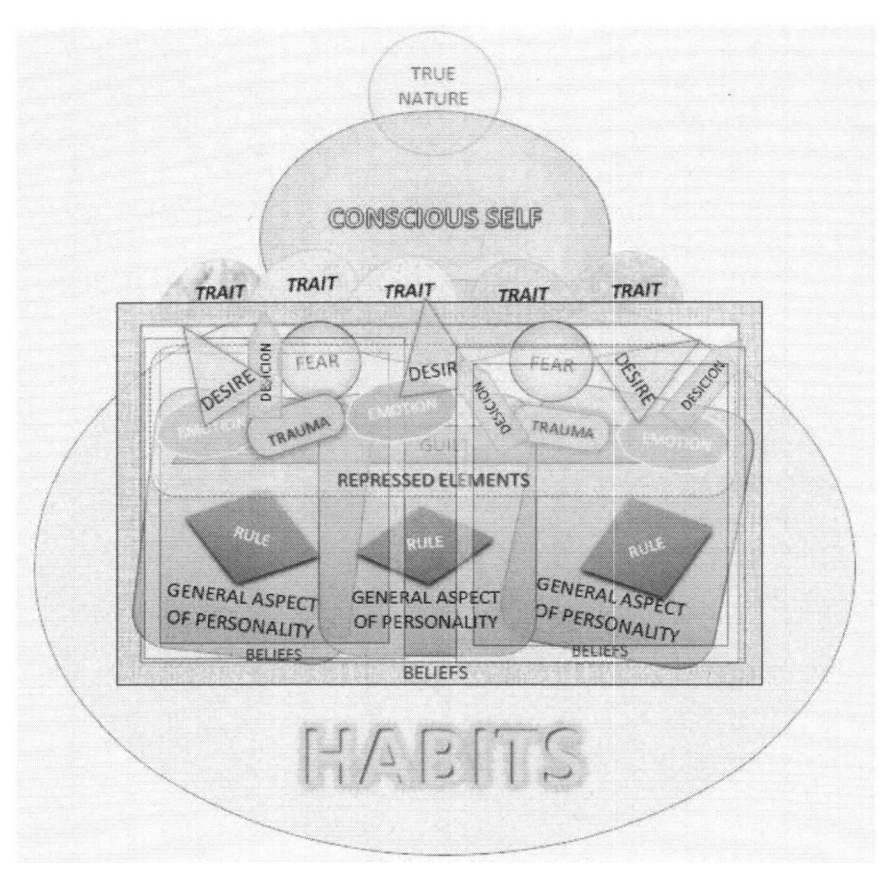

Figure 28: Symbolic Representation of the Structure of Personality

You may find that some of these parts are actually sub-sets of other, more general ones. We could classify, for example, our desires, fears and guilt under the umbrella of 'emotions', or we might instead assume that emotions are only part of traumatic memories, and beliefs are habitual thoughts backed by emotions, etc. Each could be right or wrong, depending on your point of view, but for our purposes I've tried to specify the main elements of personality according to practical reasons. To my knowledge and experience, these are simply the parts that we need to deal with the most.

There are many approaches out there for dealing with these intimate elements. Most predominantly, psychological and spiritual teachings are trying to *fight* these sub-entities of our being. Unfortunately, these unwanted behaviors naturally resist our attempts to destroy them, so they often persist no matter how hard you fight.

Our approach, though, is a benevolent one, so to speak, which is in accordance with the 4th postulate of the Reintegration System. This means that we *never fight* the unwanted elements of ourselves, but we *integrate* them instead. To be more precise, we *reintegrate* them, meaning that their intrinsic objectives have always been beneficial to us and we have only to lead them to find their positive purpose in our life again. In the Reintegration system, even if I were to state that an element would be 'removed', such a process would actually involve bringing it to its highest state: the Void or the Source of all that exist, rather than any type of banishment.

General Aspects of Personality

*"Keep your thoughts positive, because your thoughts become your words.
Keep your words positive, because your words become your behaviours.
Keep your behaviours positive, because your behaviours become your habits.
Keep your habits positive, because your habits become your values.
Keep your values positive, because your values become your destiny."*
— Gandhi

In our approach, we will consider one's personality to be able to be broken down into sub-personal entities, each of which deals with certain areas of a person's life. These sub-entities are unique to every person, but here are some common aspects that could help you in discerning your own personal aspects:

1. Family
2. Spirituality
3. Health
4. Finance
5. Career
6. Creativity
7. Relationship
8. Social
9. Rest
10. Fun

Each of these aspects of your identity is responsible for an important area of your life. For example, when you are dealing with family issues, you assume the specific identity appropriate for your family member role. If you are at work, you are taking on your identity as a boss, co-worker, or similar. So, when you are in the identity of a daughter, your behavior is pretty different from your identity as a boss.

Also, always take into consideration your self-image, or what you picture about yourself. It has the ability to pose a great obstacle to your personality's coherence and to your spiritual growth in general, so it is important. You can deal with this picture directly, or you could add it to your list of your most important general aspects.

If you can, try to consider all these general aspects as half-conscious entities, which you will have to harmonize together in order to live happily ever after. Let me be honest with you: it's not a simple task. I am still in the process of doing so myself. These general parts of personality are often complex and inhomogeneous, but we will have to do our best to reconcile them as much as possible anyway.

All *elements* of personality other than general aspects (habits, beliefs, decisions, emotions, traumatic memories, fears, accusations, desires and personal traits) are also *parts* of personality, just in a more specific form.

So: what do you have to do in order to harmonize the general parts as much as possible?

First, define what each general aspect really means to you. For example, what does the aspect "relationship" mean to you? Is that a romantic aspect of the relationship with your spouse or current girlfriend or boyfriend? Or is it maybe your romance with a secret mistress or wooer?

Or, what is the meaning of your "career"? Do you have a hidden desire to change your job? Does "career" specifically mean your current job or is it actually a more general term for a career, both the current and a possible future job?

You must be completely honest with yourself, as you are working on your most intimate things in your life.

Next, examine the mutual coherence between the general aspects. Create an "Assessment List of Mutual Coherence of General Aspects" chart, as seen on the next page, by assigning a value between 0 and 5 for every relationship between the aspects. While doing this, don't overthink it; just write the numbers as you feel them at the moment. Once you have your Assessment list done, you will have enough information to begin the subsequent reintegration work.

Since these general aspects of personality are relatively large, complex sub-structures, it is not advisable to employ the Inner Triangle or Chain techniques on them. Doing so might merge their polar aspects, yes, but we seek to harmonize these big parts of our life, not merge them... at least for the beginning of this journey.

Instead, I recommend that you use the Convergence Procedure as many times as possible. In my experience, it is most appropriate for harmonization.

You can see on the next page the list (Figure 29) made by Anna, one of my friends. The empty list suitable for your work you can find in the Appendix III.

Assessment List of Mutual Coherence of General Aspects (example)

Nr	Aspect	Support to other aspects	Family 36	Spirituality 29	Health 34	Finance 25	Career 31	Creativity 32	Relationship 34	Social 35	Rest 28	Fun 30
			\multicolumn{10}{c	}{Support from other aspects}
1.	Family	21	x	2	3	1	4	2	3	2	2	2
2.	Spirituality	43	5	x	4	4	5	5	5	5	5	5
3.	Health	45	5	5	x	5	5	5	5	5	5	5
4.	Finance	42	5	5	5	x	2	5	5	5	5	5
5.	Career	10	2	0	1	2	x	0	1	4	0	0
6.	Creativity	43	5	5	5	5	3	x	5	5	5	5
7.	Relationship	31	4	3	5	2	3	5	x	4	3	2
8.	Social	17	4	1	1	1	4	1	2	x	0	3
9.	Rest	34	5	5	5	2	3	5	4	2	x	3
10.	Fun	28	1	3	5	3	2	4	4	3	3	x

Figure 29

Marked are the lowest values, requiring immediate attention.

Anna's most problematic areas are Finance, the area least supported by the other life fields, as well as Career and Social, the areas the least supportive of other fields of her life.

There is also the *Wheel of Life*, an interesting and useful symbolic scheme which shows the general aspects of one's personality and their present status in a different way.

Below you can see a concrete example of the Wheel of Life, made by Anna (Figure 30).

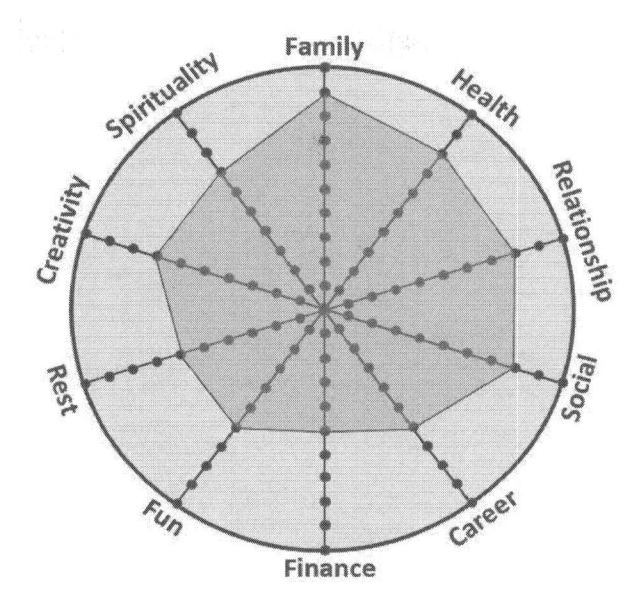

Figure 30: Wheel of Life (example)

Anna had actually created her Wheel of Life before completing the Assessment List for General Aspects. This ended up being useful, because it showed that the results of her gut feeling (regarding the main areas exhibited in the Wheel of Life) were almost identical to the results of the more thorough assessment list.

Habits

"Sow a thought, and you reap an act;
Sow an act, and you reap a habit;
Sow a habit, and you reap a character;
Sow a character, and you reap a destiny."
— Samuel Smiles

In their nature, habits are something different from other parts of personality. They are patterns through which the parts of personality and corresponding behaviors are being expressed.

In his great book "The Power of Habit: Why We Do What We Do, and How to Change," Charles Duhigg reveals the details about the scientific research that has led to a very important discovery: the so-called Habit loop (Figure 31).

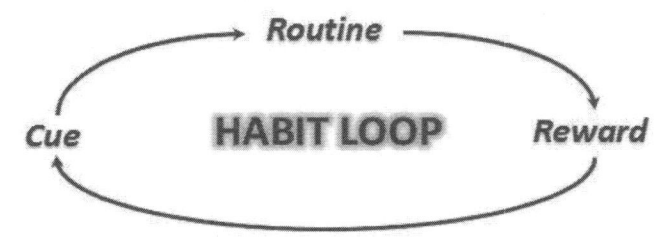

Figure 31: Habit Loop

Every habit has three components: a cue (trigger), routine and reward.

A cue is anything that triggers the habitual routine. There are five types of cues:

- Location (when you get to a particular place, the habit is triggered),
- Time (the habit is activated at a particular time of the day),
- Emotional state (for example, if one feels depressed, the habit of overeating is initiated),
- Other people (the habit is triggered if you find yourself in the presence of a particular person),
- Immediately preceding action (a specific action done by you or another person which then triggers the habit).

If the routine brings a concrete reward to the person, it could be repeated. In that case, it would continue to repeat and reaffirm itself due to some sort of reward at the end.

The reward is usually an inner state of contentment or relief that comes through the routine itself, but can also be an external pleasant event or thing.

For instance, let's say a particular alcoholic is triggered to have a drink by his inner feelings of loneliness, depression, or other kinds of negative emotions. An urge for relief appears at an often subconscious level. Initially, heavy drinking seems successful in its role as a depression-suppressor. Over time, his mind is trained to believe that alcohol brings the reward of defeating or forgetting the negative state of mind. The urge for a temporary relief has been satisfied. Heavy drinking then becomes a routine, reinforcing itself by getting a temporary reward again and again, despite the unpleasant and harmful mental or physical consequences afterwards.

In a way, every element of our psyche is a kind of habit. They are each being triggered by some internal or external cue, then run as a usual behavior, and, in the end, we get some kind of reward. So, it would be difficult to transform or remove any element of personality whatsoever, without first getting into the nature of habits themselves.

How is it possible to stop a negative habit, or change it into a beneficial one?

In Duhigg's book, the results of his research show that habits are very difficult to remove—if not impossible—due to the neurological pathways that each habit establishes. Supposedly, these paths can't be eliminated, so the corresponding habits can't be, either. They can only be changed.

Duhigg points out: *"How do habits change? There is, unfortunately, no specific set of steps guaranteed to work for every person. We know that a habit cannot be eradicated—it must, instead, be replaced. And we know that habits are most malleable when the Golden Rule of habit change is applied: If we keep the same cue and the same reward, a new routine can be inserted."*

In accordance with Duhigg's conclusions, the path for replacing habits is to determine all three elements of the habit's loop, and then to replace the routine. Here is the procedure:

1. Identify the routine. What's the thing you want to work on?

2. Identify the reward. As the reward creates an urge or craving which drives the routine, you should try to feel and determine the root urge and, based on that, isolate the reward.

You must be meticulously careful in this process, because you could easily delude yourself and come to a wrong conclusion. Test each of your assumptions on a potential reward. Try out each reward in real life a few times and honestly examine whether you still feel the urge for that routine or not. If you do, that's not the real reward, so try something else. As Duhigg says, "the reward *does* propel the habit only if you do not feel the urge to do the routine anymore."

3. Identify the cue (trigger). To do this, examine which of five possible types this particular trigger belongs to. Once you isolate its type, use corresponding questions to get more information:

- Location: ask yourself *"Where am I?"*
- Time: *"What time is it?"*
- Emotional state: *"In which emotional state am I?"*
- Other people: *"Who else is here?"*
- Immediately preceding action: *"Which action directly preceded the need?"*

4. Make a plan for changing the habit. Which positive routine could replace the existing unwanted one?

However, there are additional ways to deal with habits which—I might dare to say—can remove them completely.

First, I would recommend that you make a list of all your habits, especially the unwanted ones. That list should include information on the cue, routine and reward for each habit. We will call it *the list of habit loops*.

You may take a look at such a list created by Marta, one of my acquaintances. She had a lot of self-destructive habits, and she spent some time trying to determine all the elements of the habit loops (see Figure 32).

Habit	Cue	Routine	Reward
Overeating	*(Multiple cue)* - *Emotional state:* feeling depressed or disappointed - *Immediately preceding action:* being criticized by an authority	Overeating	Temporary relief
Internet addiction	- *Emotional state:* boredom	Spending hours on the Internet	Temporary pleasure
Social isolation	*(Multiple cue)* - *Emotional state:* fear of spotlight - *Time:* at weekends	Staying home all day long	Provisional security
Over-working	*(Multiple cue)* - *Location:* at work - *Emotional state:* feeling unworthy - *Time:* during work hours	Overworking	Feeling worthy
Laziness	- *Emotional state:* feeling overwhelmed with duties	Always procrastinate	Temporary relief
Always late	- *Emotional state:* feeling neglected	Always getting late to work or meetings	Getting attention
Poor sleep habits	- *Emotional state:* feeling inadequate	Too much sleep; irregular sleep patterns	Avoiding responsibility

Figure 32: List of Habit Loops (example)

Note that some of her habits were triggered by more than one cue.

Now, if you really want to erase a habit, you must remove all three components—cue, routine and reward. What should you do with each component? Here is my recommendation:

- *Cue:* Describe each trigger with a more detailed spectrum of concrete content. Do an appropriate Reintegration technique in order to transform it completely—Dissolving the Temporary I (DTI), Single or Double Chain (SC/DC), or the Inner Triangle (IT) technique.

  Generally, the IT works best on these types of cues: emotional states and other people; and the DTI on: immediately preceding action, location and time. If you do the Inner Triangle, it is the good opportunity to *couple the cue with the reward as two polarities* in the process.

- *Routine:* First, treat it in your mind with the Gentle Touch of Presence (GTP) technique; then, if possible, exercise the routine multiple times in real life mindfully, and for this you could use the Freshness & Acceptance (FA) technique.

  Essentially, this is the same work as suggested in the "Mindfulness" section. In this way, you are not only overcoming the bad habits, you are *using* them as portals to living more mindful, conscious life.

- *Reward:* Since your reward is usually an emotional state, the best solution is to do the Inner Triangle (with coupling it with the cue, if possible), or Single or Double Chain technique. Of course, you can always try using the DTI instead.

In one of his TED talks[21], psychiatrist Judson Brewer suggests that mindfulness can help us to break bad habits. Brewer describes an interesting idea in which you simply become curious and aware of

---

21

https://www.ted.com/talks/judson_brewer_a_simple_way_to_break_a_bad_habit/transcript

your own routines. *"Notice the urge, get curious, feel the joy of letting go and repeat,"* he said. (You may notice that, in essence, this approach corresponds to our FA basic technique.)

One participant at the TED talk who was smoking was told, *"Go ahead and smoke, just be really curious about what it's like when you do."* After that, she said, *"Mindful smoking: smells like stinky cheese and tastes like chemicals, YUCK!"*

Anyway, the sheer power of the previous habit's inertia sometimes is so strong that the habit eventually reemerges.

Related to that, Charles Duhigg adds another vital clue to this subject: *"But that ('the Golden Rule of habit change') is not enough. For a habit to stay changed, people must believe change is possible. And most often, that belief only emerges with the help of a group."*

This leads us to the next vital element of our personality—the beliefs.

Beliefs

"You are given the gifts of the gods: you create your reality according to your beliefs. Yours is the creative energy that makes your world. There are no limitations to the self except those you believe in." — Seth (As channeled by Jane Roberts) in *"The Nature of Personal Reality"*

Beliefs are of the utmost importance in a person's life and experiences. They shape one's life, especially the core beliefs, which are mostly subconscious.

For example, a person finally manages to achieve all her main life goals, and is ecstatic because of that. But, instead of having a long period of happiness and contentment, she continues to face various difficulties exactly as happened regularly in her life before the success. What is the reason? Perhaps the person has some deeply ingrained limiting beliefs like "Life is a constant battle," "Life is full of problems" or similar, which spoil all her accomplishments. She may also have a few subconscious decisions made in her early childhood about life, like that no matter how hard she tries, she 'will never succeed' in reaching a state of permanent satisfaction.

"Beliefs are like the frame of a picture. The experiential frame so to speak. When you are convinced that you are not good enough, your experience will take place somewhere within this area."[22]

In a way, beliefs are the centers of gravity for our overall behavior, and for our way of perceiving the world, thinking and experiencing emotions.

If you do not change your framework or core beliefs, any positive thing you achieve may be followed by a negative experience, in order to keep the "balance" stipulated by your existing framework of beliefs.

There are so many examples of this, such as when people win the lottery and then go on to misspend the money in a short time, or have some unexpected serious difficulties which ruin their lives. The reason is clear: they achieved an important goal, but since they did not transform their core beliefs, the level of their happiness in life stayed the same, on average. It's a self-fulfilling prophecy.

Most of our beliefs are formed in childhood, when we are extremely receptive and obedient to our parents' views. These beliefs are further self-strengthened until they become real powers that limit or defeat our potential achievements.

For instance, if a person believes she's a bad public speaker, before a presentation she will get shaky in front of the crowd and will spoil her performance. The failure in that presentation then reinforces her belief that she's a bad presenter. Even if her performance is later successful, her belief will make her feel she failed. This "feedback" always reinforces the existing belief and it will lead to more "supporting evidence."

---

[22] Citation: Ighisan, Mircea. WOW! how to create new realities. Matrix Transformation. Kindle Edition. 2012

Another example of a negative, self-reinforcing belief is the assumed fact that people start to lose their memory as they get older as a natural, unavoidable part of aging. This belief acts as a self-fulfilling prophecy. The more you believe it, the more you will behave in line with your belief, and the accuracy of your belief becomes apparent. Researchers have already proven that you can continue to become more intelligent and attentive if you use your mind extensively as you get older (barring disease or some other, unnatural contributor of course).

This is the reason why there is a saying: "Whatever you believe in, you are right." Your life experience will always support the underlying beliefs.

However, beliefs can work for both good and bad. Although we focus mostly on bad experiences and remember them more vividly, we definitely have many good aspects of our life and a lot of pleasant experiences. The reason for them does not solely lie in our casual acting from the core of our being, from the Presence, but also in the many positive beliefs we keep in our subconscious.

Beliefs are our little truths about everything. They are usually supported by underlying emotions, so they become very strong mental habits. Beliefs are often manifested as recurring thoughts (often together with emotions) on a particular subject.

Every belief has these characteristics:
1. Mental—our thoughts about something, what we believe to be true,
2. Emotional—an underlying background of emotions closely tied to the thought pattern, sometimes completely hidden from our conscious mind,
3. Habitual—recurring thoughts and emotions which are deeply rooted in our behavior.

Of course, if we want to be effective in our work, which we certainly do, we should deal with all three components of a belief.

We have two options to do so:
- *Remove* a negative belief,
- *Change* it into a positive one.

If we want to eliminate a belief, we will have to remove all three aspects, which will take a lot of effort and repetition. We would need to 1) *remove* the mental characteristics of the belief, e.g. thoughts and mental pictures; 2) *clear up* all the emotional background of it and, finally, 3) *abandon* the habitual pattern in which the repetitive thoughts have been occurring, or *assign* the pattern to some other behavior.

On the other hand, if we would like to turn a negative belief into a positive one, we should 1) *modify* the thought pattern; 2) *convert* the emotional background of it and, finally, 3) *change* the habitual pattern.

To achieve this, we have two very effective techniques within the Reintegration System: Replacing Beliefs and Dismantling Beliefs.

Replacing Beliefs

The Replacing Beliefs (RB) technique is simple, and basically involves applying the DTI+ to a negative belief. But before that, I recommend printing out and reading the list of most common beliefs (you find it can find it in the Appendix II). Circle those that you think are yours as well. Add other beliefs you think are characteristic for you. This will enable you to make your individual list of limiting/defeating (negative) beliefs.

If you are not sure whether you have a particular belief or not, just say it aloud to yourself and try to feel it. If you have some emotional feedback, either pleasant or unpleasant, you definitely have that belief.

In your search for hidden beliefs, for example, you may also ask yourself: "What is being selfish for me?" Is it to have a lot of money? Is it selfish to love yourself? Or to take time for yourself?

Each "Yes," backed with a sort of emotional feedback, means a serious self-defeating belief! If you really believe that it's selfish to love yourself, then your life is full of suffering. You are repeatedly punishing yourself on an unconscious level, and on a conscious level are wondering why that's happening to you again and again.

It is similar to a negative belief about money or about precious time just for yourself. That's the case with many other self-defeating beliefs and other detrimental aspects of your subconscious mind.

After creating your individual list, modify it by adding an opposite, positive belief next to each negative one in order to make pairs of opposite beliefs.

Once you have done that, you will be able to do the DTI+ on each negative belief from the whole list. If possible, pass through the list several times, as long as you feel any traces of negative beliefs in your psyche. For this purpose, I have created the RB Worksheet which can be found in the Appendix III.

Remember that you will have to be persistent and patient in this work. Beliefs are neither easily removable nor changeable because they are sort of mental and emotional habits. That's why it's important to go through the list as many times as possible.

Here you can find two parts of a real-life worksheet from a very extensive RB process done by one of my friends, Sean (Figure 33, Figure 34).

Temp. l Location	Beliefs — Negative Belief	Beliefs — Positive Belief	DTI+ Done?	Note
Neck	I must keep everything under control.	I let everything take its natural course.	✓	
Lower neck	Other people have power over me.	I am totally independent of the others.	✓	
Neck	I'm vulnerable.	I'm strong, sturdy and flexible.	✓	
Neck	The unknown is dangerous.	I love the unknown. The unknown is inspiring and interesting to explore.	✓	
Neck	I should not take the risk.	Reasonable risk always brings success.	✓	
Neck	If I don't obey, I'll be punished.	All my decisions are accepted and appreciated.	✓	
Upper chest	Life is unfair.	Life is always on the side of justice and truth.	✓	
Upper chest	I'm not good enough.	People love me and respect me. People always perceive me as a good person.	✓	
Upper neck	It is very important what others think about me.	It's irrelevant what other people think about me. I love myself and love others.	✓	
Head	I should always be realistic.	I have unlimited possibilities.	✓	
Upper chest	I don't deserve love.	I deserve love.	✓	
Upper chest	Others are stronger, bigger.	We are all equal.	✓	*emerged during RB*

Figure 33: RB Worksheet, part 1 (Real-Life Example)

Temp. l Location	Beliefs		DTI+ Done?	Note
	Negative Belief	Positive Belief		
Upper chest	Life is hard.	Life is beautiful and interesting.	✓	
Upper chest	My job is very difficult.	My job is easy and interesting.	✓	
Neck	I am a victim in my life.	I am strong and happy.	✓	
Lower neck	If you give them an inch, they will take a mile.	I am at the same time firm and full of love. Others respect that.	✓	*done twice*
Neck	I have to work a lot in order to gain something.	I easily attract abundance.	✓	
Neck	I have no happiness in life.	I am happy and successful in life.	✓	
Lower neck	No one should be trusted.	I harbor a deep trust in people. They also deeply trust me.	✓	
Upper neck	People are selfish and pursue only their own interest.	People are good by nature.	✓	
Lower neck	The others are to be blamed.	I am fully responsible for my life.	✓	
Neck	No pain, no gain.	Through the peace and presence all be easily achieved.	✓	
Upper neck	Money is not important.	Money is my friend; I have it always in abundance and I am happy in my life.	✓	
Upper neck	The rich are unhappy.	I am a rich and happy man.	✓	
Upper chest	I am a victim of injustice.	I am relaxed because life is always on my side.	✓	*emerged during RB*

Figure 34: RB Worksheet, part 2 (Real-Life Example)

Dismantling Beliefs

Dismantling Beliefs (DB) is a more intricate and demanding procedure than the RB. You will need to find a concrete situation which is the source of a belief or at least the first event exposing the belief that you are able to recall. The idea is to change the meaning of that event.

1. Find the source: the specific situation in the past that caused the belief.
2. Find at least one proof in your life that shows you that this belief is not true, or at least not totally true.
3. Find at least one alternative meaning of the original situation. Watch the situation from the alternative perspective. Notice that you can freely choose the meaning of that situation.
4. Do the DTI+ on the original situation; use the alternative meaning for the MH part of the DTI+.
5. State the original belief to yourself and see if there is still any emotional reaction.

Since this technique is also very important and powerful, you can find an example from real life in Part IV page 294, so you will be able to get a clearer picture how to apply the DB in reality. The empty form of this list you can find in the Appendix III.

Traumatic Memories

"The wound is the place where the Light enters you." — Rumi
"No pressure, no diamonds." — Mary Case

Painful experiences can leave deep scars in our psyche. They inevitably influence our whole life in defeating and limiting ways. They produce negative beliefs, bad habits, wrong decisions, painful emotions, and so on.

On the other hand, most of us have matured and learned tremendous lessons through painful experiences. They have strengthened us. They have driven us. The reason for that is the fact that we live in a material world whose main trait is inertia, which is also one of our main traits.

Our physical bodies are naturally submissive to the law of inertia; we're lazy, more or less. When there is nothing to push us forward, as pain does, we can sink deep into the quicksand of our lethargy. It's our nature and we must not blame ourselves for that. As a consequence, when a painful experience arises from that swamp of our inactivity, it pushes us ahead. Thanks to these shocks and traumas, we have gained depth of personality. Therefore, our wounds are blessings, too.

However, if we really want to improve our lives, we must deal meticulously with the traumatic memories. The time has come for removing the unpleasant emotional charge and all other negative elements of personality that have clustered around the painful events from our past. We can enter a completely new phase in our existence—a phase in which we don't need pain for going forward at all.

The precondition for reintegration of traumatic past experiences is to find and recognize these experiences in the first place. One of the most effective ways to do this is to make a timeline of our life.

First draw a simple timeline on a sheet of paper, with a zero point representing the year of your birth, and a point near the right arrow, indicating your present age, as shown on Figure 35.

●────────────────────────────────┼──▶

Birth   **Present**

Figure 35: Basic timeline

Now, say that you are 40 years old. Divide your lifetime into 5-year periods, which in this case means to divide the line span between birth and present into 8 parts (Figure 36).

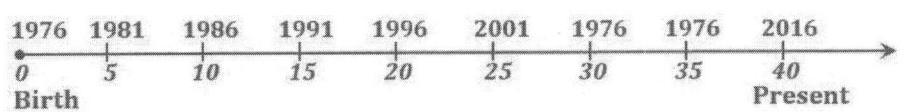

1976 1981 1986 1991 1996 2001 1976 1976 2016
──┼─────┼─────┼─────┼─────┼─────┼─────┼─────┼─────┼──▶
  0   5   10   15   20   25   30   35   40
Birth   **Present**

Figure 36: Timeline with 5-year periods

Then, try to recall a few of the most important events in your life for each 5-year period, whether they are positive (pleasant) or negative (unpleasant) to you. When I am talking about events, I mean *experiences*. They can be sudden and brief incidents, related to an exact point in time, or kind of fuzzy impressions, even stretching through longer periods of your life. They might be a mix of positive and negative feelings, rather than just one. The only criterion for the importance of events should be the intensity of emotions connected with them, regardless of their pleasantness.

So, although our intent is to clean up traumatic experiences from our past, it is necessary to search firstly for all types of experiences (positive, mixed and negative ones), because that will ease the whole process of recollection. The events will flow out from our memory more naturally.

You could also do this without drawing the timeline, but a visual representation of the concrete periods of your past is a good stimulus for your subconscious mind and smoother memory recollection.

Pleasant and mixed experiences you may put above the timeline, and the unpleasant ones below it.

It might look something like Figure 37:

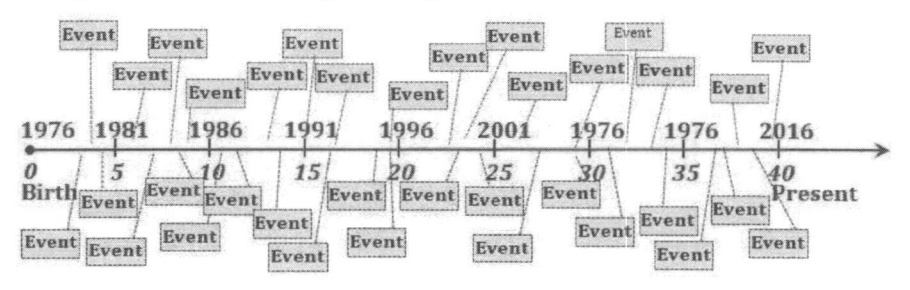

Figure 37: Timeline with Events

Of course, "event" in the above example would be replaced with abbreviations or words symbolizing each particular experience.

Very often, people recollect more unpleasant than pleasant experiences. In fact, that is not surprising, since there has been scientific research showing that negative events have a much stronger impact on our personality and memory than positive ones (the so called "negativity bias").[23]

After assigning a short name to each experience above or below the timeline, write down the emotions connected to every single event. Along with each emotion, find out which core state of being would have been an appropriate replacement for it. We will need that for the DTI+ technique.

As we mentioned before, the consequences of traumatic experiences could be negative self-imposed rules, so it is advisable in this procedure to watch for these rules as well. After defining each traumatic experience at the timeline, ask yourself: "What was my conclusion from this experience—how did it teach me to behave in my life?" Write down what emerges.

For every negative event do the following: put on paper the names of the most significant persons involved with you in the event. Now imagine that you are inside that event and try to recall and feel the negative emotions related to the event. Do the DTI+ technique on your Temporary I, with a suitable MH statement, such as: *"I am a person who dwells in Love/Peace/Joy (choose the most appropriate state)."*

After that, try to identify with each person involved in that event. Do the DTI from the points of view of those people.

---

[23] "The negativity bias (also known as the negativity effect) refers to the notion that, even when of equal intensity, things of a more negative nature (e.g. unpleasant thoughts, emotions, or social interactions; harmful/traumatic events) have a greater effect on one's psychological state and processes than do neutral or positive things. In other words, something very positive will generally have less of an impact on a person's behavior and cognition than something equally emotional but negative. The negativity bias has been investigated within many different domains, including the formation of impressions and general evaluations; attention, learning, and memory; and decision-making and risk considerations."
Source: https://en.wikipedia.org/wiki/Negativity_bias

Stay assured that this work will pay itself off. Once you are free of painful memories and immersed in Presence of consciousness, you will advance more steadily and powerfully in all aspects of your life. You will gain more and more depth, maturity and freedom.

Decisions

"At every point in time, there are infinite possibilities and a parallel reality exists for each possibility, so there are literally infinite branches..."
— the character of Daniel Jackson in the TV series Stargate, Episode: 'Point Of View'

Decisions are also very important and influential parts of our individual universe.

When making a decision, you are deciding between at least two possibilities before you. Having decided to take one concrete course of action, you actually divide the whole individual universe, made of infinite possibilities, into two parts: the one in which you have taken an action, and all the others in which you haven't. This decision-making process is being done on all levels of our existence, all the time, often unconsciously.

Small, everyday decisions made while doing chores, for example, are unconscious. When you become aware of these micro-decisions made during the normal day, you are entering the mindfulness meditation and state of Presence, which in fact clears up your mind and heart. Through that process of becoming aware of every little move, breath, thought, word and so on, you are becoming aware of these micro-decisions. In that way, you are re-uniting the countless individual universes that were previously split up in that incessant decision-making process; you are re-uniting yourself. So, don't underestimate the importance of these micro-decisions and making yourself aware of them as much as possible.

On the other hand, conscious decision-making can also have key influence over our lives, not only because they can push us onto a completely different lifeline than the one we originally wanted/expected, but because, once made, they can sink into our subconscious and become habitual. If made during childhood, those decisions could literally become our fate.

For instance, when I was 7 years old, every time I behaved noisily and extrovertly at school, I was attacked by a boy from my class who was the local bully. From that state of fear, I made a decision to completely change my social behavior and became, from then on, an introvert. Whenever I was in a group of children, that decision made me behave shyly and reclusively. The actual problem was that this decision quickly became deeply unconscious, so for a long time I couldn't find the real cause of my strong and annoying tendency towards that kind of behavior. Only recently have I been able to become aware of it and remove it.

How can we remove these negative, unwittingly made decisions from our past? Simply, with the DTI+ technique. You have to delve deeply and seriously into your past in order to do so, and the best tool for that purpose is the timeline.

When you find a negative decision, do the DTI+ on it a few times. For the MH part, either choose an opposite, positive statement/decision, or a statement with which you will surpass any new unnecessary splitting of your possibilities.

For example, in my case the decision was: "I have to be quiet in any company!" It hadn't been expressed in words at that time, as I recall it more as a feeling. It was a strong decision after which I had been noticeably less attacked, so it had served its purpose quite successfully. Anyway, the decision was soon suppressed, forgotten and moved to the subconscious level. But it continued to influence my life persistently.

I immediately did the DTI+ on that decision 5 times. For the MH part I chose this statement: "I am a completely relaxed person in any company." I did the DTI+ process again in the next few days, so I felt that the problem was definitely resolved.

Now, there are also many good decisions you've made in the past. Of course, you don't have to remove or replace them. However, since they sometimes oppose each other, they can create constant challenges and procrastination. That's why you have to *harmonize* them, and the best option is to use the Convergence Procedure. Harmonize them one by one. For that purpose, use one of the core states as one polarity, and the positive decision that you are working on as the other polarity.

You can also make completely new decisions for your life that will serve as very strong affirmations. Implement them through the MH technique. But don't be surprised if, during that process, you get distracted by some unexpected mind content. Perhaps some thoughts, emotions or sensations will get into your focus and divert it from the MH statement. As we already know, that content will be an expression of your inner obstacles to the goal you want to achieve, so you will have to remove it with the DTI+ technique. Of course, the MH part will be the same MH statement related to the decision which you are working on.

You can find more information on the goal achievement process in Part IV.

Rules
"Know the rules well, so you can break them effectively."
— Dalai Lama XIV

Rules are patterns of behavior severely imposed on us in the past, which we still subconsciously obey. Pertaining to that, there are two kinds of rules: self-imposed and externally imposed. In both cases, they come in the form of *orders* or *prohibitions*.

The most severe *externally imposed* rules most often come from our parents, other authorities, or even peers during early childhood.

Here are some examples of orders and prohibitions inflicted during childhood by parents or peers that one of my friends reported, after contemplation:

- *Shame on you!*
- *We don't have money for that!*
- *You jerk!*
- *You listen to me!*
- *Obey the elderly!*
- *Obey when I say something to you!*
- *Eat!*
- *You, sloth!*
- *Hurry up!*
- *You'll get a beating!*
- *Watch out!*
- *You could fall!*
- *You must take care of everything!*
- *You have to be careful at every step!*
- *Don't trust anyone!*
- *Be honest in your life!*
- *Study!*
- *Why are you so irresponsible?!*
- *Do not cry!*
- *You should be like him/her!*

Self-imposed rules are usually consequences of a traumatic event from our past, especially early childhood, sometimes linked to the externally imposed rules. In fact, they frequently are just aftermaths or effects of such experiences, commands and prohibitions.

These rules are indicated when we say *I have to..., I must..., I should..., I can't..., I shouldn't...*

Both self-imposed and externally-imposed rules are very powerful forces in our lives. Similar to beliefs, traumatic experiences and decisions, they can work behind-the-scenes to greatly influence our lives.

It is important to go back to your past and try to recall every single rule that you've heard or obeyed, especially in your childhood. Make an effort to evoke all imposed orders and prohibitions in as precise as possible linguistic forms. Again, it is advisable to use the timeline approach.

How can we detach from these rules? Again, you could apply almost every of the Reintegration techniques presented in this book, but, generally speaking, the quickest and the most effective way is to use the DTI+ technique. If that's not enough, you may find the IT or Chain techniques effective as well.

In any case, it would be useful to pass through all life events from the timeline and to create a list of these rules (such as the list above), write down an opposite statement next to each rule and do the DTI+ technique on every rule.

Emotions
"Anything that you resent and strongly react to in another is also in you."
— Eckhart Tolle, A New Earth: Awakening to Your Life's Purpose

Perhaps you picture emotions like clouds. No matter the color of the cloud, there is always the sun shining behind it; there is always some higher, genuine purpose behind it all. We should appreciate the presence of emotions, as well as of other parts of our being. They are trying to give us a valuable message.

To make our dealings with emotion much clearer and easier, let's examine the very nature of emotion and possible methods of classifying them.

An emotion is energy-in-motion within our being. It is our primal response to a significant situation. As Eckhart Tolle said, *"Emotions arise in the place where your mind and body meet"*[24].

---

[24] Eckhart Tolle, The Power of Now: A Guide to Spiritual Enlightenment

Definitely, the role of emotions in human life is huge. If we really want to integrate our personality and achieve inner peace and outer success, we must face our emotions in the first place.

In this system, we will use *Robert Plutchik's wheel of emotions* (as shown in Figure 38) to determine the opposite emotions.

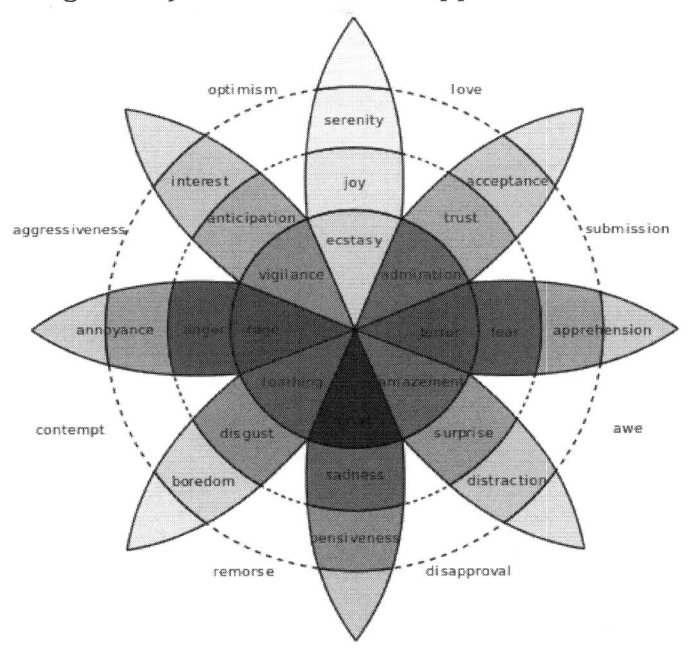

Figure 38: Plutchik's Wheel of Emotions[25]

"Robert Plutchik's psycho-evolutionary theory of emotion is one of the most influential classification approaches for general emotional responses. He considered there to be eight primary emotions—anger, fear, sadness, disgust, surprise, anticipation, trust, and joy. Plutchik proposed that these 'basic' emotions are biologically primitive and have evolved in order to increase the reproductive fitness of the animal."[26]

---

[25] Source: Wikipedia, the free encyclopedia,
https://en.wikipedia.org/wiki/Contrasting_and_categorization_of_emotions#Plutchik.27s_wheel_of_emotions

[26] Ibid.

Plutchik's wheel of emotions and theory of emotion will prove pretty useful throughout our Reintegration practice. When we work with an emotion, we can find it on the wheel (or a similar emotion under a different name), and therefore immediately determine the opposite emotion. In this way, we are able to get a pair of polarities to work with the Inner Triangle process.

Every emotion has its own trigger which launches it. It's usually a situation which occurs from time to time in our everyday life. The connection between the trigger and the emotion is very tight and habitual, which often means that we need to deal with triggers too, in order to avoid the manifestation of their emotions, unless we integrate the emotion itself. That's commonly done with anger, for example. Since anger outbreaks are common for almost every human being (and even some animals), it is one of the most basic emotions and in that sense the most difficult to integrate. That's why we also have to deal with its triggers.

But if we were able to remove all triggers of anger (or any other unpleasant emotion), we wouldn't remove the anger itself from our psyche. It would pose a dangerous situation, because that emotion would need to express itself in some way, which would lead to some uncontrolled outbreaks or even to personality disorders.

Thus, if we deal with triggers, we must deal with their emotions concurrently.

I recommend that you make a list of negative emotions together with their triggers. Go through the list and try to reintegrate all emotions as well as triggers.

Emotions are complex entities within us, with the original intention of appropriately reacting to a particular experience. They are never inherently unfavorable to us. Our experiences are usually filtered by negative beliefs or other elements of personality, which create distortions in our perception of the experiences. Therefore, if we have a negative perception of an event, an unpleasant emotion will emerge.

In this way, the emotion could be regarded as a valuable indicator of a deeper defeating or limiting element of personality which is affecting our view of reality. We must not fight emotions. We have to reintegrate them and take advantage of them as pointers to the parts of our psyche that are the real sources of our troubles.

In accordance with the above conclusion, the most appropriate procedure for dealing with emotions in this system is the Inner Triangle process. The recommended tactic is to have the unwanted emotion as the first polarity, and the second polarity as the opposite emotion which you could find on Plutchik's wheel.

If you are short on time, you may use the Single or Double Chain technique for the reintegration of emotions. However, if you use some of the basic Reintegration procedures, keep in mind that they probably won't be successful in the long run with stronger recurring emotions, though they will surely help to decrease emotional charge.

Always remember to remove their triggers as well, because even though you integrate an emotion, the trigger itself will continue to re-generate habitual reactions and, in some cases, re-create the whole structure of a negative behavior, sometimes in a new and unexpected way. Re-live the trigger, do the Dissolving the Temporary I (DTI) procedure on it and then do the Gentle Touch of Presence (GTP) technique with the same trigger as well.

There are many emotions that deserve our serious work. Fear, rage, anger, sorrow, resentment, guilt... a better and complete list of various emotions can be found on the Plutchik's wheel shown in Figure 38 for use within your work.

All these negatively perceived emotions often generate unwanted actions and unpleasant consequences, but they are inherently good. They originally have had the highest intentions for your well-being. They certainly deserve to be welcomed back to you.

Aversions and Fears

"Don't be afraid of your fears. They're not there to scare you. They're there to let you know that something is worth it." — C. JoyBell C.

A fear could be seen as an emotion, as well as an aversion. But I highlighted both aversions and fears as basic elements of our personality due to their real importance in our lives. They, together with inclinations/desires, are some of the basic life dynamisms in every living creature.

In this system, we will consider fears as a subgroup of aversions. Therefore, aversions and fears, as the basic dynamisms, are deeply ingrained in the roots of every human being, which makes them extremely important to deal with in every kind of psychological or spiritual work.

In psychology, fear is defined as an unpleasant emotion induced by a real or imaginary threat, which causes a change in our thought patterns, biological functioning or behavior (such as running away, hiding or freezing).

Unfounded fears are induced by some imaginary threats and they are responsible for undermining our health, confidence, desires, plans, hopes and relationships with others.

Aversions are strong dislikes or disinclinations. They are a means of opposition or repugnance. Fears are similar in nature to aversions, but are more amplified in extent. Additionally, anger or other negative emotions could be born out of a strong sense of aversion toward something.

The following are different forms of aversions:

1. Risk aversion
2. Loss aversion
3. Taste aversion
4. Travel aversion
5. Work aversion
6. Food aversion
7. People aversion
8. Publicity aversion

These are most common fears in people:

1. Fear of death
2. Fear of failure
3. Fear of success
4. Fear of criticism
5. Fear of ridicule
6. Fear of change
7. Fear of responsibility
8. Fear of the unknown
9. Fear of the future
10. Fear of loss
11. Fear of standing out
12. Fear of pressure
13. Fear of loneliness
14. Fear of abandonment
15. Fear of disease
16. Fear of public speaking
17. Fear of flying
18. Fear of heights
19. Fear of the dark
20. Fear of intimacy
21. Fear of rejection
22. Fear of aging
23. Fear of drowning
24. Fear of spiders

As is the case with all other parts of personality, we shouldn't be fighting fears and aversions. They have inherently positive roles in our maturing to a well-integrated, spiritual person.

We can deal with fears and aversions with the Inner Triangle, Single or Double Chain techniques, Dissolving the Temporary I Plus (DTI+, with the MH parts asserting serenity, calmness, and similar) or Gentle Touch of Presence (GTP). Just go boldly through the list of all your aversions and fears and relentlessly reintegrate them, one by one.

Once again, don't forget to remove their triggers. If you don't do that, the triggers will continue to re-create the fears and aversions. For this I recommend the use of Dissolving the Temporary I (DTI) and GTP techniques. Just do the DTI on the trigger, and when you find yourself in the vastness of Presence, bring into your focus the same trigger again and "treat" it with the GTP.

Reintegrate your fears. You will feel immense relief and deliverance. You will release yourself from an inner prison. You will sense the limitlessness.

Accusations and Guilt

"What you react to in others, you strengthen in yourself." — Eckhart Tolle
"Not forgiving is like drinking rat poison and then waiting for the rat to die." — Anne Lamott, Traveling Mercies: Some Thoughts on Faith

When we are repetitively accused of doing some bad thing, especially in childhood and adolescence, it leads us to a strong underlying sense of guilt and resentment. Furthermore, it causes us to developing anger and aggression.

A sense of guilt is one of the strongest obstacles to a healthy lifestyle. It is a self-destructive emotion, very dangerous to our health and life in general. Regardless of if the feeling is justified or not, by feeling guilt we assume that we were badly wrong about something and that we *have to be punished*. That's a dangerous thought. Whether conscious or subconscious, this emotion attracts such circumstances in which we are punished in some way.

Resentment is also a perilous emotion that works in the background of our personality, for long periods, which spoils our health and our relationships with people. It can undermine our ability to achieve goals and live a successful life in general.

We must deal with our resentment toward other people and guilt related to our own deeds. Otherwise, these feelings will continually undermine our lives.

Put on paper all the names of the people that you have had a continuous relationship with. You should examine for what concretely you criticize each person, either openly or covertly. Also, try to find any feeling of your own guilt toward these people, if you think that you did something wrong to them. It could be in a form of list, consisting of their names, accusations toward them and your guilt related to them. This list could encompass not only names of people, but general terms, like life, people, society, job, etc.

George was also working on this subject relatively recently and part of his list was this (Figure 39):

Name	Accusation	Source events	Guilt	Source events
Life	Life is so unfair to me because of my childhood injuries	The car accident when I was 4		
Society	Too many things depend on connections; injustice	When my dad lost his job, complaining about connections		
Bureau-cracy	Indolence	They refused all my requests for documents		
My company	Discrimination	I've been unable to be promoted starting from 10 years ago	I've been lazy many times	
S.	He is ridiculing me at work	From January, last year, boss' office	I offended him badly	In my office, February this year
S.	He's a liar	From May, last year, his office	I offended him badly	In my office, February this year
R.	She is two-faced	The incident at her home		
M.	He always sticks his oar in my life	His attack on me 5 years ago		
Dad	Always criticizing me	First memories of him yelling at me	I didn't listen to him when he advised me about so many things	He was asking me not to go with those boys and I was hurt badly
Mum	Worrying too much	Her desperate cry when I broke my leg at age 5	I didn't care about her love enough	The unpleasant situation when I was 8
Sister	Always distracting me	When she was crying as a baby	I was unjust to her	My yelling at her when she was a toddler

Figure 39: List of Accusations and Guilt (example)

Note that some of these accusations are actually beliefs or could also be other aspects of personality, covered in previous sections.

In order to find concrete circumstances from the past that are a source of guilt and resentment, it is advisable to use the timeline method.

Then we are ready for the next step: forgiveness. Forgive truly and wholeheartedly both those you are accusing and yourself.

"All negativity is caused by an accumulation of psychological time and denial of the present. Unease, anxiety, tension, stress, worry—all forms of fear—are caused by too much future, and not enough presence. Guilt, regret, resentment, grievances, sadness, bitterness, and all forms of non-forgiveness are caused by too much past, and not enough presence," said Eckhart Tolle in his book The Power of Now.

Of course, forgiving is sometimes difficult to do. Our Heart has been closed in a cocoon, enveloped in the many layers of elements of our persona, especially accusations and guilt. We have just started releasing it from that prison. We sometimes feel we just can't do that in some situations, to some people that we hurt, or that we can't forgive ourselves.

What to do in that case? Do the DTI+ on each hurtful memory. Let the MH part be: *"I forgive (the person's name) completely, with all my Heart."* Do this procedure several times, if needed. Remember that every person is only doing the things they believe to be helpful for their own satisfaction or happiness. They don't know better. If their deeds were harmful, even apparently deliberate toward you, it was still without *true* knowledge. They were just *taught* by miserable circumstances or ignorant people that those kinds of deeds were helpful to gain some satisfaction... just as you were. You have to forgive them! The same goes for you; forgive yourself, too!

If even this doesn't help, don't give up. You *must* release yourself from the cage of resentment and guilt. Otherwise, you can't break free and can't continue growing. The final solution is to deal with these memories or sources of resentment with the Inner Triangle technique. Or use any other spiritual or psychological technique that you know of to be helpful and effective. The urgent goal is to release all resentment, both toward yourself and others.

Inclinations and Desires
"Beyond all vanities, fights, and desires, omnipotent silence lies."
— Dejan Stojanovic, The Sun Watches the Sun

Just like aversions, the inclination or preference toward some thing or experience is one of the basic dynamisms of any living being. Here we will treat them practically and equally to the other elements of personality, because it's hard to say that their general influence on our life is stronger than the influence of other elements.

Inclinations are like aversions and fears, but the direction is reversed—instead of repelling some persons, things or experiences, they tend to attract certain parts of reality. In this way, they contribute greatly to the final shape of our subjective universe. When they are too exaggerated (like many desires are), or in disharmony with certain general aspects or elements of our personality, they actually pose a problem and have to be reintegrated or removed.

Desires are the most embellished inclinations. They usually have a long history behind them and a lot of energy invested into them over time.

There are also *addictions*, which we will treat here as a specific, neurological kind of strong desire. These desires have become habitual and repetitive and pose a sinister threat to the overall psychic and physiological health of a person.

What do we do with inclinations and desires? Of course, reintegrate them, if possible. The best approach is to apply the Inner Triangle technique.

You must first make a list of all your desires. There are your "regular" inclinations and desires that you are aware of all the time, and it won't be a problem to recollect all of those and create the list. But you have many subconscious desires as well. You could be very surprised to find that you hold desires that you'd previously thought of as inconceivable.

How do we find these subconscious desires? Thankfully, we have the holographic principle at hand. It says that our outer reality corresponds with our inner reality, and vice versa. So, if you can't find something important within you, just look around yourself—you will find it in a symbolic form.

When we deny the existence of a personal trait, or fear, desire, emotion, etc., we suppress it. After some time of persistent suppressing, that element of personality tends to find its way out in any possible way. If it can't find a way to express itself, it passes through the boundaries of our being and goes outside—it becomes embodied in another person. In that way, it says to us: "Hey, look at me, I'm still alive! Face me; take care of me!"

These embodying persons are usually close to us, their presence always reminding us of the trait we have suppressed deep inside. All our personality elements are embodied in our environment in one way or another, though most generally in the people around us.

Therefore, the very existence of significant people in your surroundings carries some deeper meaning to you. Of course, keep in mind that they have their own lives and you also have some deeper meaning to them. But every single person in our life does have at least a few personal traits that are actually ours.

How can we recognize these people and the personality elements in them?

Since we already have the names of the people involved in our traumatic experiences from the past, we can extensively use that information in this section.

Ask yourself for each person: "What are his/her desires or inclinations that are annoying to me?" Write it down. Along with each desire, find out which core state of being would have been an appropriate replacement for it. When you have put everything down on paper, imagine that *you* have that desire and do the DTI+ technique, using core states as replacements.

Also, try to find the situations in your past when you *had* that same desire. If you find it, first accept it fully as yours. Do the DTI+ on that situation or event. Do the DTI+ on the main persons involved in that event. If you can't find the initial situation, that's OK. Just do the DTI+ on that desire and that person a few times and the desire or inclination should be transformed into the core state.

If it still persists, you have to do the Inner Triangle technique or at least one of Chain techniques. The desire should be the first polarity. The second polarity should be an entity or state that you feel is an opposite of the desire. It could be the corresponding core state, some fear, or even another emotion.

Personal Traits

"There are times when I am so unlike myself that I might be taken for someone else of an entirely opposite character." — Jean-Jacques Rousseau, Confessions

Another part of our personality that we will have to seriously consider integrating is our personal traits or qualities. Of course, as there is no perfect human being, there are both positive and negative traits in every person. Fortunately, both are important in our extensive inner work.

It's advisable to create yet another list, this time of your personal traits, both positive and negative. Here are some things you might consider yourself to be: a shy person or reserved, dominant, restless, impatient, emotional, aggressive, honest, serious, independent, passive, optimistic, self-defeating, self-doubting, domineering, arrogant, stubborn, attractive, benevolent, perfectionistic, realistic, reliable, responsible, kind, loyal, eloquent, ambitious, fearful, negativistic, naïve, undisciplined, submissive…and on and on.

A more complete list of possible personality traits you can find in the Appendix III.

As we already have the list of names of people that are important to us, we can use that information in this section as well.

Ask yourself for each person: "What were his/her negative traits that were annoying to me or were the source of that unpleasant experience?" Along with each negative trait, find out which positive trait or core state of being would have been an appropriate replacement for it. When you put everything on the paper, imagine that *you* have that trait and do the DTI+ technique, using positive traits or core states as replacements.

As mentioned before, the elements of our personality that we consider as "good" or "positive" are usually our personal traits that we are most proud of (honesty, reliability, efficacy, decisiveness, perfectionism, etc.), but even a positive trait can hamper important aspects of your life. For example, *honesty* can hamper your desire for wealth, if you have a belief that rich people are not honest. Thus, you have to harmonize the positive traits as well, and the best approach for that is the Convergence Procedure.

Here you can see an example of integrating Honesty with Double Chain technique, a personality trait that Melissa was so proud of. The process was initiated by her insight that her own version of Honesty had hindered her other goals. It is presented with answers and entity's descriptions only.

Example of Integrating Honesty using the Double Chain

(Initial description of the entity: It's a big, dark blue diamond within and all around me.)

> *Inclination 1:* I want to be as honest as my father was.
> *Aversion 1:* I don't want to steal and lie, as rich people usually do.

(The diamond has become light blue.)

> *Inclination 2:* I want to follow the example of my father.
> *Aversion 2:* I don't want to gain anything to the detriment of others.

(The diamond has shrunk to the size of a ball in the chest and has become bright.)

> *Inclination 3:* I want to achieve an ideal of perfection.
> *Aversion 3:* I don't want any imperfection.

(The diamond is in the Heart.)

> Peace and Perfection. *(This was the highest state of the entity.)*

In a Nutshell

Main Elements of Personality

These are the main elements of personality for dealing with in our work:

- General aspects of personality
- Habits
- Beliefs
- Decisions
- Traumatic memories
- Emotions
- Aversions and Fears
- Accusations and Guilt
- Inclinations and Desires
- Personal traits

This classification is for practical reasons only—they are the elements we will probably deal with in our Reintegration work the most.

Our approach will be not to fight them, but reintegrate and, if possible, lead every single element to its highest state, to the Source.

General Aspects of Personality

We will consider the main areas of our life as the key parts of our personality and we will be reintegrating them as separate sub-personal entities, so called General Aspects.

For example, they could be the following: Family, Spirituality, Health, Finance, Career, Creativity, Relationship, Social, Rest and Fun. For better insight into the problematic areas, you could picture the perceived level of your satisfaction with these aspects through the Wheel of Life.

In order to harmonize these elements of personality, you may use the "Assessment List of Mutual Coherence of General Aspects." Do your estimation of their mutual support and use the Convergence Procedure several times.

Habits

Habits are patterns through which the parts of personality and corresponding behaviors are being expressed regularly. Every habit has three components: a cue (trigger), routine and reward. These components make the so called "habit loop."

According to recent exploration, the best way to deal with unwanted habits is to *replace* the routines. To do that, you have to identify all three elements of the habit loop. Then make a plan for changing the habit, by replacing the unwanted routine with a preferred one.

If you want to erase a bad habit, you must erase all three of its components (cue, routine and reward) by doing this procedure:

– *Cue:* do the DTI, SC or DC, or the IT technique. Use the IT on these types of cue: emotional states and other people; do the DTI on: immediately preceding action, location and time. If you do the Inner Triangle, you may form two polarities of the cue and the reward.

– *Routine:* re-live the routine in your mind with the GTP technique. Then, do the routine multiple times in real life mindfully, using the FA technique.

This way, you are not only overcoming the bad habits, you are *using* them as portals to living a more mindful, conscious life.

– *Reward:* do the IT, SC, DC or DTI.

Beliefs

Beliefs are our little truths about everything. They are usually supported by underlying emotions, so they become very strong mental habits.

Replacing Beliefs (RB) technique

Create your individual list of negative beliefs and put it into the RB Worksheet. Do the DTI+ procedure on each negative belief from the list. Pass through the whole list several times, as long as you feel any traces of those beliefs in your psyche.

Dismantling Beliefs (DB) technique

1. Find the source: the specific situation in the past that caused the belief.

2. Find at least one proof in your life that shows you that this belief is not true, or at least not totally true.

3. Find at least one alternative meaning for the original situation. Watch the situation from that alternative perspective. Notice that you can freely choose the meaning of the situation.

4. Do the DTI+ on the original situation and the alternative meaning for the MH part of the DTI+.

5. State the original belief to yourself and see if there is still any emotional reaction.

Traumatic Memories

In order to find and remove traumatic memories, use a timeline divided into 5-year periods. Recall a few most important events from each period. The only criterion for the importance of events should be the intensity of emotions connected to it, regardless of their pleasantness.

After assigning a short name or abbreviation to every experience on the timeline, write down any emotions connected to each event. Along with each emotion, find out which core state of being would have been an appropriate replacement for it, which will be used within the MH part of DTI+ technique. Ask yourself after defining each experience on the timeline: *"What was my conclusion from this experience—how did it teach me to behave in my life?"* Write down what emerges.

For every unpleasant experience do the following: note the names of significant people involved with you in the event. Imagine that you are inside that happening and try to recall and feel negative emotions related to the event. Do the DTI+. Then try to identify yourself with every significant person involved. Do the DTI from the points of view of those people.

Decisions

Use the timeline you already have created. Try to recall significant life decisions you made in each life event. In some events, you won't find any particular decisions, but in others you may find several of them. Do the DTI+ on every negative decision a few times. For the MH part, choose a positive statement at your will—that could be an opposite, desirable decision or positive emotion—but the best solution is almost always to choose a core state.

When it comes to positive decisions, you have to harmonize them, one by one, using the Convergence Procedure. Use one of the core states as one polarity, and the other polarity will be the positive decision that you are working on.

Rules

Rules are the patterns of behavior severely imposed on us in the past, which we still subconsciously obey. Rules are expressed in the form of orders or prohibitions.

In order to find and remove your rules, first pass through all the life events from your timeline and try to find related rules for each event. From that you can create a list of rules, then write down an opposite statement next to each rule and do the DTI+ technique on each. In more difficult cases, you may apply more complex techniques, like the IT or Chain techniques.

Emotions

Since all emotion's original intention is to enable us to appropriately react to a particular experience, they are never inherently unfavorable to us. On the contrary; they are valuable indicators of deeper defeating or limiting elements within our personality which distort our perception of reality. Therefore, we must not fight our emotions; we have to appreciate and gently reintegrate them.

For reintegrating emotions, you can use the IT process, or Chain techniques. If you use the IT, your unwanted emotion may take the role of the first polarity, and the second polarity you could find on Plutchik's wheel.

You also have to remove each emotion's trigger, by re-experiencing the trigger, doing the DTI on it and then also doing the GTP technique on it.

With basic Reintegration techniques, in most cases, you will only be able to partially release energetic charge from a particular emotion.

Aversions and Fears

As is the case with all other emotions, for reintegrating fears or aversions you have the IT procedure at your disposal, and the SC or DC techniques as well.

Application of the basic Reintegration techniques on fears and aversions will usually only result in discharging the energetic load of these emotions.

When you are reintegrating a fear, don't forget to remove its triggers. If you don't do that, the triggers will continue to re-create the fear. To do this, you may use DTI and GTP.

Accusations and Guilt

Resentment toward other people and guilt related to our own deeds are very dangerous feelings that continually undermine our health, relations with people and everything else in our life.

In order to reintegrate resentment, first you should put on the paper all the names of important people in your life. Examine whether you feel resentment toward each of them and for what concretely. Also, try to find any feeling of your own guilt toward these people.

Then you have to forgive all of them, truly and wholeheartedly, one by one. Forgive yourself, too. Remember that every person is only doing the things they believe to be helpful for their own satisfaction or happiness. They don't know better. If their deeds were harmful, even apparently deliberate toward you, it was still without *true* knowledge. The same goes for you, and that's why you have to forgive yourself, too.

But if you still can't forgive, do the DTI+ on each hurtful memory. The MH part could be: *"I forgive (the person's name) completely, with my whole Heart."* Do this procedure several times, if needed.

If you still can't release your resentment or guilt, the final solution is to do the IT process on these emotions. It should be related to the particular people that are the most problematic in your life.

Inclinations and Desires

Make a list of all inclinations and desires you are currently aware of. Then, proceed to finding your subconscious desires. For that purpose, use your already created list of important people that are present in your life at this time and for each person ask yourself: "What are his/her desires or inclinations that are annoying to me?" Write everything down.

Along with each desire, find out which core state would have been an appropriate replacement for it. Feel that desire and do the DTI+ technique, using core states as replacements.

Additionally, try to find situations from your past in which you had that same desire. If you find it, first accept it fully as yours. Do the DTI+ on that situation or event. Do the DTI+ on the main persons involved in that event. If you can't find these situations, don't worry.

For stronger or more persistent desires you can do the IT, SC or DC procedures.

Personal Traits

Use the list of names of important people in your life that you already have. Ask yourself for each person: "What were his/her negative traits that were annoying to me or were the source of that unpleasant experience?" Do the DTI+ technique on each of their traits, using positive traits or core states as replacements.

You also must mutually harmonize your positive traits, because they can hamper some important aspects of your life. For this harmonization use the Convergence Procedure.

Meditation

"The key to meditation is to exist one hundred percent in the here and now." — Ilchi Lee, Human Technology: A Toolkit for Authentic Living

Meditation is one of the pillars of this whole system. If you want to have stable and lasting results in your work with all these techniques, it is essential to discipline yourself and have at least one, 15-minute meditation session every day. Do not limit your practice to only these fixed sessions; expand your consciousness into your everyday life.

Therefore, Reintegration Meditation actually consists of two components: sittings (regular meditation sessions) and mindfulness.

If cautiously practiced (more on this later), Reintegration Meditation will surely positively affect your whole day and, if done regularly, your whole life.

Sittings

*"Keep your heart clear
And transparent,
And you will
Never be bound.
A single disturbed thought
Creates ten thousand distractions."
— Ryokan*

In this section I will briefly describe the procedure for a meditation sitting. You should schedule these sessions for every day in the morning, and if possible, in the evening, too, roughly at the same time of day.

You can practice all kinds of meditation. If you prefer to stick with traditional approaches, there are many varieties of Buddhist or Yoga meditation you could practice along with other aspects of Reintegration work. Keep in mind, though, that some of these methods require the practitioner to stick with all other practices within that particular system.

In this book, I will explain a variant of meditation that utilizes some basic Reintegration techniques, which, in my opinion, significantly improve the profoundness of meditation and its benefits. After all, this meditation was designed to resonate completely with the entire Reintegration system.

The goal of this kind of meditation is simply to stay in the state of Presence or pure consciousness as long as possible. Whenever something comes into your mind and disturbs your Presence, you just apply the Freshness & Acceptance (FA) technique on it and return to the Presence. That's it.

First, you enter a state of full awareness, without thoughts or any other mind content, i.e. the state of Presence. The easiest way is to do a *multi-layered DTI* on your current state of mind, then on your body, and lastly on your impression of the external reality around you.

Then you just do the FA on everything that disturbs your peaceful state of awareness. In this way, you bring your mind again into the Presence. And this is the whole circle.

But if there are some heavy emotions that keep arising and distracting your peace severely, you should do the *multiple layered FA* on the content, then body, then on your external reality, each time doing the FA on your Temporary I as well.

The Reintegration meditation consists of these steps:

1. **Relaxation**
2. **Entering the state of Presence** using the multi-layered DTI procedure as well as the MH technique
3. **Occasional removal of distracting mind content** using the FA technique

Relaxation Phase

First you relax completely, using either the Relaxation Technique described in this book or some other procedure that works for you. It is strongly recommended that you sit with your spine straight up, whether on a chair or in one of the "lotus"[27] positions. Whether you keep your eyes open or closed depends on your preference, but I would suggest doing the meditation with half-open eyes, in order to keep yourself awake more easily.

Entering the State of Presence

In this stage, we are shifting from a normal state of consciousness, with a lot of thoughts, emotions and other content, into a deeper, meditative state, which is less "contaminated" with content of the mind. To reach that state, we have to dissolve our identification with mind content, body, and surroundings.

Thus, the entering stage consists of these parts:

- At the beginning, do the DTI on your current state of mind.
- Do the DTI for your body.
- Do the DTI for the external reality that you perceive at the moment.
- Do the Moving to the Heart technique.

Turn your focus inward. Feel your current state of mind. Maybe you are overwhelmed with thoughts or emotions, maybe you are tired or anxious, but if you did the first stage (relaxation), it shouldn't be an effort for you to do the next step: a multi-layered DTI.

At the beginning, become aware of whatever you are experiencing at that very moment, your anxiousness, thoughts, emotions or anything else. Find your Temporary I and do the DTI on it. Wherever

---

[27] https://en.wikipedia.org/wiki/Lotus_position
http://www.yogajournal.com/meditation/everything-need-know-meditation-posture/

your Temporary I is located at the moment, do the expansion of it. You will find yourself in the vast field of Presence.

After a while, feel your body and its energy field, as a whole. Again, locate your Temporary I from which vantage point you are experiencing your body. Do the DTI on it.

Next, feel the space around you and everything within it. Find your Temporary I from which standpoint you are seeing and feeling your environment. Do the DTI. You may have difficulty finding the Temporary I, but try anyway. You can even consider a blurred field of your being as your I at that moment. In any case, do the DTI with whatever you find.

Then, do the Moving to the Heart technique. Again, if you can't precisely locate your Temporary I, try to feel a "center" of the fuzzy sense of your being and move it to the Heart. Your MH statement could be just *"I am."* Stay in that Presence or pure existence, and if there is any "center" or "core" of your being from which you are experiencing the "I am"-ness, may it be in your Heart only.

Stay within that vastness of pure consciousness as long as you can. You don't have to come back to the "I am" state, just be in the pure consciousness. This is the aim of meditation. It doesn't often last long, not only for the beginners, but even for the majority of experienced people. A few seconds only or, at most 10 to 15 seconds, probably. Some mind content will surely arise and kick you out from your Presence. You will probably not even be aware that you are out of your pure consciousness. But eventually, you will become aware of that fact and you will try to bring yourself back into the original blissful state. You can do so with the FA technique.

Occasional Removal of Distracting Mind Content

Sooner or later, a content of the mind will pop up into existence and pull you out from the bliss of pure consciousness. But that content could be vastly different in its nature. It may be just one light thought, or, on the other side, it can consist of heavy and repetitive emotions.

For **light mind content**, you do only this:

- Do the FA on the Temporary I which perceives the distracting mind content.
- Repeat the same for any light mind content that comes up, until the end of session.

Now, you are going to use the Freshness & Acceptance (FA) technique whenever an ordinary thought or other common content of mind comes up and distracts you. Since the FA is a softer and perhaps subtler technique than DTI, you can easily fall asleep as you are doing it if you are tired. Therefore, if you get drowsy during meditation, switch to the DTI instead of the FA.

So, when a thought, light emotion or sensation arises in the mind, you simply do the FA on the Temporary I from which vantage point you are experiencing that mind content.

Find where your Temporary I is located. While being focused on your Temporary I and its location, ask yourself: "Am I really this?" Feel surprised that "you" are "condensed," and that you are "located" at that area of your body (e.g. in your head, neck, chest or somewhere else). Feel as if it's the first time for you to have this kind of experience, like you know nothing about that "compression" of your I. Feel curious about that.

Then, fully accept your Temporary I with your whole Heart. Be completely okay with it.

Note that this process should be brief. Of course, you should practice first, and the procedure is explained more in detail in Appendix I, within the section of "Alternative DTI" technique. There you will find some suitable exercises too.

So, this was the first layer of FA applied to the light mind content only, and it's usually absolutely enough to bring yourself into the state of Presence, of pure consciousness. Stay in that state as long as possible; that's the goal of meditation.

Some **heavy mind content** will often appear, disturbing your peace completely. You might even forget that you are meditating altogether. It usually consists of strong and persisting emotions coupled with bits of various thoughts, sometimes even with unpleasant bodily sensations. But when you remember that you are actually meditating, you should do a more comprehensive FA process applied to your mind content, body and environment.

So, in the case of heavy content distracting your Presence, you should do the multi-layered FA plus MH procedure, as following:

- Do the FA on the Temporary I which perceives the distracting mind content.
- Do the FA on the Temporary I which perceives your body.
- Do the FA on the Temporary I which perceives the reality around you.
- Do the Moving to the Heart technique.
- Repeat the same for any heavy mind content that comes up, until the end of the session.

As is the case with light mind content, you first do the FA procedure on the Temporary I which perceives the actual content. Stay a while in the Presence, but not too long.

The next step is to do the process on the Temporary I which perceives your body, which is similar to the "Entering the State of Presence" stage, but this time you are doing the FA instead of DTI.

The following step is related to the Temporary I which perceives the reality around you. You also apply the FA as a replacement for the DTI procedure.

Finally, do the MH procedure, with the simple statement *"I am."*

If this multi-layered FA approach doesn't work and you are again overwhelmed with the same strong thoughts and emotions, you can even shift into the multi-layered DTI, and then return back to the FA if everything settles down.

If you experience an avalanche of emotions or thoughts during your meditation, don't hesitate to switch to the Inner Triangle or Chain technique. Stay assured that in these cases of facing strong contents of mind, doing some of the main Reintegration techniques on them is the best way of spending your meditation time. Once you reintegrate the subconscious structure which caused the emotional flooding, your sitting sessions will probably become smoother, even if only for a few days.

Inevitably, as you continue with the practice, different previously unconscious structures will be surfacing into your consciousness. Of course, this whole process is a great opportunity for you to reintegrate your being as much as possible. If you avoid dealing with any of these structures which can be revealed during meditation, they will inevitably manifest themselves in your external reality, most likely in a very unpleasant way. They can bring about some hostile people, diseases or problematic situations into your life. So, face boldly every mind content which comes into your field of consciousness immediately; don't avoid dealing with it at any cost.

There are countless other resources out there about meditation, but this particular one is quite a new approach which you may not find a lot about elsewhere. I believe it's enough for your regular practice.

Additional Notes

Note that you may, occasionally, find yourself becoming drowsy or falling asleep. That's not something to be worried about. That only shows that you are entering some deeper levels of your subconscious. You are beginning to bring up the long-forgotten and suppressed elements of your personality, from the depths of your unconscious mind, which is great news.

Thus, when sleepiness arises, try to stay awake; change your posture, rub your eyes, switch to the DTI, but don't fight it too much. You are maybe just too tired and your body needs sleep more than meditation. So, if nothing helps, sleep for a while. But don't always give up. Sooner or later, you must face the subconscious elements that are revealing themselves and reintegrate them.

Give yourself a promise that you will do the meditation session every single day, at roughly the same time. If you have to strengthen that decision, use a "good old" treaty with yourself. Write it down thoroughly, describing when and what you will be doing every day. Also, note what you will do if you miss a scheduled session (for example doing two sessions the next day or doing a prolonged session). Sign it and keep up with it.

I cannot stress enough how important consistency in your meditation practice is. Regular meditation is the very basis of your spiritual development. It's the foundation of your personal transformation. It will naturally lead you into having more mindfulness within your daily life, and it will direct your efforts in reintegration of the elements of personality as well. It will give you additional love, health, strength, calmness, creativity and smoothness in your life.

And, ultimately, it could lead you straight to enlightenment. No kidding.

In a Nutshell

Sit with your spine straight up, whether on a chair or in one of the "lotus" positions. You can keep your eyes open or closed.

Reintegration Meditation consists of these steps:
1. Relax—you can use the Relaxation technique described in this book to do so.
2. Enter the state of Presence using the multi-layered DTI technique:
   a. Do the DTI on your current state of mind.
   b. Do the DTI on your body.
   c. Do the DTI on the external reality that you perceive at the moment.
   d. Do the Moving to the Heart technique, with statement *"I am."*
3. Occasionally remove distracting mind content using the FA technique:

For light mind content, you do only this:
   a. Do the FA on the Temporary I which perceives the content.
   b. Repeat the same for any light mind content that arises, until the end of the session.

For heavy mind content, you do the multi-layered FA:
   a. Do the FA on the Temporary I which perceives the content.
   b. Do the FA on the Temporary I which perceives your body at that moment.
   c. Do the FA on the Temporary I which perceives your external reality at that moment.
   d. Do the Moving to the Heart technique, with statement "I am."
   e. Repeat the same for any heavy mind content that comes up, until the end of the session.

If same mind content keeps recurring, do the multi-layered DTI on it and then return to the FA. If needed, don't hesitate to do even the IT or SC/DC procedures.

If you are sleepy during the meditation, try to stay awake by changing your posture, rubbing your eyes, switching to the DTI, etc. but don't fight it too much. If nothing helps, just give in and sleep. Next time, be fresher for the session and fight off the sleepiness, in order to face the mind content arising from the subconscious.

Be consistent with your sitting sessions. Schedule them for every morning, and, if possible, every evening too, roughly at the same time.

Mindfulness

"Everything real is in the present moment. Only here can we find happiness and harmony, feel alive and do something that will change our future. Only here can we be with the people we love, enjoy the things we like and see beautiful places." — Lidiya K., This Moment

The term "mindfulness" is accepted in various Buddhist traditions, as well as in many modern-day spiritual teachings. Basically, it means to live consciously in the moment; in the Now.

In his book "Stillness Speaks," the German author Eckhart Tolle[28] says: *"On the surface it seems that the present moment is only one of many, many moments. Each day of your life appears to consists of thousands of moments where different things happen. Yet if you look more deeply, is there not only one moment, ever? Is life ever not 'this moment?' This one moment—Now—the only thing you can never escape from, the one constant factor in your life. No matter what happens, no matter how much your life changes, one thing is certain: it's always Now. Since there is no escape from the Now, why not welcome it, become friendly with it?"*

Numerous scientific explorations have proven that the value of mindfulness for overall physiological and psychological well-being of people could be immense.

It is very nicely described in Wikipedia: *"The practice of Mindfulness involves being aware, moment-to-moment, of one's subjective conscious experience from a first-person perspective. When practicing mindfulness, one becomes aware of one's 'stream of consciousness'. The skill of mindfulness can be gradually developed using meditational practices that are described in detail in the Buddhist tradition. (...) The term 'mindfulness' is derived from the Pali-term 'sati' which is an essential element of Buddhist practice, including vipassana, satipaṭṭhāna and anapanasati. It has been popularized in the West by Jon Kabat-Zinn with his mindfulness-based stress reduction (MBSR) program. (...) Clinical studies have documented the*

---

[28] Wikipedia: https://en.wikipedia.org/wiki/Eckhart_Tolle; official site: https://www.eckharttolle.com/

physical and mental health benefits of mindfulness in general, and MBSR in particular. Programs based on MBSR and similar models have been widely adapted in schools, prisons, hospitals, veterans' centers, and other environments."[29]

James Baraz has also beautifully described it: *"Mindfulness is simply being aware of what is happening right now without wishing it were different; enjoying the pleasant without holding on when it changes (which it will); being with the unpleasant without fearing it will always be this way (which it won't)."*

Mindfulness dissolves your inner conflicts softly and almost imperceptibly. It ultimately leads to a permanent state of expanded consciousness which is similar or identical to the state labeled in this book as Presence. However, in this book, and especially in this section, the words "mindful," "present" and "aware" are interchangeable.

Another important note is that when you are present, you may actually be centered in your Heart. In fact, when you are experiencing the world from the Heart, you are deeply mindful, really present here-and-now. It's also possible that you are present without any particular anchor, existing and observing the reality as a non-local consciousness, but still, even in that case, your observing mind with its senses are subtly connected to your Heart, which is your direct channel to the non-local consciousness.

For that reason, you will never make a mistake if you swiftly do the Moving to the Heart (MH) technique in any situation you find yourself in, and start observing your world from the Heart. Centered at the Heart, all your actions will be perfectly appropriate for that particular situation, as is the case with doing anything from the state of non-local consciousness. So, all triggers and approaches I will be presenting you in this "Mindfulness" section

---

[29] Source: Wikipedia, the free encyclopedia; https://en.wikipedia.org/wiki/Mindfulness

lead either to the sublime state of non-local awareness or to the state of being centered in the Heart (which is ultimately the same).

How does one experience everything from the Heart?

Well, it's the most natural way of perceiving reality. The problem is that we aren't used to that mode of experiencing the world. If we find it difficult or unfathomable to be centered in the Heart, which is often the case at the beginning of the practice, we just have to *feel* the Heart. Sense the Heart area within your body as much as you can. As you feel your Heart for a while, you will eventually start perceiving your reality from it. You will find yourself centered in the Heart. Try to stay in that state as long as possible, but don't feel you have to force it; just stay and enjoy it.

Whether you feel centered in the Heart or you are in a state of pure non-local consciousness, you will be at perfect harmony with the world; your body will move lightly and flawlessly; your mind will function impeccably whenever needed, and all your actions will be done in the most effective way. Thus, if you drop a thing or stumble upon something unexpectedly, it is a clear message from your divine core: awaken, be present, feel your Heart.

In order to increase awareness in everyday life and make it stable, I suggest you make a list of your typical activities during the day, with small characteristic details or brief actions within them. Those details shall be your *triggers* for becoming present in the here and now. This will be your mindfulness list for setting up the triggers.

The triggers could be, for example, walking along a usual path, cleaning teeth, opening or closing the door, sitting down or getting up from a chair, arriving at a specific location or even thinking a particular thought. You can actually make *anything* a trigger.

Now you will be introduced to some of the most common daily activities, along with possible triggers that you could use in these situations for "waking up," and with detailed explanation on how to maintain and develop your awareness.

Immediately After Waking Up
"Let the breath lead the way."
— Sharon Salzberg, Real Happiness: The Power of Meditation

Possible trigger: the very act of opening your eyes.

As soon as you wake up in the morning, become fully mindful of your breathing with the very act of first opening your eyes. Feel the air as it enters your nose and lungs, as well as when it goes out from them. Try being mindful in this way for a few minutes. This will clear up your mind and could positively influence your whole day ahead, giving you fresh energy and necessary focus.

Morning Routines
"No ideals. No illusions. Just reality—but more perfect than you've ever imagined. That's what being mindful and living in the present means."
— Lidiya K., This Moment

Possible triggers: putting toothpaste onto your brush; putting the shaving foam on your face; switching on the shaver; touching various parts of your body while taking a shower.

The very act of squeezing toothpaste onto your toothbrush could trigger your mindfulness. When you "wake up" into the Presence, slow down every movement and try to maintain the awareness of every motion of the brush inside your mouth; sense mindfully the friction between the brush and teeth with gums. Feel the movements of your hand. Enjoy mindfully every motion.

When it comes to a shaving routine, the act of putting the foam onto your face could elicit your awareness, or the action of switching on a shaving device. Maintain awareness of every movement of the brush or shaver on your skin. Slow down each motion.

As with all other morning routines, taking a shower could also be amazingly enjoyable when you are present. As you initially touch any part of your body with your hand, let that act trigger your Presence. Keep up with this awareness as long as possible. Be mindful of every part of your body and its motions, of every stream of water rushing onto it. Enjoy the sense of this bathing in freshness, while being fully aware of every moment and everything that comes to your attention. Slow down everything and delight in your Presence.

Meals and Drinks
"The present moment is filled with joy and happiness. If you are attentive, you will see it." — Thich Nhat Hanh, Peace Is Every Step: The Path of Mindfulness in Everyday Life

Possible triggers: the act of chewing or swallowing; preparing meals, tea, coffee or juice; the act of taking up a spoon, fork, cup or glass and bringing it to your mouth.

Let these triggers initiate your mindful eating or drinking. Feel mindfully all your motions during the meals: the movements of your hands, tools, your tongue, mouth, gut, and all other sensations. Smell thoroughly the meal from time to time. Enjoy its taste. At the same time try to maintain the awareness of your own Presence. Eat slowly and immerse yourself completely in the Now.

When you are drinking, first be mindful of bringing the cup or glass full of liquid to your mouth. Sense its weight, determine how cool or hot the cup is. Smell the coffee or tea deeply before the act of drinking. Feel the liquid in your mouth: its taste, its passage down your throat. Experience fully all subsequent motions of your hand, mouth, tongue, together with all related bodily sensations. Be in the Now, while maintaining the awareness of your own presence.

"Don't drink your tea like someone who gulps down a cup of coffee during a work break. Drink your tea slowly and reverently, as if it is the axis on which the whole earth revolves-slowly, evenly, without rushing toward the future. Live the actual moment. Only this actual

moment is life. Don't be attached to the future. Don't worry about things you have to do."[30]

Dressing
"Patience requires a slowing down, a spaciousness, a sense of ease."
— *Allan Lokos, Patience: The Art of Peaceful Living*

Possible triggers: the acts of putting on or taking off items of clothing.

Whenever you begin dressing, or more precisely, as soon as you start putting on any item of clothing, you should be brought directly into the Now.

Try to sustain the state of Presence at least until you finish your dressing. Be in the moment. Feel the weight of the clothing on your skin. Stay conscious of every motion of your body and parts of clothing, together with accompanying bodily sensations. Slow down, enjoy the Now.

Driving/Commuting
"Wherever you go, there you are" — *Jon Kabat-Zinn*

Possible triggers: opening or closing the doors of your garage and car; red light on the traffic lights.

If you have a garage, immediately upon opening its door, you should become fully conscious of yourself and everything around you. Or, as you open the door of your car, your mindfulness is being triggered. Then you become completely aware of every motion and sensation.

Sit in the car; feel the sensations of the comfortable seat. Don't start the engine straightaway. Wait for a minute; relax and be fully conscious of your breathing. Then start the engine. Continue being

---

[30] Thich Nhat Hanh. The Miracle of Mindfulness (Kindle Locations 272-274). Kindle Edition.

present while driving. Melt yourself into the traffic flow, the engine's sounds, sensations of moving the wheel, pushing the gas pedal, touching any button, while keeping the awareness of your own being. Drive slowly and carefully.

Whenever you are waiting at a red traffic light, don't be anxious. Instead, take advantage of it. Pause with any thoughts and become aware of your breathing, then of all other sensations and sounds. Become aware of the Now.

To me personally, driving is one of the best opportunities to bring myself into the Now. Moreover, I drive almost impeccably when I'm completely present in the Now.

Walking

"Walk as if you are kissing the Earth with your feet." — Thich Nhat Hanh, Peace Is Every Step: The Path of Mindfulness in Everyday Life

Possible trigger: the act of standing up and beginning the first step of a walk.

When you become mindful while walking, your objective is to be fully aware of the sensations caused by your walking, together with the awareness of your own presence.

For the beginning of your practice, walk slower than usual in order to be able to follow consciously your steps. Act as a toddler who is walking for the first time, re-create the feeling of awe as you are watching the miracle of walking. Witness your first step, sense your foot lifting up, moving forward, descending, touching the ground. Follow its movement. Do the same with the other foot, and repeat this until you are fully immersed in the walking. All the while, be in the moment.

Whenever you walk, even from your office to your colleague's workplace, take advantage of this walking meditation, however short it is. Turn your every step into a small poem. Slow down, feel each step as it comes, each motion of your feet, legs, arms, all sensations of touching the ground with your shoes, your breathing, your Heart and your whole body. Enjoy the wonder of walking in the Now.

Emotions

"Feelings come and go like clouds in a windy sky. Conscious breathing is my anchor." — Thich Nhat Hanh, Stepping into Freedom: Rules of Monastic Practice for Novices

Possible triggers: any hint of a developing emotion.

All emotions, for example anger, fear or sorrow and their many variations, could also be mindfully experienced. As we meet the emotion with Presence, its unpleasantness declines dramatically. But if we succeed in intercepting its *trigger* with full awareness, we will completely avoid "the attack" or surprise of the emotional response, and the energy "assigned" to that attack will be released in a pleasant way.

It may be easier to spend some time doing the Inner Triangle or similar technique, rather than to wait for the emotion to express itself in real life. In the section "Emotions" (Part III) we have covered the most important points on dealing with emotions.

So, when we catch an emotion at its very beginning, the best approach is to simply become aware of the emotion's trigger. If possible, do quickly the FA or DTI on the trigger. If not, just accept it and become fully aware. This will often completely stop the emotion's manifestation.

But when you become conscious in the midst of its manifestation, the best way is to immediately begin conscious breathing. That will relatively quickly abate the emotion itself and allow you to do some basic Reintegration techniques on it.

Conversations

"Instructions for living a life. Pay attention. Be astonished. Tell about it."
— Mary Oliver

Possible trigger: catching the eyes of your friend; pauses during conversation.

To be honest, staying present during a conversation is pretty hard to do, but it's feasible. To achieve this in such situations you can't rely on your remembering "Oh, I should be mindful!" You must create and use your own triggers, and my above stated ideas on this are just food for thought. For example, you may create triggers from some specific words or phrases spoken during conversations, some gestures or anything else.

So, as you become aware in the middle of a discussion with a friend (or any person), first you have to become conscious of yourself and, at the same time, of the subject of conversation. Slow down the pace of the talk itself and stretch the small pauses between sentences. Try to be aware of these micro-pauses. Listen carefully to your friend, while you are staying aware of your own consciousness. Immerse into the totality of yourself and the conversation you are involved in. Feel that totality and let the flow of the dialog lead you, as you keep up with being Present.

From time to time, think silently toward your companion, whoever they are: "I wish you to be truly happy, my dear friend," or something similar. Feel love for them. It doesn't matter whether you know that person or not. It matters not if you have a great or difficult relationship with them. But if you take my advice, you certainly should be prepared for this: the current talk, as well as your whole relationship with that individual, could be transformed in beautiful, unexpected and sublime ways!

Using Electronic Devices
"Choiceless awareness—at every moment and in all the circumstances of life—is the only effective meditation." — Aldous Huxley

Possible triggers: opening the lid of a laptop; pressing the "Power" button; pressing the "Home" button; clicking or scrolling of the mouse...

I find that activities on a computer, tablet or smartphone are very demanding when it comes to maintaining Presence. These activities, especially video-games, are often draining and soak up one's attention and energy. The person is frequently completely immersed in the game or other actions within the virtual world. That's why it's advisable to set up not one, but several different mindfulness triggers. Some of them will have the role of bringing you into the Presence at the beginning of each "e-session." Others will be bringing you back into awareness occasionally during the session. It's so easy to entirely lose yourself in these kinds of activities.

Once you get back to the state of Presence during the sessions on electronic devices, keep the awareness of yourself. As you're doing your tasks, retain the awareness of your Self, of your being-ness, of your Heart, all the while. From time to time, you may also practice conscious breathing, simultaneously with your work.

Keep practicing. Be persistent. Mindfulness requires persistence and never-ending expansion of your practice.

Talking on a Phone
"The little things? The little moments? They aren't little."
— Jon Kabat-Zinn

Possible triggers: specific words or phrases, like "Hi," "Well," "How are you," etc.

This is another hard "case," particularly for engaging the triggers. You must be creative in finding those that work for you. But when you succeed in making them functional in real phone conversations, the same advice applies for talks face-to-face: be conscious of yourself and, at the same time, of the subject of talk. Reduce the speed of the dialog. Be aware of small pauses between sentences. Be in the flow of the conversation, while you retain your self-awareness.

As with in-person conversation, occasionally direct a compassionate thought or feeling toward the person on the other end of the line. Send them love.

Watching TV

"The whole present moment was a celebration; it always had been; all I needed was fresh eyes to see it." — Narissa Doumani, A Spacious Life: Memoir of a Meditator

Possible triggers: turning on the TV set with the remote; seeing particular scenes, specific images, concrete people or your favorite advertisements on the screen.

Again, one of the most demanding activities for maintaining mindfulness. You are completely passive while watching TV and are normally totally immersed in whatever happens on the screen.

The goal here is to become aware of yourself and maintain that self-awareness as you are watching television. Try some tricks. You can occasionally move your sight from the screen to the frame of the television set, all the time being aware of yourself. When the pre-determined scenes or images (designated for triggering awareness) appear on the screen, use them to strengthen your self-awareness.

Daily Errands
"Each act is a rite, a ceremony."
— Thich Nhat Hanh, The Miracle of Mindfulness

Possible triggers: the acts of putting a kettle on the burner, releasing tap water, sweeping the floors or dusting, grabbing the door handle, etc.

Daily errands could mean a lot of various regular activities, like cooking meals, washing dishes, cleaning the house and so on, which are usually considered a burden. These kinds of activities are widely accepted in many approaches for developing mindfulness. Try to be aware of every motion of your body, sensation, sound, and smell. From time to time, pause and direct attention to your breath, and then to your sense of self. Sustain that state of self-awareness during every activity. You will enjoy every errand; it will become somehow light and almost transparent.

Every conscious moment in the Now will gradually accumulate and add up to all the previous ones. The effort to become mindful of your everyday errands will make your whole life easier and abate or even prevent many future challenges.

Reading
"Even just taking 20 seconds to truly appreciate your surroundings makes a world of difference." — Russell Eric Dobda

Possible triggers: the act of browsing the pages; seeing any images; coming across a certain word or expression.

Whether you are reading a book, newspaper, a magazine, or reading something on an electronic device, you are always browsing pages or articles, seeing images or encountering some specific words. For instance, my favorite mindfulness triggers for reading are several concrete words or expressions like "therefore," "however," "for example," "et cetera." ... I have "programmed" my subconscious, more or less successfully, to launch me into the state of Presence whenever I come across these words.

Staying present while reading can be difficult. As with watching movies, you are often completely identified with the characters or the plot itself. Immediately upon becoming mindful, you have to find a delicate balance between self-awareness and attachment to the story. You will undoubtedly need to try this many times before you finally succeed in remaining stable in that state for some time. But when you make it, you will find astonishing, divine inner peace while reading and that peace will not negatively influence your reading at all. On the contrary, it will provide you with greater focus and better reading experience.

Observing Thoughts
"You can't stop the waves, but you can learn to surf." — Jon Kabat-Zinn

Possible triggers: specific thoughts.

Staying mindful during thinking actually means observing your own thoughts while you think them. You may wonder how it's possible to notice any thought in the first place, when it seems you *are* that thought as long as it stays in your mind. Luckily, we have triggers that will help us to do this.

Assign to some typical and frequently reoccurring thoughts the role of trigger for your mindfulness. That could be thoughts like "I like it," "I'm determined to...," "This is so beautiful," "I really enjoy this," "Great," "Love," "True," "Peace," and so on. Whenever these thoughts come into your mind, they should automatically induce your Presence.

The triggering thoughts can be even negative ones. As they usually initiate a stream of other negative thoughts and emotions, your Presence will abate and even transform that stream into a positive one or into pure awareness.

Now, you've become aware of your thoughts and you should know how to face them. Yet, there's a myriad of circumstances in which you could become conscious of your thoughts. In some situations, like when you are meditating, resting, or simply doing nothing, you will be perfectly able to deal with every thought that comes into your field of attention. The best way is to meet them as was explained in the "Regular Sessions"—to do the FA technique.

So, a thought arrives, like a cloud over a clear sky. You immediately notice it, but you stay fully conscious, not allowing it to overwhelm you. Next, you do the FA technique on the Temporary I which perceives that thought. As your Temporary I vanishes, so will the thought itself. Repeat this process with every single thought, as you do in meditation. After some practice, you will even be able to observe thoughts that come and go, while you are still deeply rooted in the divine emptiness of your Being. Thoughts will rarely arrive in your consciousness, and when they do, you will be completely still, despite them.

But, when you are engaged in some other activity and are having an avalanche of thoughts, it's very difficult to apply any method or technique. You should just accept each thought as soon as you notice it, regain mindfulness which includes self-awareness and continue with your main activity.

Following the Breath before Sleep
"Breathing is our participation with the cosmic dance. When our breath is in harmony, cosmos nourishes us in every sense." — Amit Ray

Possible trigger: relaxing before going to sleep.

Lying in your bed, and after doing a recapitulation of the whole day, you may finally get your well-deserved sleep. Getting ready for sleep should be a mindfulness trigger on its own and you may consider it to be a kind of meditation. But, this bed-time session should not be the kind of meditation described in the "Regular Sessions," with all those "multiple-layered" or simpler techniques, because after only a few days, such practice will get you into a habit of falling asleep while doing regular sessions. You could unconsciously transform that practice into a trigger for getting asleep.

Therefore, you should do something else. I recommend following the breath and this is a nice opportunity for a brief explanation of that well-known mindfulness technique.

If you forget to be mindful before falling asleep, let some triggering thoughts launch your awareness, or bring you back into awareness. Then you continue with following the breath. But if you are tired or have your normal sleeping routine, don't force yourself to return again and again to your breath awareness. Let yourself naturally sink into sleep. You must have enough sleep in order to be healthy, energized and mindful in your life.

Mindfulness of Breath
"Stop, breathe, look around and embrace the miracle of each day, the miracle of life." — Jeffrey A. White

There are several variations of the mindfulness of breath. In all of them you should consciously follow the movement of air into your body and out of it, along with any sensations that the movement produces. But you could focus on different areas of your body.

For example, you might prefer concentrating on the sensation of the air, moving in and out of your body in its entirety, however you feel it. Personally, I prefer this variation because it brings me more easily into a state of self-awareness. In this approach, you are trying to be fully conscious of your chest's motions during inhaling and exhaling, of the whole volume of air going in and out from you, and of the entire feeling of its gentle contact with your inner organs—nostrils, throat and lungs.

You may also practice breath mindfulness by focusing only on the sensations within your nostrils during inhale and exhale circles. Alternatively, you could orient your attention to the sensation of the air filling and emptying the inside of your lungs.

Try out all these approaches. Use whichever one is most suitable for you and enjoy mindfulness on many occasions—immediately after waking up, during driving, walking, working on the computer, while doing various daily errands, in the midst of emotional bursts, before sleep, or many other situations, at your will. Mindfulness of breath can bring you deep peace in every situation, help you in releasing stress and raise your overall level of consciousness.

Triggers
"Mindfulness isn't difficult; we just need to remember to do it."
— Sharon Salzberg, Real Happiness: The Power of Meditation

Of course, you can change any of the previously noted triggers or create more concrete ones for each of the suggested situations. You can tailor them to the specific activities which are characteristic for your own day life.

Visualize yourself in each of these trigger scenes, one by one. Imagine that in every single trigger you are becoming completely aware of both *yourself* and your *environment*. You have to visualize the most common concrete scenes from real life, in order to transmute them into functioning triggers for becoming present. Imagine the very moment in which you become fully aware.

If possible, immediately after each imagined scene, do it in real life and really become mindful. Do this a few times for every scene, the more the better. This will definitely "cement" these situations as the triggers for your mindfulness.

Remember that you are trying to create new habits for triggering mindfulness. Although mindfulness by its nature is kind of opposite to all habitual behaviors (because habits are usually unconscious actions), we still can make their *triggers* habitual. In order to create a completely new habit, we have to create its three elements: a cue, routine and reward. You have the cue for each small habit—that's the corresponding trigger. You know what the "routine" should be—*becoming* mindful. But don't forget the last, but equally important part: the reward.

What should be your reward for each of these small habits? That depends on you. Despite the fact that mindfulness itself can be regarded as a reward, you could also designate the role of reward to a small, pleasant or healthy thing that you can afford to do for yourself. One option could be to simply congratulate yourself and give yourself some love.

Designate some time every day to setting up your mindfulness triggers. You could do the visualization of 3 to 5 triggers in one session. As already noted, each visualization should be followed by exercising the trigger in real life a few times.

When you become aware that you haven't been present, you can do various things in order to get back easily to the state of Presence. There are many gates to that state. For example, stop completely your breathing for a while. You will notice that your thoughts have also stopped. No breathing, no thoughts. And that thoughtless state is actually pure consciousness. Of course, don't stay in that breathless state too long, for it's not healthy to disrupt the breath too much. You can stop breathing for 5 to 10 seconds only, enter the thoughtless state and then continue normally with breathing, while staying in the state of Presence.

Eckhart Tolle often recommends another gate to the state of pure consciousness: feeling your body. Just sense your physical body as a whole entity. Be aware of it. This will bring you into the state of Presence.

You could also tell yourself some of these words: *Now; Here; I Am; Am; I exist; Where am I?; Attention!; Stop!, I don't know.* Feel the meaning of these words; they will bring you here and now, into the state of mind without thoughts. That's mindfulness.

Distractions

"I don't need anyone else to distract me from myself anymore, like I always thought I would." — Charlotte Eriksson

OK, we are holding our mindfulness, but what should we do with distractions that will inevitably occur? They could be inner events, like unnecessary thoughts, emotions, sensations, or they could be external happenings, like people approaching or interrupting you, or any other outer event. In both cases, unless you are attacked or jeopardized in some way, you shouldn't react to them, nor should you be angry at yourself because of that.

For example, while sitting and not being engaged in a demanding activity, you should be able to remove or reintegrate any distraction with the Dissolving the Temporary I, Dissolving the Temporary I Plus, Gentle Touch of Presence or Freshness & Acceptance procedures. That's the best-case scenario.

In other circumstances, you won't be able to apply any technique. You will have just to let go of the interruption and gently return to the state of Presence. Simply tell yourself "OK" and continue with your activity, while being fully conscious. If distractions are repetitive, do this all over again, until you are finally firmly rooted in inner peace.

After everything being said here on mindfulness, you might get a feeling that mindfulness is all about creating lists, defining triggers, discipline, and so on. It is not. In his book "Mindfulness: Living in the Moment—Living in the Breath," Amit Ray tells us: *"Mindfulness is not a mechanical process. It is developing a very gentle, kind, and creative awareness to the present moment."* A very good point.

Be patient and persistent, as there is no other way, and remember: rushing kills mindfulness.

In a Nutshell

Being mindful means to do any activity fully conscious of yourself and of the activity itself. It means to live in the present moment.

Mindfulness dissolves your inner conflicts softly and almost imperceptibly.

A great way to develop the practice of everyday mindfulness is to set up triggers for various situations or activities that you are usually engaged in during the day. These triggers should become habitual "launchers" of mindfulness.

Generally, you should try to be aware of every motion of your body, sensation, texture, sound, taste and smell. From time to time pause and direct attention to your sense of self. Sustain that state of self-awareness during every activity. You will enjoy every task, you will become light and, in a strange way, even transparent.

Every conscious moment in the Now will gradually accumulate and make your whole life easier and abate or even prevent challenges.

Anything that distracts you, or pulls you out of mindfulness, you should accept as such, and not react to it at all (unless you are threatened somehow). Then continue with the activity, being fully conscious of it and of yourself simultaneously. Also, if you are in an appropriate situation, you could reintegrate the distracting mind content or your reaction to an outer distraction by using one of the basic Reintegration techniques.

Importance of Pacing
"Difficult roads often lead to beautiful destinations" — Melchor Lim

Many people have reported some unusual, often upsetting symptoms after periods of rigorous application of meditation. After an initial decision to start meditating, they immediately began very intensive practice, which led to disturbing symptoms, often after a few weeks only.

So, if you are a beginner, I would strongly recommend that you avoid overdoing meditation during the initial period at least, otherwise you could begin having difficulties or strange sensations as follows:

- Vibrating, tingling, stinging, itching or crawling sensations
- Changing sleep patterns: restlessness, night sweats, waking up two or three times a night
- Periods of fatigue
- Increase or decrease in appetite
- Weight gain, typically around the belly
- New allergies to certain foods
- Blurred or foggy vision
- Occasionally seeing flashes of light, shimmering or glittery objects
- Occasionally hearing strange voices or sounds
- Flu-like or allergy-like symptoms (high temperatures, sneeze attacks, runny nose, sore throat, neck pains, night sweats, headaches, aching bones and joints)
- Concentration difficulties and dizziness
- Involuntary bodily movements, like muscle spasms, jerking, tremors, shaking
- Heart palpitations and fluttering
- Enhanced senses of smell, touch or taste
- Lucid or vivid dreams
- Occasional breathing difficulties
- Depression for no reason, feelings of loss or isolation
- Emotional outbursts or mood swings

I don't want to scare you off. These sensations never happen all at once. You could experience only one or two of them, or maybe even five to six at the same time, or maybe none. However, this is the reason why you should be cautious in practicing meditation, even including mindfulness.

What is the cause of these unpleasant phenomena?

Neither our mind nor body is ready for a sudden start with very intensive practice. Since meditation induces relief inside us on every level, internal energies could start flowing too vigorously and our body would react defensively. The strong flow of life energies (in some traditions it is called chi or prana) produces a biological chain reaction in our organism, which results in more robust generating of toxins and the whole body reacts. Of course, these toxins are usually not too dangerous and in some cases the energy flow is not followed by production of toxins whatsoever, but they are often just a temporary issue for our health.

For example, when I finally disciplined myself and started my everyday routine of practicing meditation, I began with 40 minutes of meditation every morning and every evening. Since I decided really firmly to sustain that routine, eventually it became a habit, and that makes me very pleased now. But meanwhile, roughly one month after commencement of that steady practice, I began sensing some of the above-mentioned symptoms—energy rushes, frequent high temperatures with sore throat (even once a week, lasting one or two days, often only in my hands and feet), occasional muscle spasms, and some emotional outbursts.

Initially, I was disturbed mostly due to those flu-like symptoms and thought that somehow my immune system had deteriorated. I wasn't aware that these sensations were maybe just a consequence of my over-excessive spiritual practice and I kept on practicing in the same manner. My physicians couldn't find anything particularly wrong. After about two months, these symptoms slowly started to diminish. Meanwhile, I learned about these effects and didn't change my routine for a few more months. After that, I stretched practice five more minutes every half a year and stopped with this increasing when I reached one hour in the morning and one hour in the evening, which is still my routine. I have never experienced similar symptoms again.

Don't be discouraged by the long list of possible difficulties above. If you get some of these, do not worry too much. Of course, some of these symptoms you should check with your physician anyway, but if they are consequence of your practice, they will almost certainly pass relatively quickly if you slow down your practice.

So, what should you do?

Despite all these warnings, I would still strongly encourage you to establish a daily practice of meditation (if you haven't already), both in the morning and evening, somewhere between 15 to 30 minutes for each session. That's for the beginning. After a few months, when your newly established meditation practice stabilizes and becomes habitual, it is advisable to extend this time with 5 additional minutes to each session. If there are no negative effects, you could then add 5 more minutes to your morning and evening sessions every two or three months.

After starting the sitting meditation practice, if you notice some of these negative effects, just shrink every session down by 5 or 10 minutes, depending on the roughness of side-effects, but *do not discontinue your practice*. It is very important to stay with your meditation sessions in order to strengthen this habit. When the habit is formed, you will always feel an urge for meditation and for finding a time window in your busy day to do it.

Steady practice of mindfulness also could produce some of the side-effects stated above. Nevertheless, practicing mindfulness is also vital to your spiritual growth and your whole life as well.

Both regular sitting sessions and mindfulness will inevitably reintegrate many portions of negative energy in your psyche, layer by layer. As your practice goes on, many repressed traumas, fears, or other unpleasant elements of your personality will be revealed, just as they have been exposed to a strong, unexpected light. They will express themselves or try to hide again. Therefore, this process will probably lead you to occasional and surprising bursts of anger, sorrow, pain, or fear. You could be involved in interactions with some people you consider adverse or annoying, and these interactions may ignite your negative reactions.

Don't be discouraged, as there is no real reason for worry. Moreover, despite all these possible obstacles, you must be persistent with your practice. In the next section, "Morphic Fields," you will learn some concrete ways and methods to deal with these kinds of challenges. Therefore, I still strongly recommend practicing both regular meditation sittings and mindfulness. They are mutually supportive and practicing both of them could dramatically improve your everyday life. Once again, be cautious of pacing.

In a Nutshell

Avoid overdoing meditation during the initial period of your everyday practice. Steady, daily practice of sitting meditation is recommended due to its various benefits. However, one may experience emotional or physical difficulties to some extent in the beginning. These difficulties may manifest as vibrating, tingling or itching sensations, periods of fatigue, increase or decrease in appetite, flu-like or allergy-like symptoms, heart palpitations and fluttering, dizziness, emotional outbursts, etc. Although less likely, mindfulness practice could also induce some of these effects.

This is only a temporary challenge. As your practice continues, these phenomena will gradually subdue. It happens usually if you have never practiced meditation before, or if your sitting periods are too long in the initial phase of practice.

The above-mentioned unpleasant manifestations mostly occur as a consequence of too strong flow of life energies within our body, which is unprepared for that and reacts defensively for some period of time.

Some unpleasant experiences will also arise because during your practice many previously suppressed emotions, traumas, fears, beliefs or other elements of personality will be inevitably revealed. They may express themselves either during sittings or mindful periods, or in "normal" state of consciousness.

It is advisable to start your everyday meditative practice with sitting sessions that are no longer than 30 minutes. After every couple of months of such work, you may extend each session by 5 minutes.

If you still experience some of the unpleasant phenomena, just shrink down periods of sittings by 5 or 10 minutes.

Morphic Fields

"People who deny the existence of dragons are often eaten by dragons. From within." — Ursula K. Le Guin, The Wave in the Mind: Talks & Essays on the Writer, the Reader & the Imagination

There is a somewhat unsettling thing I have learned about in my life and spiritual practice, and I give credit for that to the books "The Power of Now" and "Transurfing."

Although I knew that ultimate responsibility for all aspects of my life lied within myself, I doubted for a long time that there were strange forces inside or outside of me that perpetually and tenaciously hindered my spiritual growth.

In your life, have you ever noticed that right after you achieved something good, or had finally raised yourself to a higher level, you then had some setback come smashing down, or an unexpected reaction force that struck back? What is that? Why are there such disappointments in our life?

Eckhart Tolle frequently refers in his books to a "pain-body" inside every human being. The pain-body is a conglomerate of negative energy within us which is half-conscious, or sometimes a self-conscious entity. Numerous spiritual practitioners around the world believe that this disturbing concept actually has a very firm foundation in real life.

As all physical objects with a certain mass mutually attract with gravitational force, there is also a strange kind of attracting force among energies that are similar in their nature. As positive energies or human experiences attract each other and tend to attract more and more like experiences, so the negative energies and experiences tend to coalesce and unite into an ever-bigger energetic entity. There is another name of these energetic entities: the morphic fields.

These fields develop not only in individual human or other living beings, but also on a collective level.

As is the case with living organisms, morphic fields have a strong tendency to survive and grow. What's more important, they "feed" themselves with the like energies. So, negative morphic fields will try to survive and grow by feeding with negative energies, which are usually produced in fights, battles, wars, accidents, diseases, etc.

Additionally, which could sometimes pose a real problem to us, these entities have a vague consciousness. After eons of development and accumulation of like energy, some of these entities seem to have clearly defined themselves as completely self-conscious beings.

There are countless types of morphic fields. For example, there are morphic fields of every family, group of people, sport clubs, organizations, companies, countries, nations, state administration, schools, particular religions, specific human behaviors, emotions of all kinds, and so forth.

Equipped with some sort of consciousness and mind, negative morphic fields will always try to *induce* destructive thoughts or emotions in individual people or harmful events on a collective level, in order to feed themselves with energies produced in such states or events.

Of course, positive morphic fields will always try to bring about some pleasant state or circumstance that will be beneficial to us and them as well. Many prayers of religious people are actually feeding these positive entities formed around particular positive ideas, angels or passed individuals considered as saints. In many cases, these benevolent energetic beings, as conscious entities, respond positively to the believers with fulfilling their prayers and even miraculous events.

The sad thing is that we don't see all these beings. We are rarely aware of them. However, in many mythologies and religious traditions, the morphic fields of both kinds are pictured as angels or demons.

In his book "Transurfing," the Russian author Vadim Zeland describes many aspects of human spiritual growth, and among other things, he explains his concept of "pendulums." He elaborates much more extensively on the subject of these negative morphic fields than Tolle. While the German author focuses mostly on individual pain-bodies, Zeland emphasizes the negative collective morphic fields, which he labels as pendulums.

He calls them pendulums due to their tendency to swing relentlessly, like the pendulum on a clock. If we want to stop its movement, it's not so easy. If we hit it at the wrong time, that will only amplify its swinging. Thus, if we fight against these collective (or individual) negative entities, we will probably only strengthen them. If we act positively toward them, we will also strengthen them.

One of the ways to stop the pendulum's swinging is to raise our awareness, ignore its movement and leave it to die off. In other words, when its attack strikes, you have to become present as much as possible. If you are fully aware in such a situation, the proper action (or non-action) will arise from you. Of course, becoming present in these circumstances is quite difficult, especially if something hits us straight on our head every time. It's hard to stay present and consciously ignore the negativity around us... but it *is* possible.

In the "Power of Now," Tolle gives us some very useful advice related to the very moment when the "pain body" attacks: *"If you are able to stay alert and present at that time and watch whatever you feel within, rather than be taken over by it, it affords an opportunity for the most powerful spiritual practice, and a rapid transmutation of all past pain becomes possible."*

He adds another concrete instruction: *"Focus attention on the feeling inside you. Know that it is the pain-body. Accept that it is there. Don't think about it—don't let the feeling turn into thinking. Don't judge or analyze. Don't make an identity for yourself out of it. Stay present, and continue to be the observer of what is happening inside you. Become aware not only of the emotional pain but also of "the one who observes," the silent watcher. This is the power of the Now, the power of your own conscious presence. Then see what happens."*

Another way is to "hit" the pendulum just at the right moment, when it is approaching us, with a mild and properly directed force. Translated into real life, we should apply some of the Reintegration or other spiritual or psychological techniques on them, but we must do it cleverly and carefully. We have an arsenal of effective tools for that: for negative states of mind that have just started developing, the best technique could be the Freshness and Acceptance; we could also use the Dissolving the Temporary I Plus or the Gentle Touch of Presence. For already developed negative circumstances and states of mind, we could apply either the Inner Triangle, Single Chain or Double Chain Technique.

Along with the Reintegration work, we have to have a proper general attitude, firmly rooted in moral behavior. Otherwise, our misbehaving may attract a related pendulum, and will start falling into the spiral caused by its gravitation.

Additionally, when you feel the pendulum approaching, when you notice that the situation is getting worse, try to totally and unexpectedly break the string of events. It's similar to calming a child: when it gets angry and starts screaming often without any apparent reason, you could calm it down by suddenly and quickly pointing to something in the room totally unrelated to the child's attention. Being unexpectedly interrupted in its tirade, in awe, the child rapidly calms down.

The same approach works with pendulums: in negative circumstances, full of rising rage, fights or disputes, try to break the morphic field's momentum by abruptly and suddenly turning the attention of all involved onto an entirely different subject. It could be a ridiculously normal thing, some good joke, pointing to a scene or person on TV, or maybe something else. It depends on your creativity. This will stop the pendulum's swing and the atmosphere will most probably calm down immediately. You can even feel a sort of soothing energy flooding onto you and your group. That energy was initially "intended" by the pendulum to be put into the fight. However, in this way you will win the battle, but not the "war" yet.

We should definitely be persevering in this work. There will be many setbacks; pendulums are very persistent, sometimes even crafty.

Please keep in mind that we live in a holographic universe. The negative elements of our personality are kind of pendulums' "agents" inside us. Pendulums mirror our internal challenges. When we succeed in reintegrating our negative personal parts, we actually leave the pendulums without their roots in our being. They can't influence us anymore, since they are just outer projections of our inner negative elements. Of course, this would account for our own individual reality, not for that of others. Those same pendulums will continue to lurk and feed on other people that haven't solved their own internal problems.

If you miss the right moment to break the pendulum's attack at the beginning, you may face a challenge, but don't give up! When you think you are in its deepest darkness, without any exit, in the middle of a crisis—you have already fed the pendulum enough, and it will release you soon. When that deliverance comes, immediately take action. Use that attack to reveal a hidden cue: the cause. Begin preparations for the next attack. Try to dive into your subconscious; ask yourself: "What caused this attack (problem)?" Try to find a suppressed trait, emotion or another element of personality that caused the issue. That personality element is the pendulum's "agent" or root within you.

Sooner or later, you must find that cause. It could have multiple sources. When you find the root of the problem, apply some of the main Reintegration techniques and reintegrate it forever. You will finally free yourself from that problem and its related pendulum.

In a Nutshell

As with positive energies within human personality, negative energies and experiences tend to coalesce into an ever-bigger energetic entity. We call these entities morphic fields or pendulums. They grow in individuals, groups, or even in the whole humanity, on a collective level. Normally, we are not aware of their existence at all.

The morphic fields have a strong tendency to survive and grow. They also have consciousness of a certain level and feed on energies of their similar kind. These entities will always try to induce positive or negative psychological states or external events (depending on their own nature), in order to feed themselves.

We must not fight negative morphic fields, as that will only give them an additional momentum, and that's the reason why we can call them pendulums.

One of the ways to stop the pendulum's swinging is to be present during its activity and consciously ignore generated negativity, something like being transparent. If we were persistent each time in this, that specific morphic field will abandon our individual life.

Additionally, whenever we notice that a problematic situation is arising, we can try to do something completely unexpected and different, to turn the attention of all involved people onto a totally different subject. This will stop the development of the problematic event, though we will only get a temporary relief, as the roots of the morphic field's attacks are still existent.

In order to extinguish the pendulum's roots within our personality, we have to apply some of the Reintegration techniques on a negative behavior or event which represents the pendulum's influence.

Healing

"The secret of health for both mind and body is not to mourn for the past, nor to worry about the future, but to live the present moment wisely and earnestly." — *Gautama Buddha*

First of all, let me be absolutely clear here. Although you may find some parts of this material not firmly rooted in science, I am a firm supporter of science and do not advise anyone to do any treatment of an illness with an alternative approach if they have not already tried an appropriate medical treatment. So, if you haven't already, please consult your physician if you are suffering from a serious illness. If he or she agrees, you may use Reintegration processes to aid in your recovery on top of your existing treatment. These processes should be considered only as a supplement, and not a replacement for proper medical treatment.

As you reintegrate all aspects of your personality, your health will greatly improve. Your personality will become amalgamated and your inner True Being will shine through. The True Being is the source of Presence and Love.

What actually is health? It is the perfect state of our body and mind. Our organism depends on internal physical and chemical processes. These processes rely on the energetic blueprint of our body. That whole energetic structure rests on underlying currents of energy which have their own habitual paths and patterns. These currents' proper flow directly depends on your personality's integrity.

Any disharmony or collision among the parts of your personality reflects on your energetic body's stability and ultimately on the overall functionality of your physical body.

How can we achieve this perfect state of mind and body?

There are many ways to heal yourself or somebody else, but we will focus on prayer, Love, Presence and healing through Reintegration techniques.

We should be aware that disease is a kind of strange phenomenon. There are countless examples of times that people did everything they possibly could to heal themselves, and the recovery just never happened; and vice versa, where many people did virtually nothing in order to heal themselves, and yet, miraculous recoveries happened. We just can't be 100 percent sure about the recovery process.

Prayer

"Perfect prayer does not consist in many words, silent remembering and pure intention raises the heart to that supreme Power."
— Amit Ray, Om Chanting and Meditation

For those of you that believe in God, healing with prayer can be of great importance and value. Personally, I found that practicing psychological techniques alone was too dry, so the addition of occasional prayer was helpful to me. My inner relation to the Source, Being, Allah or God (whatever you wish to call it/Him) has become of utmost importance to me. That connection has only been strengthened by the meditation and prayer in my life. However, each person's spiritual connection with the Supreme Being is completely intimate to themselves, so I can only express some of my personal impressions about it.

Though I have often felt that God already knew my intentions and wishes regardless of prayer, the very act of praying is valuable in itself. It is important to form and express your inner needs as a kind of spiritual practice from time to time.

Certainly, there must be corresponding morphic fields for each religious belief or ideology. For example, there would be a morphic field for the Christian Church and its numerous subdivisions, for each of its saints and angelic entities, as well as fields for all other spiritual movements or even cults. They may be invisible and beyond the reaches of our everyday senses, but the fields are there.

After hundreds or thousands of years of intensive praying and worshipping, many of these morphic fields will have become very powerful, self-conscious beings. There are the negative energetic beings, called pendulums, and the benevolent ones which can help people. So, you could pray to those benevolent morphic fields, but be careful in that practice. It's a bit of a slippery terrain area, as there are so many entities and energies that are not as benevolent as they may seem at first. Keep in mind, also, that any inner inadequacies or hidden conflicts within you would be reflected by this world of invisible energies.

So, if you are not yet experienced in prayer, I would recommend sticking to praying to your Supreme, benevolent Being, whichever one you adhere to. The only important thing is to be completely honest in the prayer and with yourself. Personally, I try to keep my wording minimalistic, all the while filling my Heart with pure intention, without any attachment. Just be in the Presence, centered in the Heart, and filled with clean, honest intention supplemented by a few words or sentences; that's all.

It's up to you whether you will be praying to God or not, or in which way will you pray to Him. There have been many accounts of miraculous recoveries in human history so far. Divine help might not be in a form of miracle at all; it may normally be invisible and incomprehensible to our minds. It may even come to us through an inner impulse to do some work on our internal barriers, hindrances, fears or other problems.

Though He may or may not help us, we must trust that He will do what is best for us. In praying to God, we strengthen our connection with Him, after all. We simply have to be completely honest in that deed. Our prayers must originate from our hearts, and be motivated by truth and love.

After all, any honest act, if done from the Heart, has the power of true prayer. As Mahatma Gandhi said, *"The simplest acts of kindness are by far more powerful than a thousand heads bowing in prayer."*

Love

"What happens when people open their hearts?"
"They get better."
— *Haruki Murakami, Norwegian Wood*

The topic here is not a romantic kind of love. Not wanting to underestimate or demean romantic love, I would say that pure Love is something immensely glorious and powerful, yet immeasurably gentler than romance. The Love we are talking about here is the ultimate divine force in the universe. It is not an emotion, nor is it a state of mind. It is the true state of the Heart and its union with oneness.

If our Hearts were as pure as that, we wouldn't need any techniques; our minds would be one with our Hearts and we would all have a perfect existence filled with Love and Presence. But, as we all know, that isn't the case. We are all still working toward that goal.

Love, as well as Presence, is incredibly important. Despite the occasionally dry, scientific language of some of the techniques in this book, Love is an underlying theme of the Reintegration System. We have to purify our Hearts to be able to really emanate Love. In order to cleanse our Hearts, we need to be reasonable, resourceful, and persevering in our everyday work on ourselves. We must continuously apply techniques, while being guided by our Hearts and reason at the same time.

Love dissolves all negativity in us. We can heal ourselves and other people as well, just with Love. If we were able to open up our Hearts entirely and lastingly, I believe it would be absolutely enough for complete healing.

Healing with Love can be one of the most powerful methods of healing work. Yet, for the majority of people, it is the most challenging way. Why is this so? It's because our Hearts are often closed and wrapped in many layers of mind content.

However, all of us occasionally feel Love, often without any apparent reason. Sometimes we see a little child and our Hearts can't help but open to the pure innocence which is emanating from that being; or we see a dog or some other animal that simply wants to play; or we meet with an old friend; or there is no reason whatsoever. Love just springs out from us and it's invaluable. It makes barriers disappear, suffering diminish, and fears vanish. The power of pure Love is undeniable to any negativity in us or outside of us.

I would certainly recommend the approach of many spiritual and psychological teachings that encourage us to develop Love in our hearts, both toward ourselves and others—but first toward ourselves! It is not selfishness. It is like the safety instructions on commercial planes: a parent must put their own oxygen mask on before helping their child. The same is true in life. If we aren't able to help ourselves first, we aren't able to help others, which we seek to do so much.

If you are able to open your Heart entirely, at least for a while, the flow of Love will pour out of you. First it will fill your being completely, then it will flow to others, without exception… even to our enemies!

Enemies, (if we have them at all) are in fact our greatest teachers. They are often a concentration of many traits and behaviors that bother us, which in turn tells us about ourselves, and our own long suppressed parts. Although being unaware of this, they show us clearly which traits in our personality we should work on. We should love those persons because of this! They are projections of our inner suppressed parts.

It's time to take a completely different position in your life—to get wisdom not through pain anymore, but through nurturing Love and Presence within you, in every situation, with every being. So, inside your mind you can always tell those people or your corresponding inner parts: *"I love you. Thank you for all your valuable lessons. You have always taught me how to gain wisdom and maturity through suffering. From now on, give me your help through Love and Presence."*

I believe Love can heal any part of life. It can heal any illness, any dysfunction, challenge or problem. Sometimes, when I had a cold, I would remind myself that the best thing I could do would be to open up my Heart and feel Love for myself, for all people around me and toward the whole world. Whenever I succeeded even a little bit in that "opening" endeavor (though it shouldn't had been an endeavor at all), in a matter of hours I was up on my feet again, feeling completely renewed and healed.

How can you wake up Love in your Heart?

I can recommend only some of the numerous ways to do that. For example, imagine that a little child, or toddler, is approaching you. It's smiling innocently at you, wobbling in its walking. It's so cute, with bright, smiling eyes staring at you. The child is giggling with its sweet voice, telling you "I love you!" You are embracing it with warmth. How couldn't you feel Love toward such an innocent being? Let Love rush out from your Heart.

When you open your Heart, let Love fill you completely. Extend it also to yourself. Love yourself with your whole Heart! Feel that you deserve the deepest Joy and Happiness. After all, you have always been giving the best you could. You, as that child, need only to be happy. You only want to be happy in your life and you definitely deserve that! Love yourself, your body, and your whole being. Wish yourself all the best.

Love all parts of your being and personality, all traits, flaws, mistakes and imperfections; love the body that has served you so dutifully your whole lifetime; love your life, your past, present and future, anything that comes to your mind.

Let Love amplify and expand to encompass all people around you. Love your family, your children, spouse, parents, friends, colleagues; love your job, your errands and annoying things; love your enemies, too; let Love pour out from your Heart toward all of them. Extend your Love to all humanity. Feel yourself as a part of it. Love your darling pets; love all animals, plants and all living beings. Love your Mother Earth, the entire Universe, the entire Existence. Feel the fact that countless beings exist within Creation, and all of them are trying to be happy in some way. Wish them all true happiness with your whole Heart.

This is Love and it is miraculous. It can potentially heal, harmonize and mature everything. Try not to expect healing, but love yourself and all beings around you. If the healing should come, it will come, to both you and inevitably those around you. Something wonderful will surely happen, although you cannot know what it will be.

If you want to heal other people, the answer is simple: grow Love within your Heart, express it, and you will be healing yourself and the people around you in the best way. I will touch on the subject of helping others in Part V, section "Additional Areas of Application" as well.

Presence
"Every star was once darker than the night, before it awoke." — Dejan Stojanovic, The Sign and Its Children

The state of Presence is one of the aspects of Supreme Happiness. Presence encompasses Peace and Joy, but in its nature, it's the same as Love, so its effects are similar too.

Gentle Touch of Presence (GTP), as you may remember from earlier in the book, is one of the most important techniques. The Presence is the source of perfect intelligence in our body and mind. When we are in the state of Presence, anything we do, we do impeccably and effortlessly.

You can delve into the state of Pure Consciousness or Presence in many ways. Here we will achieve that through the first step of the GTP technique:

"Feel from which Temporary I vantage point you are experiencing the present moment. Do the DTI. You will find yourself in a state of pure consciousness, the Presence. Stay in that state for roughly ten to fifteen seconds."

Then, the second step:

"Now, softly bring the issue you are dealing with into that Presence. Be that Presence, while gently experiencing the issue. Envelop that issue with your Presence. It is important to have them both together, the Presence and the issue, simultaneously. Keep that 'togetherness' as long as possible, until the issue completely disappears, or at least your unpleasant 'gut feeling' related to the issue, vanishes."

In this case, that issue is a disease, or more concretely, the unpleasant feeling or bodily sensations produced by that disease.

When the unpleasant feelings completely disappear or at least significantly weaken, do the Moving to the Heart technique. The announcement should be something like: "I am a person who is completely relieved, comfortable and healthy."

The results of healing with Gentle Touch of Presence are similar to those of healing with Love, because Presence and Love are only two aspects of the same—the Supreme Happiness, the Supreme Being.

Healing others is also covered at the end of this book, within the section named "Additional Areas of Application." However, you can use this same technique both for healing yourself and for others.

Healing through Reintegration Techniques
"Change, like healing, takes time." — Veronica Roth, Allegiant

This aspect of healing relies more on the relationship between cause and effect. If the psyche is in disharmony, or there are numerous conflicts in our personality, it may effectually cause a disease.

The work I present to you in this chapter—reintegration of general aspects, breaking bad habits, letting go of limiting beliefs, decisions, rules, emotions, traumatic memories, fears, desires and traits, meditation with pacing—can help prevent diseases and keep your health in great shape. Of course, regular physical activity, healthy nutrition and lifestyle are of great importance to one's health as well.

With the Reintegration techniques, you will be able to heal yourself (and others, through yourself), although this approach to the healing work is more for intellectual-type people. Nonetheless, it can bring about great results, just as Prayer, Love or Presence can.

When it comes to healing others through these techniques, I would strongly recommend that you not apply them directly on the ill person, but rather find a corresponding part of your own personality and do the technique on it.

First, you have the basic techniques (DTI and DTI+) at your disposal. If you need to find the cause of the disease as soon as possible because of pain, you could try to find the ill organ or part of your body by applying the manual muscle testing (MMT).

In order to simplify things, make a few assumptions as to which organ or body part is the source of the illness. Usually it's the one which is most painful. Check it with the MMT. Use the statement "This part/organ is healthy." Go over a few body parts and determine which ones are ill. Do the DTI+ on that body part and the unpleasant feeling of it first, with the MH phrase "I feel that this body part (state its name/location) is healthy."

Then, do the DTI+ on the general symptoms of the disease and the overall unpleasant feeling or pain, with the MH phrase "I feel relieved, comfortable and completely healthy." You could use a different statement if it's more suitable for you, just be aware of formulating the announcement positively, without mentioning the pain or illness (if possible). It should also be expressed in the present tense. If you can't find an appropriate statement without using the words related to pain or disease, use formulations like "I am completely free of pain (or disease) and I feel relieved and comfortable."

Go over all negative beliefs, rules, traumatic memories, fears, guilt feelings, etc., and try to determine what could be the concrete inner cause of that illness. Create a list of possible "candidates." Then, go over each personality element from that list and check it with the MMT. While doing the MMT, state: "This personality element (state its name) is the cause of my illness (state the name of the illness)." If that statement shows as true, then you have the cause, but make sure you check all the possible elements, because some diseases have multiple inner sources.

At least do the DTI+ on these problematic elements. I say 'at least', because you have much more powerful tools at hand. These are the Inner Triangle (or its alternative version), Simplified Inner Triangle, Single Chain or Double Chain. As you know, the most comprehensive and often most effective technique is the Inner Triangle. Sometimes the cause could even be some positive element of personality which you don't want to dissolve or change a lot. In that case, you could also use the Convergence Procedure with the positive element as one polarity and the goal "I am perfectly healthy," as the other polarity.

When it comes to mere pain relief, we have to do the DTI technique on the pain directly. First, we mentally give a concrete location and shape to the pain as it is a living entity. It is advisable to attribute as many features as possible to it and to observe it from the outside for a couple seconds. Then enter it. Feel it "from the inside." Find the Temporary I from which vantage point you are experiencing the pain entity. Do the Dissolving the Temporary I. Repeat the procedure as long as you feel the pain. You will probably notice that the position of your Temporary I changes as you are repeating the DTI procedure.

In a Nutshell

In your dealing with an illness, always seek appropriate medical treatment first. The methods of treating ailments described here should be considered and implemented only as supplements to modern medical treatment. Always consult your physician.

Prayer

The power of an honest prayer can be immense, especially for those who deeply believe in a Supreme Benevolent Being, or God. It is a way of sincere relationship with the Source. Since God already knows all your deepest longings and fears, prayer does not need to consist of too many words and should be supported by our genuine feelings. It must be completely honest, motivated only by unselfish intentions, truth and love.

Love

Love, similar to Presence, dissolves all negativity in us. I believe we can heal ourselves and others with just Love. If we were able to open up our Hearts entirely and lastingly, it would be enough for a complete recovery, though we are far from that goal right now.

You can easily open your Heart by imagining an innocent, cute being that induces Love in you. That could be your child, or any toddler, pet, or even a mature person who you love immensely. Feel Love toward that lovely being.

Also, feel Love for yourself. Let it fill your being completely. Love all parts of your being, all traits, flaws, mistakes and imperfections; love your life, your job, your past, present and future, anything that comes to mind. Extend Love to all your family, friends, people, humanity, animals, plants, all living beings, and to the whole of Existence.

If the healing should come, it will come. Don't expect anything. Just love yourself, everybody and everything. Something wonderful will surely happen, we just can't know what it will be.

Presence

Presence is the source of perfect intelligence in our body and mind. When we are in that state, anything we do, we do impeccably and effortlessly. As with Love, the Presence dissolves and integrates all negative aspects of our personality, improves our external life and can exert positive influence on diseases, too.

Here is a concrete procedure for healing with the Presence:
1. Bring yourself into the state of Presence. You can use DTI for that.
2. Bring gently the feelings or sensations related to the disease into your consciousness, while persistently keeping yourself in the state of Presence. Keep that unity of Presence and unwanted sensations as long as possible.
3. Do the Moving to the Heart technique, with the statement: "I am a person who is completely relieved, comfortable and healthy."

Healing through Reintegration Techniques

This way of healing is based on the relationship between cause and effect. If there are numerous conflicts in our personality, they may cause a disease, so we must do reintegration work as much as possible to harmonize them and bring back our health again.

You can follow these steps in your reintegration work on a disease:
1. Determine the probable ill part of your body by using the Manual Muscle Testing technique (MMT).
2. Do the DTI+ on the general symptoms of the disease and on the overall unpleasant feeling or pain, with the MH phrase "I feel relieved, comfortable and completely healthy."
3. Determine which negative elements of personality are probable psychic causes of the illness. You can use the MMT technique to assist you in that process.
4. Treat those elements with DTI+, Inner Triangle, Chain techniques or Convergence Procedure.

Moral Behavior

"When you think yours is the only true path you forever chain yourself to judging others and narrow the vision of God. The road to righteousness and arrogance is a parallel road that can intersect each other several times throughout a person's life. It's often hard to recognize one road from another. What makes them different is the road to righteousness is paved with the love of humanity. The road to arrogance is paved with the love of self." — Shannon L. Alder

The Reintegration System—or any other psychological or spiritual system, for that matter—*cannot* be effective in the long run without moral behavior.

Real, moral behavior should naturally spring from an enlightened person, who acts from their true being, from Love and Presence, and from a pure Heart. That's a rare case, though. Who among us is really enlightened? A small number of people, at best. Personally, I don't know anybody. Maybe you do, but if you were already enlightened, you probably wouldn't buy this book.

However, you may have had many moments or even periods of living from your true being, or Presence. If we were to act from the Heart, here and now, fully conscious, we would do everything perfectly, and it would be perfect moral behavior.

But meanwhile, what do we do with the majority of our everyday life when we can't sustain our Presence? We must be firm and resolute—to live ethically and honestly.

Why is it so important? Well, if you behaved unethically, you will have spoiled everything you've done in the Reintegration so far. Immoral conduct inevitably produces remorse inside you, at least on a subconscious level. It also yields resentment in others. Remorse and resentment generate anger and suffering. This will result in major setbacks to your work on yourself and in your life, generally.

Moral behavior is a matter of pure decision and firmness, assisted by Love, Presence and Reintegration techniques. Whenever you find yourself on the verge of immoral conduct, if you feel a temptation to act dishonestly, bring yourself into the state of pure Love. It dissolves dishonest inclinations, anger, resentment, fear, pain and other negative emotions at their roots.

If you can't open your Heart and reveal Love inside yourself, try to dive into the state of Presence. It's also a divine state, the same in its roots as Love, and it will help you to behave perfectly in any situation.

However, if you still have trouble getting yourself into the states of Love or Presence, do some of the basic Reintegration techniques, for example Dissolving the Temporary I Plus (DTI+) or Gentle Touch of Presence (GTP). Whenever you recognize a temptation or urge to behave dishonestly, do these techniques on it as soon as possible. If you've already done something bad, use them more extensively on that as mind content, and, if needed, treat it with Inner Triangle or Chain techniques.

When you have some free time, try to find all your selfish traits, beliefs, thoughts or other parts of your character. You can also use your timeline in order to become aware of some of your selfish and immoral behaviors. Be completely honest and admit to yourself in what situations you behaved egotistically. Make a list of these traits and behaviors, and meticulously reintegrate all of them using some of the Reintegration techniques. My recommendation for this would be the Inner Triangle, Single Chain or Double Chain techniques.

What is truly moral behavior? It is honest conduct in any situation, which always takes into account the feelings of others, while led by the highest ideals of Love, Peace and Joy for the person conducting the deed, for all others involved and for the whole of humanity.

It is a positive ideal, stemming from inner truth. It doesn't forbid specific harmful deeds, although in many situations one should limit oneself in that sense, too.

However, it is much better to avoid an immoral deed, even at the price of suppressing it temporarily, than to commit the deed and regret it forever. A suppressed bad deed you could handle later anyway, and for that you would have at your disposal various Reintegration procedures or techniques from other psychological or spiritual systems. On the other hand, the committed wrong-doing would have generated regret, guilt, resentment, anger and other negative strong feelings in yourself and others, which would be much harder to heal and integrate later.

In a Nutshell

True moral behavior is honest conduct in any situation, which always takes into account the feelings of others, while led by the highest ideals of Love, Peace and Joy for the person conducting the deed, for all others involved and for the whole of humanity.

It stems from your inner truth—Love and Presence. Although it is positive by its nature, and it should not impose limitations onto your conduct; if you are not in the state of Presence and Love, you should force yourself to always behave honestly.

It is important to reintegrate your repetitive selfish behaviors from the past and of all the selfish elements of your personality as well.

Immoral conduct produces regret and guilt within yourself, and resentment and anger in others. This leads to suffering. The results are major setbacks in your work on yourself.

You should avoid an immoral deed, if necessary, by suppressing it temporarily, so as to deal with it later using Reintegration techniques. Whereas, if you commit the deed, guilt and other negative emotions in you and others will be much more difficult to overcome later.

Part IV
Achieving Goals

PART IV: ACHIEVING GOALS

*"Hold fast to dreams,
For if dreams die
Life is a broken-winged bird,
That cannot fly."*
— Langston Hughes

You may be wondering why this chapter is put after the previous chapters, when goal achievement is the most attractive practice for many people, and there are certainly lots of extremely effective approaches to attaining goals. The reason is the following: if you do not transform your framework beliefs and clear up your main subconscious life decisions, any big goal attained may eventually lead to a big disappointment or, even worse, to misfortune.

Accordingly, I would strongly recommend that you practice clearing and integrating the most limiting parts of your personality first, and only then do any serious work on your goals.

If you really learn to live in Presence and accept life as it is, your life will spontaneously become more and more joyful. You will achieve many of your present or previous goals and desires without any effort, often in completely unexpected ways.

Eckhart Tolle beautifully explains that: *"To offer no resistance to life is to be in a state of grace, ease, and lightness. This state is then no longer dependent upon things being in a certain way, good or bad. It seems almost paradoxical, yet when your inner dependency on form is gone, the general conditions of your life, the outer forms, tend to improve greatly. Things, people, or conditions that you thought you needed for your happiness now come to you with no struggle or effort on your part, and you are free to enjoy and appreciate them—while they last. All those things, of course, will still pass away, cycles will come and go, but with dependency gone there is no fear of loss anymore. Life flows with ease."*

Therefore, the best way for you to live a joyful life is often not to fulfill your goal, but merely to learn how to live in the Now. This word "merely" is different than "easily," though. To those of us who live in a modern, busy society full of turmoil and stress, it can be very challenging to attain a permanent state of living in the Now. So, if you want to achieve goals, you have to ensure that these goals are attained in a safe, sustainable and comprehensive manner, and in a way that will prevent most of the possible negative side-effects.

Through the goal achievement processes that will be presented here, you will not only achieve your goals, you will reintegrate many parts of your personality and improve the quality of your whole life.

Here are two main methods for achieving goals:
- Comprehensive Goal Achievement Process
- Determination Technique

The Comprehensive Goal Achievement Process is a really broad and thorough method. It allows you to avoid most of the possible pitfalls of "usual" goal achievement work, because it leads you through the process of wide-ranging integration of your personality.

The Determination Technique is one of the "usual" approaches, and is, in my opinion, best for those who are short on time for inner work, but desperately need to accomplish some goals. Yet, after you achieve the goal through this technique, you should do a systematic integration of the most limiting element of your personality, as described in the previous part of this book, in order to avoid any unexpected problems in other areas of your life.

Types of Goal Structures
"If you don't know where you are going, you'll end up someplace else."
— Yogi Berra

Yes, we can turn our dreams into reality, but how? First, we must define a goal from our dream. What should the goal look like? Should it be in form of a detailed picture or just a sort of vague, pure intention?

When we talk about goals in general, we could say there are two types of goal structures: *general* and *detailed* ones.

The *general goal structure* is a vague picture or feeling about the desired state, but with a clear intention toward it. This type of goal has some advantages: it is easier to find a specific way to achieve the desired state, because there are many more possible combinations for successful achievement. Depending on our state of consciousness, we can either consciously or subconsciously select the best one for the moment.

Regardless of potential obstacles, there is always some way to achieve the goal (Figure 40).

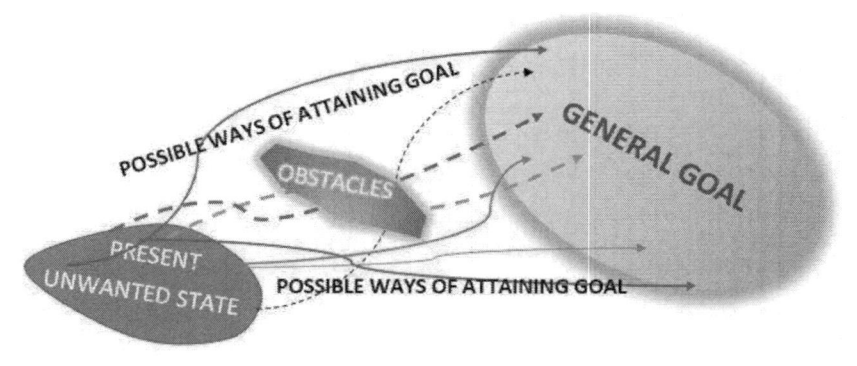

Figure 40: General Goal Structure

However, if we have a strong subconscious fear of the unknown (and almost all of us do, more or less), it hinders the largest number of possible outcomes (Figure 41). Many subconscious, hindering parts of our personality could interfere. That is one of the reasons I insist that we have to get rid of the obstructing parts of our personality first, and only then begin working on our goals.

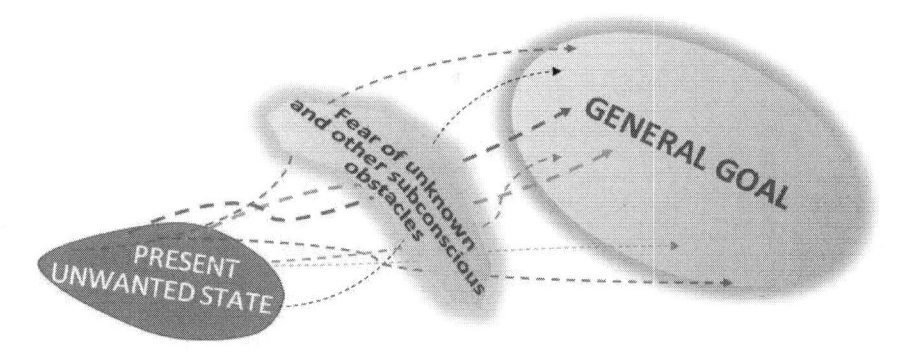

Figure 41: Interfering Subconscious Obstacles toward a General Goal

Once we integrate all the main hindering fragments of our personality, though, we have immensely more possibilities in front of us.

A *detailed goal structure*, on the other hand, has a much narrower target area (see Figure 42). You define almost everything, coming up with a precise picture that you're able to visualize every so often, precise feelings that you need to generate, wording, schedule, date of achievement, even ways, means or methods you have to use in order to achieve it, and so on.

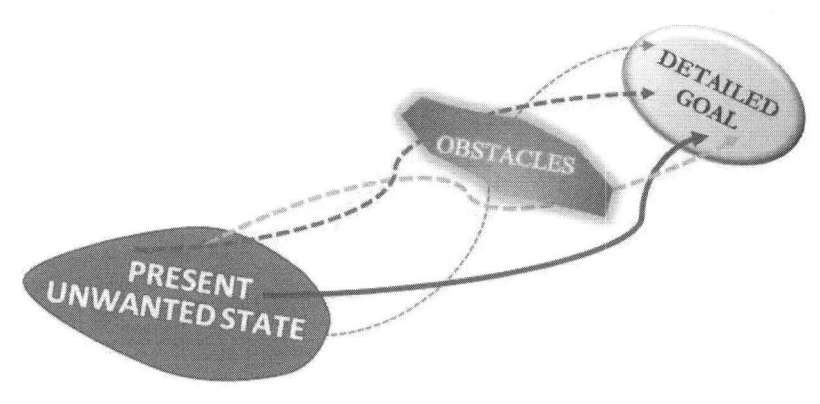

Figure 42: Detailed Goal Structure

As you can see in the symbolic picture, the number of possible ways of attainment has been significantly reduced—perhaps even to only one, in this case. Still, while this may be a pretty certain way, you will have to invest big amounts of time and energy in this practice. Moreover, the detailed goal structure is often inconsistent with what is good for us in the long run.

Nevertheless, this is often pretty effective methodology just because it prevents the expression of fear of the unknown, thanks to the fact that the target state is precisely determined.

Whichever way we choose for goal attainment, we should always keep elevated feelings of Peace, Joy and Love as a framework state of mind. In this manner, we will make sure that the process of achieving the goal unfolds in the best and easiest way.

I won't recommend either the first or second option. However, you will either have to:

1. Find a general goal, eliminate at least the fear of unknown, and then go through the process of achieving the goal by strictly keeping a positive frame of feelings, or
2. Find a detailed goal, define a comprehensive and precise goal structure within it, and invest a lot of time and energy to achieve that precise goal.

This is only an introduction to our wide-ranging and effective approach to the process of goal achievement.

Comprehensive Goal Achievement Process

"If you want the benefits of something in life, you have to also want the costs." — Mark Manson

Now we have come to the main procedure of achieving goals that will be presented in this book. The Comprehensive Goal Achievement Process (CGAP) is definitely comprehensive, and pretty demanding. It can consume a lot of your energy and time. On the other hand, it will pay itself off in many ways. Through it, you will not only attain your goal very effectively, but, which is even more important, you will harmonize many elements of your personality and that will lead you to many other improvements of your life.

Within the Comprehensive Goal Achievement Process, you will:

- Discover and define all your intrinsic goals,
- Pick up one goal and harmonize other goals and parts of personality with it, and
- Work on its attainment by doing the subset of the Process called "Reaching the Goal Procedure."

There are several concrete steps that the CGAP leads you through. First, it is recommended that you find your own excellence. That is the skill or field in which you are your best. Then, you will define your main life goals, starting with the highest states of happiness and ending with a few dozens of concrete goals. If, after that, you have not ended up with your excellence among these goals, you can simply add it to the goals list.

Next, you will choose one concrete goal and do the Goal Harmonization process. As many parts of your personality are not aligned with your goal, or are actually opposing it, you will have to harmonize them all mutually and in relation to your goal. It is an all-encompassing process which yields many side-benefits.

After this step, you will be ready to decide between a detailed or general goal structure for use on that goal.

For the detailed goal structure, you will develop a Detailed Target State to strive for, that will serve as a thorough and concrete goal. You will then define the Mid-Stages, which are the intermediate phases and states that will lead you to your final target. The Detailed Target State and the Mid-Stages will help you come up with Concrete Actions to undertake, so you can accomplish all in-between goals leading up to, and finally including, your ultimate goal.

You will have to reserve some time every day for inner work on your goal (Reaching the Goal Sessions), which will involve visualization and feeling the Mid-Stages and the Detailed Target State.

Meanwhile, you will be undertaking the Concrete Actions, whatever you have discovered them to be.

The general goal structure, on the other hand, does not involve defining any Detailed Target State, Mid-Stages or Concrete Actions. Instead, you would work on removing the fear of the unknown so as to ready yourself for many possible outcomes. This also includes doing Reaching the Goal Sessions, though they will be different from those in the detailed goal structure.

Within the general goal structure, you may have visualized a much more blurred or abstract target, therefore your actions may be more spontaneous, stemming from your Heart and state of Presence. The final outcome could be quite surprising for you, but the chances are that you will be much happier with it in the long run.

Regardless of which goal structure you choose, if you remain steadfast, do all the steps, and are flexible and persevering, you will surely achieve your goal.

If you prefer a more structured portrayal of the procedure, here it is. The CGAP consists of two parts: preparations and the actual goal achievement process (Reaching the Goal procedure), as follows.

1) *Preparation for Reaching the Goal procedure:*
   a) Find your excellence *(this is optional; if you have already chosen the goal which you want to work on—you can skip this step for now)*;
   b) Define your life goals and choose a specific goal to work on *(if you have already chosen the goal on which you want to work, you can also skip this step for now)*;
   c) Do the Goal Harmonization (GH) process;
   d) Choose the goal structure: detailed or general.
2) *Reaching the Goal procedure:*
   (Option 1—if you have chosen a detailed goal structure)
   a) Define the Detailed Target State (DTS);
   b) Define the Mid-Stages (MSs);
   c) Define the Concrete Actions (CAs);
   d) Regularly perform Reaching the Goal Sessions (RGSs) on the DTS and MS while letting go of the goal completely between the sessions;
   e) Execute the Concrete Actions and, if needed, do all the necessary corrections along the path.

   (Option 2—if you have chosen a general goal structure)
   a) Define the goal in a general form;
   b) Remove the fear of the unknown (and other, similar fears) by doing the DTI+ process on them;
   c) Regularly perform Reaching the Goal Sessions (RGSs) on the general idea of the goal (meanwhile you have to let go of the goal completely);
   d) Take appropriate actions, whenever you feel an urge for them, and do all the necessary corrections along the path.

For clarification, here is an illustration of the whole Comprehensive Goal Achievement Process (Figure 43):

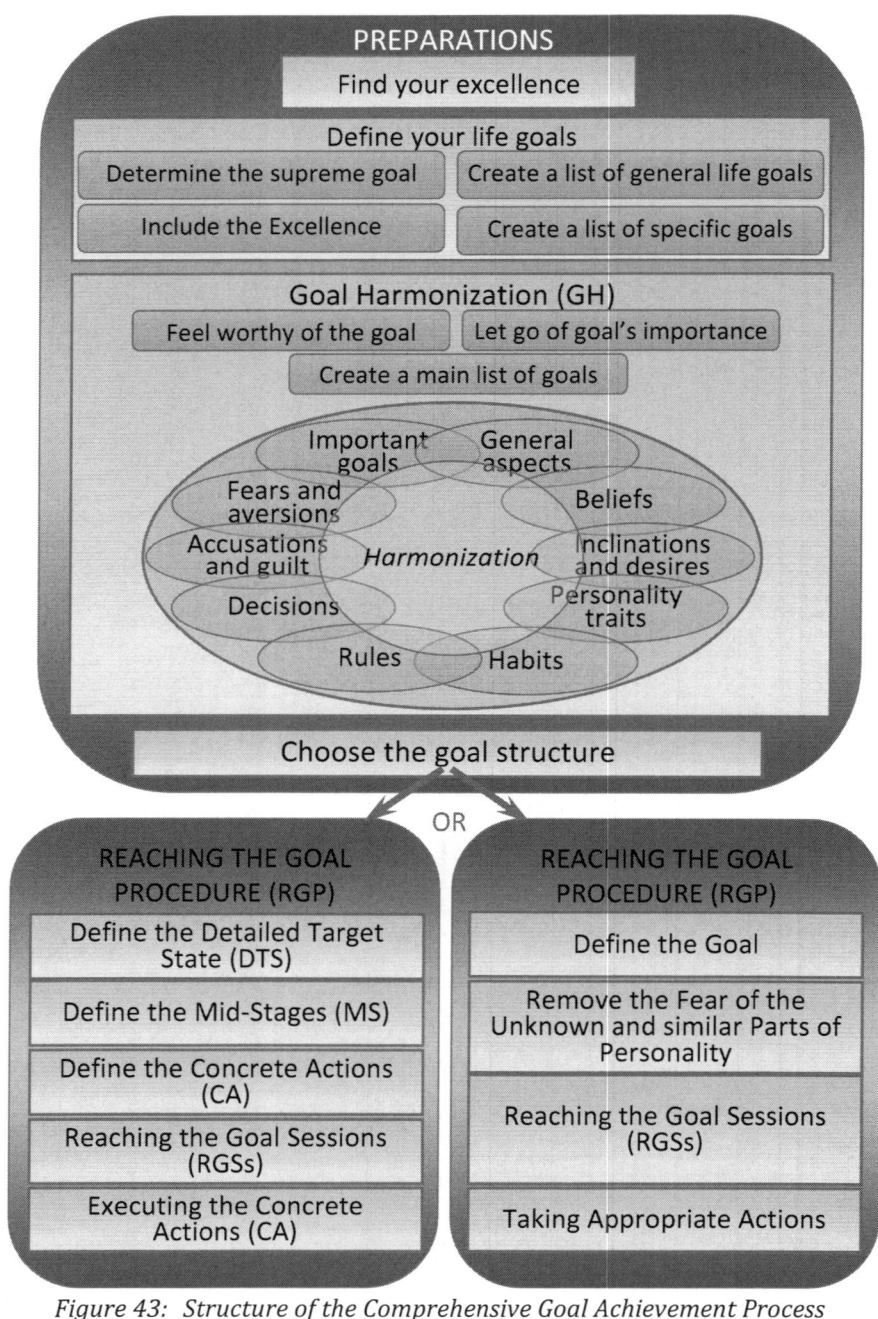

PREPARATIONS

Find your excellence

Define your life goals

- Determine the supreme goal
- Create a list of general life goals
- Include the Excellence
- Create a list of specific goals

Goal Harmonization (GH)

- Feel worthy of the goal
- Let go of goal's importance
- Create a main list of goals

Harmonization:
- Important goals
- General aspects
- Fears and aversions
- Beliefs
- Accusations and guilt
- Inclinations and desires
- Decisions
- Personality traits
- Rules
- Habits

Choose the goal structure

OR

REACHING THE GOAL PROCEDURE (RGP)

- Define the Detailed Target State (DTS)
- Define the Mid-Stages (MS)
- Define the Concrete Actions (CA)
- Reaching the Goal Sessions (RGSs)
- Executing the Concrete Actions (CA)

REACHING THE GOAL PROCEDURE (RGP)

- Define the Goal
- Remove the Fear of the Unknown and similar Parts of Personality
- Reaching the Goal Sessions (RGSs)
- Taking Appropriate Actions

Figure 43: Structure of the Comprehensive Goal Achievement Process

Finding Your Excellence

"Don't believe what your eyes are telling you. All they show is limitation. Look with your understanding, find out what you already know, and you'll see the way to fly."
— Richard Bach (from 'Johnathan Livingstone Seagull')

Every human being has their unique excellence. It is a particular talent, skill or ability possessed deep inside. Inhibited by the chores and pressures of everyday life, people often forget about it. They may not even be aware they have true excellence at all.

Once we are able to reclaim that lost power, though, we can redirect our lives toward any path. We can find a unique purpose on Earth and make our lives immensely happier.

How do we achieve that? I believe the techniques and procedures presented in this book can help us do so, and here is one direct method for finding your excellence.

Start by using, again, the timeline method described in Part III.

From our previous work with cleansing any traumatic experiences from the past, we already have written down valuable recollections of both pleasant (above the timeline) and unpleasant experiences (below, see Figure 44).

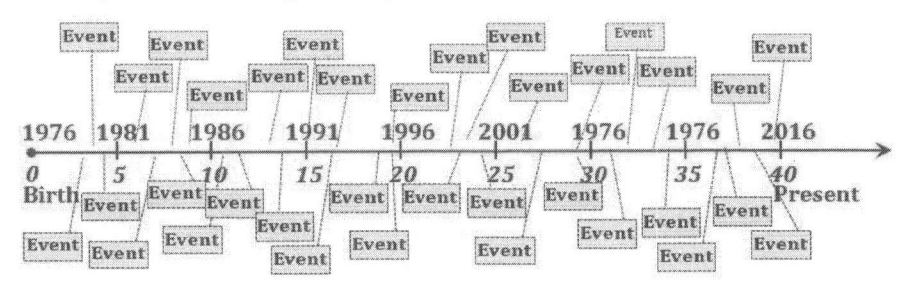

Figure 44: Timeline with Pleasant and Unpleasant Events

We should also have written down the labels for every experience, together with which emotions are connected with each event. We have recollected the groups or rows of experiences, as well as names of the most significant people involved in the life events.

With all this in front of you, you will begin the process of finding your excellence by making a new list out of all these pleasant experiences. It will just be a starting point for this purpose. These positive events will be a basis for a much broader list. Following each period from the timeline, write down every single achievement in your life that you can recall. Both your big and small achievements should be written down.

Important criteria for these attainments are only two qualities: first, you loved doing them, so they were easy or natural, and second, you were happy with the result.

Next, analyze and compare these achievements by passing through the whole list. Write down which traits and skills you had during those moments, or periods of time, which were required for achieving those feats. To each accomplishment you should attach at least two to three personal qualities.

Next, go over all your newly written skills on the list. Find the most frequent and significant skills. If you can, it is best to extract only one or two of them. These are your abilities and talents that you should use for all your future endeavors; taken jointly, they are your excellence.

Finally, write down your goals based on your re-discovered excellence.

Defining Your Goals

"You cannot expect to achieve new goals or move beyond your present circumstances unless you change." — Les Brown

In order to find your intrinsic life goals, it is advisable to begin from the core state of being: happiness and its three aspects of Peace, Love and Joy. Then, you should derive more and more concrete goals from the initial state (see Figure 45).

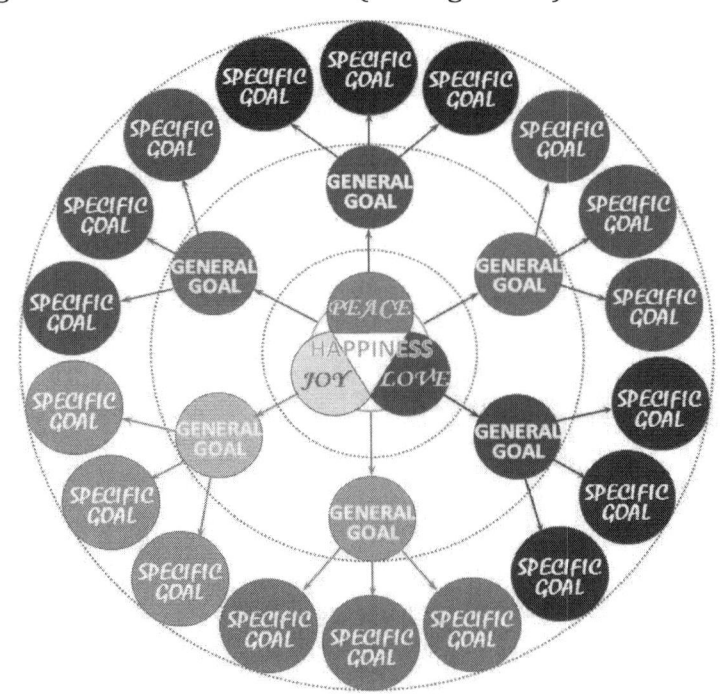

Figure 45: Deriving Goals from the Core State of Being

To define your concrete goals and then work on their achievement, follow these steps:

1. Decide on an ultimate, supreme goal for your life. Usually it is some form of lasting, ultimate *Happiness*.

2. Create a list of general life goals arising from that supreme goal. They are usually derived through the main three aspects of Happiness: Peace, Love and Joy. For example, your general

goals could be: spiritual enlightenment, perfect health, harmony in family, wealth, artistic achievements, etc.

3. Modify your list of general goals in accordance with your rediscovered excellence. For example, if your excellence is *creative work*, add it to your list or emphasize it for your further decisions regarding goals.
4. Distill a list of your specific goals from the list of your general goals. This should encompass all your main, long-term goals in life.
5. Define one, specific goal on which you want to apply the CGAP procedure.

Now that you have defined your life goals, it is time to pick one of them up and work on its accomplishment. For this initial goal achievement work, it is best not to choose one of your most difficult or far-fetched goals, nor the easiest to accomplish target. Try to find a happy medium.

Although you will be a novice in this practice, you will be able to achieve it relatively easily by applying the appropriate, significant amount of effort. In doing so, you will gain a lot of confidence for your future work.

Goal Harmonization Process

"Surround yourself with people who believe in your dreams, encourage your ideas, support your ambitions, and bring out the best in you."
— Roy Bennett

With the Goal Harmonization (GH) process you will align all main elements of your personality with the goal you want to achieve. You will also minimize the chances for any possible negative effects or subsequent setbacks occurring in your life, which are often the consequences of an "ordinary" goal achievement procedure.

Before performing the Goal Harmonization process, the elements of your personality in relation to your goal might look, symbolically, like Figure 46:

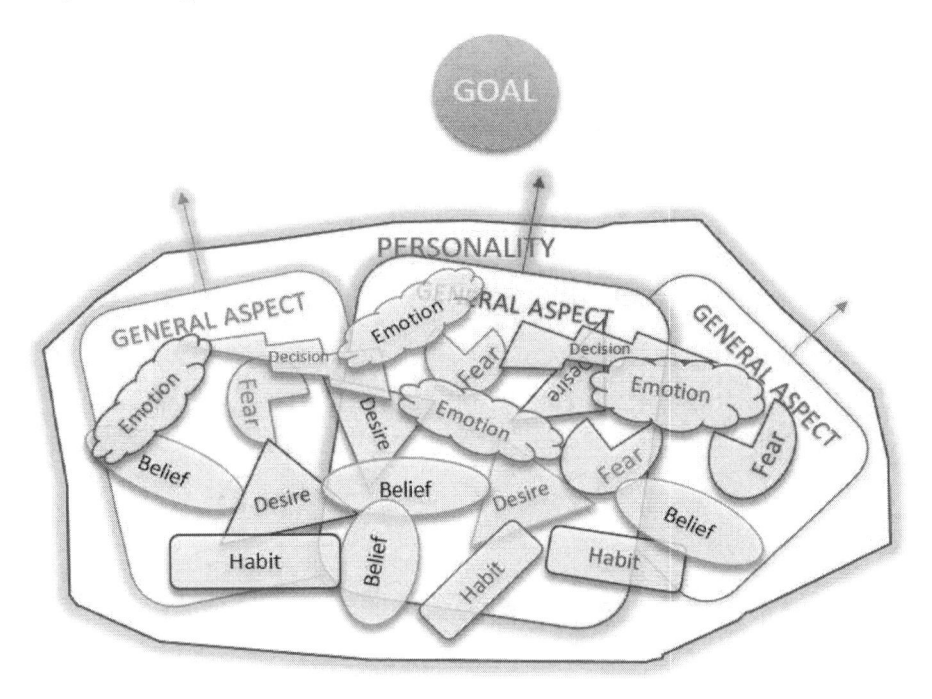

Figure 46: Personality before the Goal Harmonization Process

To sort this all out via the GH process, you will do this:

1. Feel that you are worthy of the goal you want to attain.
2. Let go of the goal's importance and of your desire for that goal.
3. Create a Main List of Goals, consisting of three core states, all general goals and all specific goals, with indicators about mutual support of all goals.

Then, you may commence harmonizing various parts of your personality:

4. Mutually harmonize your *goals*.

5. Harmonize your *general aspects of personality* with the chosen goal.
6. Harmonize your *fears and aversions* with the goal.
7. Harmonize your *beliefs* with the goal.
8. Harmonize your *accusations and guilt* with the goal.
9. Harmonize your *inclinations and desires* with the goal.
10. Harmonize your *decisions* with the goal.
11. Harmonize your *personality traits* with the goal.
12. Harmonize your *habits* with the goal.
13. Harmonize your *rules* with the goal.

In more detail, the Goal Harmonization process includes the following steps:

1. Make sure that you truly believe yourself worthy of the goal. If necessary, apply one of the basic or main Reintegration procedures, for example, you may do DTI+ technique a few times. The MH part should be *"I am worthy of... (state the goal)."*

2. Let go of your perceived importance of and desire for the goal. In order to achieve that, do the DTI procedure for both the feeling of importance and the very desire.

    Allow yourself to be completely open to the possibility of both attaining the goal, and failing to attain it. Fully accept this possibility of failure, while remaining decisive to attain the goal.

    If your desire is too intensive, you may get an opposite, completely unwanted outcome, due to your strong attachment to the wanted result. In this way, you are striving severely toward one pole of reality within your inner life, forcing the outer reality to reflect the opposite pole to restore balance. Thus, you should let go completely of the goal's importance, but still remain resolute in your decisiveness to achieve the goal.

3. Create the Main List of Goals, consisting of three core states, all general goals and all specific goals. For a visual aide, you can find a Main List of Goals worksheet in the Appendix III.

   Assign a value from 0 to 5 to each goal, rating them in relation to these three ways: *importance* (how important this goal is to you, considering your feelings), *level of resistance* (how strong you feel the outer resistance is to this inner goal), and *distance to the goal* (are you 'far away', i.e. at the very beginning of the achieving process, or do you feel close, as though you've practically already completed it). Create three columns for this information, filling in the values under their corresponding header as you go.

   Now, create a fourth column labeled *difficulty*, in which you will sum up the values of the other three columns. This will give you a rough estimation of how far away or close to the attainment of that goal you really are.

4. Mutually align your goals in this way:

   Write down the goal you want to achieve. You have already determined all goals that are not fully aligned with it. Just take all of them out from the list and make a new, smaller list just for this goal. Assign values from 0 to 5 to all intersections of goals, with 0 meaning no support for the goal, and 5 meaning full support.

   Note that all goals assessed with less than 5 should be processed because we want full harmony of all goals.

   Do the *Convergence Procedure* with the main goal and the first opposing goal from your list. Repeat the whole procedure until all the goals that are not fully supportive to the main goal are processed. If at any point you feel that you should reformulate a goal, you can do it and continue the process with that redefined goal.

5. Align the *general aspects of personality* with the goal. Since every *general aspect* is a wide-ranging and often complex entity, it will be relatively useless to treat it as a polarity on one side, and your main goal on the other side within the IT procedure (although you can try it out). The best approach is to work on them with the *Convergence Procedure*.

6. Then, move on to the *fears and aversions*, both collective and individual. Repeat the same procedure by creating and analyzing a similar list called *Assessment List of Goals-Fears Relations* and extract those that are the most harmful to the main goal. In order to completely eliminate fears opposing the goal, I would recommend you integrate each fear/aversion, one by one, using either the Singe/Double Chain technique or the Inner Triangle (IT), through coupling fears with their opposites.

If you don't have enough time, do the DTI+ technique a few times on each fear/aversion. For an MH statement, try not to mention the words "fear" or "aversion." Instead, say something like: *"I feel that this part of my personality fully supports this goal (state its name) and helps it. Both entities lead to the Supreme Happiness."*

7. A very important part of this work is dealing with all undermining *beliefs*. Create again a list, this time labeled *Assessment List of Goal-Beliefs Relations* and extract the most harmful beliefs to the main goal. You could do this by going through the Dismantling Beliefs (DB) process, with checking again and again all the undermining beliefs and repeating the DB process if needed, until you really feel there are no more of those beliefs. Alternatively, you may do the Replacing Beliefs process, but this would demand a few more times going through the whole list of undermining beliefs.

8. Another important part of this work is dealing with *accusations, resentments*, and sense of *guilt*. Treat them exactly the

same as fears/aversions, which means using the Inner Triangle, Singe/Double Chain or the DTI+ technique, just appropriately adjust the terminology.

9. Continue with *inclinations and desires*. Treat them exactly the same as the goals: use the Convergence Procedure, just slightly adapt the terminology.

10. Then, work with the *decisions*. If they are negative, use the DTI+ to dissolve them one by one and replace them with their opposite decision or state. If they are positive, treat them similarly to goals, just again modify terminology.

11. After that, go through your *traits* in a similar way—use the DTI+ technique on negative traits, and do the Convergence Procedure on the positive ones.

12. *Habits* should be treated with DTI+ procedure, replacing an unwanted habit with an appropriate firm decision.

13. *Rules* should also be treated with the DTI+ procedure, replacing an unwanted rule with an appropriate firm decision.

So, once again, what is being harmonized? These elements: goals, general aspects, fears & aversions, beliefs, accusations & guilt, inclinations & desires, decisions, traits, habits and rules, as shown in Figure 47 below:

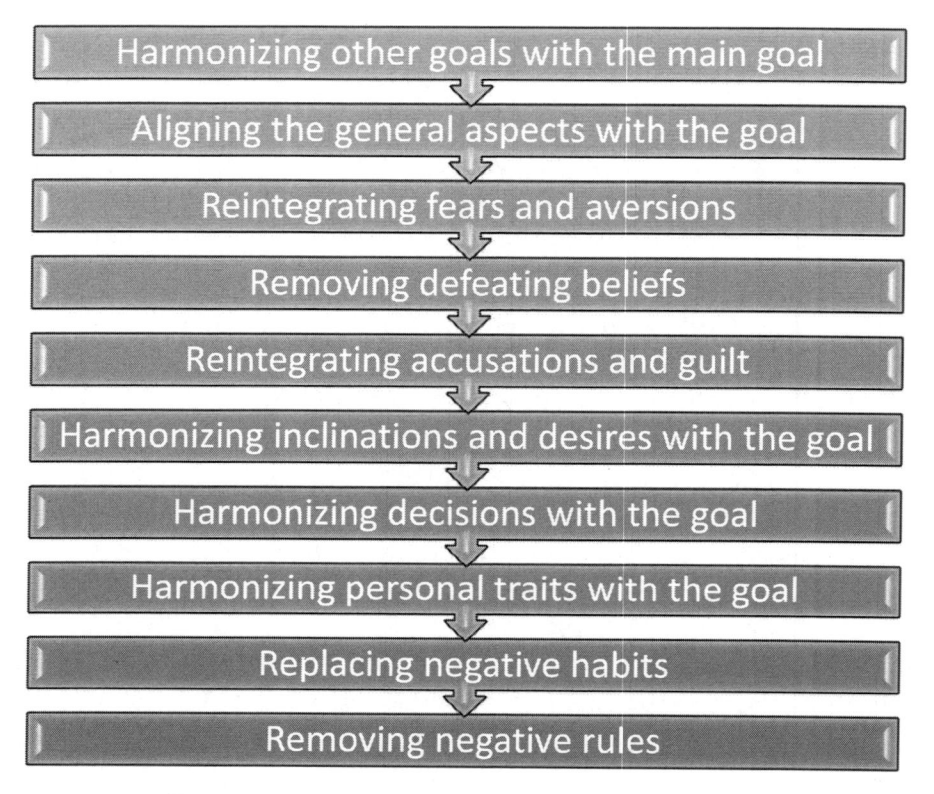

| Harmonizing other goals with the main goal |
| ↓ |
| Aligning the general aspects with the goal |
| ↓ |
| Reintegrating fears and aversions |
| ↓ |
| Removing defeating beliefs |
| ↓ |
| Reintegrating accusations and guilt |
| ↓ |
| Harmonizing inclinations and desires with the goal |
| ↓ |
| Harmonizing decisions with the goal |
| ↓ |
| Harmonizing personal traits with the goal |
| ↓ |
| Replacing negative habits |
| ↓ |
| Removing negative rules |

Figure 47: Harmonizing the Elements of Personality

After the GH process all the parts of your personality are aimed at the goal unanimously, which is symbolically shown on Figure 48:

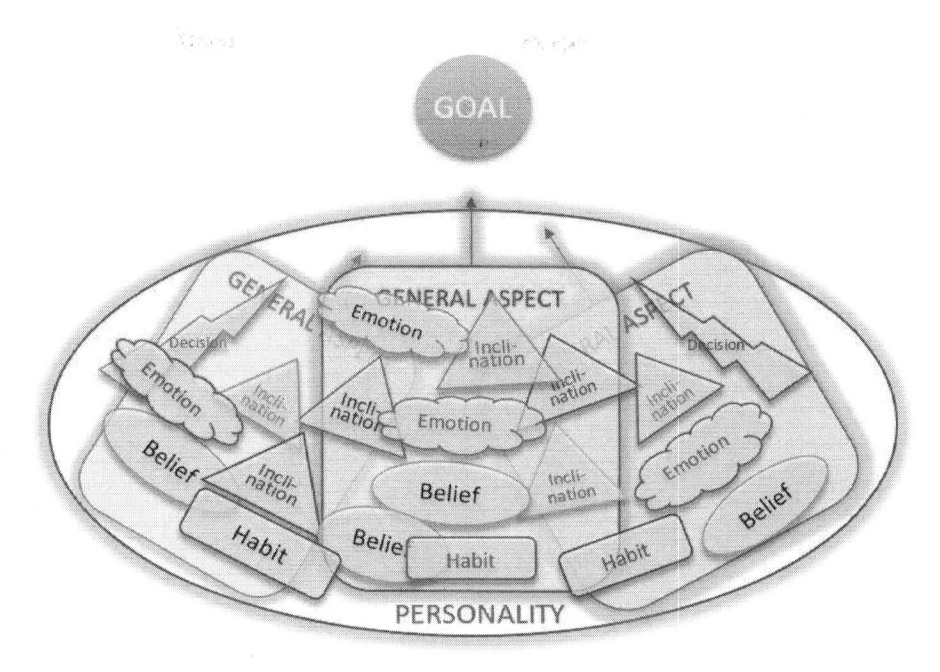

Figure 48: Personality after the Goal Harmonization Process

Now all the elements are coherent and harmonized. Some fears have disappeared; others have been changed into inclinations. All desires have also been transmuted into inclinations (a much "softer" form of desire), and all other elements have been transformed into positive ones.

Your whole being is articulated and aimed at the goal. Since you are in internal harmony, there should be no negative effects or setbacks after your external attainment of the goal.

Now, you could ask, "but, what if I decide to work on a totally different goal, either simultaneously or after having achieved the first one? Wouldn't all these elements of personality be oriented the wrong way? Do we have to work again on these elements and re-orient all of them somehow?" The answer is no. Remember that we've already mutually harmonized main life goals in the Goal Harmonization process. Therefore, work on any new goal would not demand the same work again. Your personality is now much more coherent and reintegrated and work on any new goal would definitely claim less energy than it did the first time.

Of course, when you choose to work with one goal you will not have to deal with all other goals, or other personality's elements in one CGAP cycle. It would be an overwhelmingly complex and long process. Instead, I will show you later in a real-life example how to make an estimation of what the most opposing elements of your personality are, so you will be able to pick only a few of these elements from each category and harmonize them with your goal. But if you want to be sure that you will safely achieve your goal, you shouldn't skip any of these categories. It's a wide-ranging and thorough process, but in the end, you will see that it's absolutely worth the time and energy you spent.

Reaching the Goal Procedure
"A goal without a plan is just a wish." — Antoine de Saint-Exupéry

This is the second part of our work on goals. When you've done all the steps of the previously described preparations, you are completely ready for the next stage, the actual process of attaining the goal: *The Reaching the Goal procedure*.

Now, you can go into two different directions, depending on the goal structure that you have chosen for this objective:
    a. You decided to orient yourself toward a <u>*detailed*</u> *goal structure*.
    b. You decided to orient yourself toward a <u>*general*</u> *goal structure*.

a. These are the next steps for the <u>*detailed goal structure*</u>:

1) Create your Detailed Target State (DTS).

2) Make a Plan for reaching the DTS, by splitting the path toward the Detailed Target State into Mid-Stages (MSs), going *from* the achievement *backwards* to the present time.

3) Define all the Concrete Actions (CAs, as the elements of the Mid-Stages) for attaining the DTS, with deadlines. The CAs should be created by going from the present time to the DTS (*not* going backwards).

4) Keeping your mind still, occasionally do the *Reaching the Goal Sessions (RGS)*, by doing this:

    a) At the beginning of each session, do the DTI at least 3 times in order to bring yourself into the state of deep Presence, and then do the Moving to the Heart (MH) procedure with your current Mid-Stage (the next Mid-Stage you have to reach in your Plan for reaching the DTS). At the same time, try to remain aware of the background sense of Presence.

        i) Gently immerse the Mid-Stage scene into the Presence, while being settled in the Heart, and go back to the MS scene. Immerse it into the Presence again, and do so repeatedly.

   ii) This step should last no less than 5 minutes. The longer it lasts, the better. If any distracting thought or other mind content appears, do the DTI and gently return back into the process, without blaming yourself for that.

b) Return back into the state of Presence. If necessary, do the DTI. When you are rooted deeply in the state of Presence, do the MH procedure with your DTS. While visualizing and feeling the DTS from the Heart, try to remain aware of the background sense of Presence.

   i) Gently immerse the DTS scene into the Presence. Enjoy the Presence for a while. Then, go back again to the DTS scene, while being settled in the Heart and immerse it into the Presence (similarly to the Gentle Touch of Presence technique), and stay in the Presence. Repeat this a few times.

   ii) This step should also last at least 5 minutes. The longer it lasts, the better. If any distracting thought or other mind content appears, do the DTI and gently return back into the process, without blaming yourself.

c) Meantime, between every session, just let go completely of the goal. Don't think about it at all. *This step is equally as important as steps 4a and 4b.*

5) Execute Concrete Actions in real life, in accordance with the plan, and, if needed, do all the necessary corrections along the path. In the meantime, let go completely of your goal. Be completely open for both possibilities of having the goal attained or not.

b. These are the next steps for the *general goal structure*:

1) Define the goal. It does not have to be very concrete—just an idea of it is enough.

2) Remove or integrate the fear of the unknown and other similar hindering parts of personality (if you haven't done this yet during the preparation part). For this purpose, you may use the IT or DTI+ techniques.

3) Keeping your mind still, occasionally do the *Reaching the Goal Sessions (RGSs)*, by giving your attention to the idea of the goal, together with a suitable vague feeling. You can also do the MH procedure with the idea of the goal. If any distracting thought or other mind content appears, do the DTI and gently return back into the process, without blaming yourself for that.

4) Take any action that you feel is appropriate, whenever you feel an urge for it. Do all the necessary corrections along the path. In the meantime, let go completely of the goal. Remember that you must be completely open for both the possibility of having the goal attained or not.

Note that many distracting mind contents may appear during the process, especially in the Reaching the Goal Sessions. That's absolutely normal and even expected. The thoughts, emotions or sensations arising in the process are in fact expressions of inner hindrances related to the goal.

The distracting mind contents could also have a very valuable role—they could be considered as indications of how far we are from an actual accomplishment.

Don't try to "overdo" this procedure—in the beginning you may feel confused and overwhelmed with how many steps there are to be followed in the process. If you are doing it alone, I recommend that you use a paper with the printed steps. Do as much and as best as you can, but don't try too much to be perfect in that. It will all come naturally with practice.

Detailed Target State and Mid-Stages

"Don't tell me the sky's the limit when there are footprints on the moon."
— Paul Brandt

The Detailed Target State (DTS) is your goal represented in a thorough target situation, with your concrete feelings, in a realistic future. You might imagine it as a short 'movie' in your mind, including within it key 'scenes' of a situation that could really happen as a result of achieving the goal. That movie must be accompanied with feelings you would really feel as a result of achieving the goal. In it you should have a clear awareness of a deadline date for the achievement.

It is also advisable to include in the movie at least one scene in which you see yourself from an exterior view point, like you are outside of your body, watching yourself. Doing it this way, you will create more positive tension between your present situation and the DTS.

Also, the DTS should include a "securing statement," in which you clearly declare that you will achieve the goal in real life; that you will achieve this exact goal or one even more favorable to you and your loved ones, for the highest good of yourself and all other people that will be involved.

The DTS is much easier to develop when you are free of all your obstacles represented in your fears, false beliefs, guilt, etc. Therefore, completing each and every one of all the previous steps of the Goal Harmonization process is strongly recommended for the successful development of the Detailed Target State.

You should describe the DTS thoroughly in a textual form. Develop it on a computer or tablet, polish it and then put it on a real paper.[31]

In short, the Detailed Target State:

- Should be written down on paper (or at least written in an electronic form);
- Should be in the form of a short movie which includes crucial scenes of a real situation that will be a result of achieving the goal;
- Must be accompanied by the positive feelings you would feel as a result of accomplishing the goal;
- Should have a clearly defined deadline for the achievement;
- Should include a "securing statement"—you will achieve the goal in real life, or a goal even more favorable to you and your loved ones, for the highest good of yourself and all other people that could be involved.

Regarding the whole detailed goal structure process—if possible, you should define the Mid-Stages (or MSs) and Concrete Actions (CAs) mentioned in the previous section in steps a.2 and a.3. They should be developed in a similar way as the Detailed Target State (DTS).

---

[31] Here is an example of DTS that is also described in the real-life example:

"It's September 25th, 2016. I'm sitting in front of my computer, browsing the Internet for my self-published Sci-Fi books. I see two titles with my name below. I see a lot of 5 star reviews and the label 'Bestseller.'

My whole family is sitting next to me and I'm telling them that my monthly income from these titles has just reached over $10,000. They are thrilled and hugging me. I'm explaining that I have doubled my income in the last three months.

I'm describing to them my enjoyment while I'm writing and that I generally feel so relaxed and confident about this work because I've found effective ways to write and sell my books successfully.

I will achieve this target in real life, or one even more favorable for me and my family, before October the 1st, 2016, for the highest good to me and all other people that could be involved."

I say "if possible" because there will be situations where you will have no clue about what an MS or CA that leads to the achievement of goal should look like. In that case, you should define at least a few Mid-Stages with deadlines in which you would feel happiness or other kind of enjoyable feelings. These Mid-Stages don't have to have any other elements, like any visual features or clear ideas of what they look like. However, the feelings are very important in this process. With them, you are virtually clearing the way ahead to the achievement of the goal.

If your MS does have a visual part, don't forget to include into it a scene in which you see yourself from an exterior view point.

There are many methods available out there to assist you, if you are unable to develop Mid-Stages and Concrete Actions. I would recommend brainstorming and mind maps. You can find tons of material about these on the Internet. However, if you still can't find enough ideas for these steps, don't make a problem out of that. You can just proceed without stages and actions and do the process on the DTS only.

Anyway, if you have Mid-Stages, they should have these attributes:

– To be written down on paper;
– If possible, to be in the form of a short movie which includes one or more crucial scenes of a real situation that will be a result of achieving the intermediate target state, characteristic for the particular Mid-Stage;
– Must be accompanied with appropriate positive feelings;
– Should have clearly defined deadlines;
– Should include a clear vision of what to do next;
– *(Optional)* Should include a "securing statement"—you will achieve the intermediate target state in real life, or a state even more favorable to the achievement of the goal, for the highest good of yourself and all other people that could be involved.

In a Nutshell

In any goal achievement process, we have to be aware that we must reintegrate our main negative beliefs and other limiting subconscious structures first, and only then proceed with goal attaining techniques. Otherwise, any big goal that we achieve may activate those negative parts of our personality and lead us to a big disappointment or even disaster.

There are two types of goal structures: *general* and *detailed*.

By using the *general goal structure*, we create a vague perception of a desired state, but with a clear intention toward it. Within this type of goal, there is many possible ways for attaining the final target. Also, the outcome may appear completely different than expected.

In the *detailed goal structure*, we define the specific way to achieve the goal and the final outcome, including the timeline.

<u>*Comprehensive Goal Achievement Process:*</u>

1) *Preparation* for Reaching the Goal procedure:
   a) Find your excellence (if you have already chosen the goal which you want to work on—you can skip this step for now);
   b) Define your general life goals (if you have already chosen the goal which you want to work on—you can skip this step for now);
   c) Do the Goal Harmonization (GH) process;
   d) Choose the goal structure: detailed or general.
2) Do the *Reaching the Goal procedure* suitable either for a detailed or general goal structure.

Finding the Excellence

In order to find your individual excellence, it is recommended that you use the timeline with your positive events on it. On the basis of those events, create a comprehensive list of all achievements in your life that you can remember. All these achievements should have these attributes: you enjoyed doing them, and you were happy with the results.

Analyze and compare these accomplishments. Write down traits and skills you had in that time to achieve these feats. Attach at least two or three personal qualities or skills to each of these accomplishments.

Go over all these skills. Find the most frequent and significant skills. Try to distill only one or two of them. These are your abilities and talents that you should use for all your future endeavors. Taken jointly, they are your excellence.

Defining Your Goals

1. Determine the ultimate, supreme goal of your life. It is usually *Happiness*.
2. Create a list of general life goals arising from the supreme goal. For example, your general goals could be: spiritual enlightenment, perfect health, harmony in family, wealth, artistic achievements, etc.
3. Modify your list of general goals in accordance with your rediscovered excellence.
4. Create a list of specific goals from your list of general goals. The list of specific goals should encompass all your main goals in life, generally long-term goals.
5. Define the specific goal on which you want to apply the CGAP.

Goal Harmonization Process

With this process, you will align all main elements of your personality with the specific goal you want to achieve. This is the GH process in short:

1. Feel that you are worthy of the goal you want to attain.
2. Let go of the goal's importance and of your desire for that goal. Fully accept the possibility of failure, while remaining decisive to attain the goal.
3. Create a Main List of Goals, consisting of three core states, all general goals and all specific goals. It will indicate mutual support of all goals.

(Then you have the "harmonization" part of the procedure.)

4. Mutually harmonize your *goals*. Use the Convergence Procedure.
5. Harmonize your *general aspects of personality* with the chosen goal. Use the Convergence Procedure.
6. Harmonize your *fears and aversions* with the goal. Use the Inner Triangle, Singe/Double Chain or the DTI+ technique.
7. Harmonize your *beliefs* with the goal. Use the Dismantling Beliefs or Replacing Beliefs process.

8. Harmonize your *accusations and guilt* with the goal. Use the Inner Triangle, Singe/Double Chain or the DTI+ technique.
9. Harmonize your *inclinations and desires* with the goal. Use the Convergence Procedure.
10. Harmonize your *decisions* with the goal. Use the DTI+ technique on negative decisions, and the Convergence Procedure on the positive ones.
11. Harmonize your *personality traits* with the goal. Use the DTI+ technique on negative traits, and the Convergence Procedure on the positive ones.
12. Harmonize your *habits* with the goal. Use the DTI+ technique.
13. Harmonize your *rules* with the goal. Use the DTI+ technique.

Reaching the Goal Procedure for a Detailed Goal Structure

1. Create your Detailed Target State (DTS).
2. Create a list of Mid-Stages (MSs).
3. Define all the Concrete Actions (CAs).
4. Keeping your mind still, occasionally do *Reaching the Goal Sessions (RGSs)*, by doing this:
   a) Do the DTI at least 3 times. Do the Moving to the Heart (MH) procedure with your current Mid-Stage, while repeatedly immersing it into the Presence.
   b) Return back into the state of Presence. If necessary, do the DTI. Do the MH procedure with the DTS, while repeatedly immersing it into the Presence.
   c) Meantime, between every session, let go completely of the goal. Don't think about it at all.
5. Take Concrete Actions in accordance with the list. Do the necessary corrections along the path. In the meantime, let go completely of your goal. Be completely open to the possibility of both attaining the goal, or not.

Reaching the Goal Procedure for a General Goal Structure

1. Define the goal.
2. Remove or integrate the fear of the unknown and other similar hindering parts of personality.
3. Keeping your mind still, occasionally do the *Reaching the Goal Sessions (RGSs)*, by giving your attention to the idea (or notion) of the goal, together with a suitable vague feeling. You can also do the MH procedure with idea of the goal.

4. Take action that you feel is appropriate, whenever you feel an urge for it. Do all the necessary corrections along the path. In the meantime, let go completely of the goal. Be completely open for both possibilities of having the goal attained and not.

Detailed Target State

It is your goal represented in a concrete, detailed target situation, with your concrete feelings, in a concrete future. The DTS's main points are:

— Should be written down on paper (or at least written in an electronic form);
— Should be in the form of a short movie which includes crucial scenes of a real situation that will be a result of achieving the goal;
— Must be accompanied by the positive feelings you would feel as a result of accomplishing the goal;
— Should have a clearly defined deadline for the achievement;
— Should include a "securing statement" verbalizing that you will achieve the goal in real life, or a goal even more favorable to you and your loved ones, for the highest good of yourself and all other people that could be involved.

Mid-Stages

In fact, the Mid-Stages are intermediate Detailed Target States, like in-between stages from now to the DTS. They should have these attributes:

— Should be written down on paper or electronic form at least;
— If possible, should be in the form of a short movie which includes one or more crucial scenes of a real situation that will be a result of achieving the intermediate target state, characteristic for that particular Mid-Stage;
— Must be accompanied with appropriate positive feelings;
— Should have clearly defined deadlines;
— Should include a clear vision of what to do next;
— *(Optional)* Should include a "securing statement" verbalizing that you will achieve the intermediate target state in real life, or a state even more favorable to the achievement of the goal, for the highest good of yourself and all other people that could be involved.

Real-Life Example

"Marco," as we'll call him, decided to dedicate as much time as was needed to complete the whole Comprehensive Goal Achievement Process. He knew he had a few very strong desires, but was adamant about completing the procedure, even if that might mean redefining or renouncing some of his present desires.

Unfortunately, Marco had not yet done any of the previous work on the various elements of his personality that were recommended in Part III. If he had, it would certainly have made his work on the Comprehensive Goal Achievement Process much easier.

He went through the entire process alone, working almost every day for at least half an hour—even up to two hours—doing the so-called solo-processing.

First, he went through the preparation steps for the Reaching the Goal procedure:

1. Finding his excellence;
2. Defining his life goals and choosing a specific goal to work on;
3. Doing the Goal Harmonization (GH) process;
4. Choosing a goal structure of either detailed or general nature.

To *find his excellence* he created a life timeline and thoroughly filled it out with his most important experiences. It was a transformative work by itself. During the process, any time he recalled an unpleasant event, he immediately did the DTI or DTI+ on it and sensed more and more relief.

His focus was of course on pleasant events, marked in his memory as successes. It wasn't important whether they were big or small; he examined them all equally. He made a list of these events and scrutinized each one. He wrote down the related praises he'd heard from the people in his environment during those times. He searched for which of his individual traits were praised most often, and which of his personal qualities had steered him toward each remembered accomplishment.

The result of this investigation was a revelation to Marco. He realized that one specific quality led him to most of his attainments: *creative work*. Whether it was the articles and reports he'd submitted at work that garnered great appraisals, his brilliantly written graduation work at the University, several short science fiction stories he'd written as a teenager, or the beautiful landscapes and portraits he'd painted in his childhood, it was all connected to his *artistic skills*. That was his excellence.

The next step was to define his goals: one supreme goal, then general and specific goals.

He came to conclusion that his supreme goal was Happiness, and derived his general life goals from its three core states: Peace, Love and Joy. From Peace he aimed for *spiritual enlightenment, health* and *tranquility*; from Love he decided on *family love* and *love in relation to others*; from Joy he wrote down *family progress, wealth* and *exploration*.

He then moved to the next stage and created a list of specific goals, which was quite an easy and natural process (you will see an example of this on Figure 46, later).

On the basis of his rediscovered excellence, he added one more general goal to the list derived from Joy: *creative work*, and from that goal he defined two specific goals: *successful Sci-Fi writing* and *programming*. His list of goals was finally complete.

He decided to work on the goal he had labeled "successful sci-fi writing." Writing science fiction had been an old childhood dream and somehow he felt now was the time to re-ignite it, just with the addition of "successful."

Marco was finally ready to start the Goal Harmonization (GH) process. He did these GH steps:

1. Felt that he was worthy of his goal.
2. Let go of the goal's importance and of his desire for that goal.
3. Created a Main list of goals, with indicators on mutual support of all goals.

4. Used Reintegration procedures to harmonize numerous parts of his personality with that specific goal: *other goals, general aspects, fears, beliefs, accusations, desires, decisions, traits, habits* and *rules*.

For the first step, he considered his emotional reaction toward his personal worthiness of the goal. Did he currently feel deserving of being a successful Sci-Fi writer? Actually, he discovered, he didn't. He felt that this may be a part of a bigger, underlying problem of his own unworthiness, so did the Inner Triangle procedure with the first polarity "my unworthiness of being successful," and the second polarity "successful person."

He was surprised with a few new insights about his childhood and relationship with his parents. He revived some deeply buried feelings of resentment and injustice, and eventually reintegrated them. He felt better already.

The next step was to check how important the goal was to him. He concluded that it hadn't been too important before, because it had just felt like a dream for which he wasn't too hopeful. After several days of intensive goal achievement preparations, though, it had become a most central thing for him. Marco knew that assigning high importance to a desired goal could obstruct the achievement process, so he did the DTI several times on that feeling of importance. Eventually, he felt a kind of relief, as he was almost completely indifferent to whether he would attain it or not.

He then began creating the Main List of Goals (Figures 49, 50 and 51), consisting of three core states, all general goals and all specific goals. He assigned appropriate values, from 0 to 5, to each goal concerning its importance, resistance and distance. He didn't think too much—he just put the values he felt at that moment. From there he got the values for the "difficulty" column. In this way, he got a rough estimation of how close he really was to the attainment of each goal.

As he had already decided to work on the goal labeled "successful sci-fi writing," he did the assessment of its "difficulty" and found it was 9, which showed him that writing the books could be pretty hard to achieve. Nevertheless, he was determined to continue because he had a strong desire to achieve it.

Main List of Goals (example)

	Core state	General Goals	Specific Goals	A Importance (0-5)	B Resistance (0-5)	C Distance (0-5)	Difficulty (A+B+C)	Note
1.	Peace	Spiritual enlightenment	Permanent bliss	2	5	4	11	
2.			Constant presence	3	5	4	12	
3.			Regular meditation	2	0	0	2	Already regularly practicing, need only to continue
4.			Freedom from inner limitations	4	5	3	12	
5.		Health	My health	4	3	1	8	Occasional flu
6.			My fitness	1	4	4	9	
7.			My son's health	4	3	2	9	Occasional anxiety outbreaks
8.			My daughter's health	4	0	0	4	
9.			My wife's health	4	0	1	5	
10.		Tranquility	Tranquility in my life	2	3	2	7	
11.			Tranquility in the life of my family	3	4	3	10	
12.			Peace in relationship with all the people	2	1	1	4	Already achieved, need to improve

Figure 49: Goals Related to Peace

	Core state	General Goals	Specific Goals	A Importance (0-5)	B Resistance (0-5)	C Distance (0-5)	Difficulty (A+B+C)	Note
13.	Love	Family love	Great relationship with my wife	4	3	2	9	
14.			Great relationship with my son	4	3	3	10	
15.			Great relationship with my daughter	2	0	0	2	Already achieved
16.		Love in relation to others	Great relationship with the M. couple	5	5	4	14	
17.			Great relationship with my bosses	3	2	2	7	
18.			Great relationship with my colleagues	2	1	1	4	
19.			Great relationship with my parents	1	1	1	3	
20.			Great relationship with my friends	1	0	0	1	Already achieved

Figure 50: Goals Related to Love

	Core state	General Goals	Specific Goals	A Importance (0-5)	B Resistance (0-5)	C Distance (0-5)	Difficulty (A+B+C)	Note
21.	Joy	Family progress	General progress of my family	4	3	3	10	
22.			My wife's job	5	5	4	14	
23.			My son's success in school and life	5	4	3	12	
24.			My daughter's success in school and life	1	1	1	3	
25.			My happiness with job	3	3	3	9	
26.		Wealth	Stable monthly income of at least $10,000	5	5	4	14	
27.			New flat	5	5	5	15	
28.			New house	3	5	5	13	
29.			Another car	1	5	5	11	
30.		Creative work	Successful Sci-Fi writing	4	2	3	9	The first chosen goal
31.			Programming	5	4	4	13	
32.		Explorations	Lucid dreaming	3	4	5	12	
33.			Mental powers	1	5	5	11	
34.			Broadening perception	1	5	5	11	
35.			Speed reading	1	4	4	9	

Figure 51: Goals Related to Joy

The next task was to examine mutual support among the goals.

Marco created an *"Assessment List of Mutual Goal Support"* (Figure 52) in which he compared all his most important goals from the Main list, meaning goals of the importance level of 4 and 5.

How did he compare the main goals' mutual influence?

First, he made estimations of how his possible attainment of the goal "freedom from inner limitations" would influence all other main goals, assigning values from 0 to 5, where 0 meant extremely hindering and 5 completely beneficial.

For example, he estimated that the completion of that goal would have a fully beneficial influence on all the other goals, so he put fives all down the row. For the "support to other goals" space, he summed up those values (5 x 14, in this case) and got 70. Finally, he filled in the previously determined value of 11 for the "difficulty" of that goal, from his work on the Main List of Goals.

Then he did this for all the other goals on the list. It took him around 20 minutes to do this, and after that he had a much clearer picture which goals were actually obstructing his main objective which he called "successful sci-fi writing." There was really only one such goal: "great relationship with the M. couple," a couple that had been influencing his life for a long time. He felt that the goal labeled "great relationship with my wife" was also not absolutely supporting the main goal, so he decided to work on it as well.

How were these two goals obstructing his wish to be a successful sci-fi writer? He *felt* that he didn't have support from these two sides for this life objective. That didn't mean it was actually true, but he held the impression it was, and that was what was subconsciously hindering him from any improvement in that field.

Assessment List of Mutual Goal Support (example)

Nr	The Goal	Difficulty	Support to other goals	Freedom from inner limitations (64)	My perfect health (66)	My son's perfect health (65)	My daughter's perfect health (67)	My wife's perfect health (66)	Great relationship with my wife (67)	Great relationship with my son (63)	Great relationship with the M. couple (45)	General progress of my family (61)	My wife's job (67)	My son's success in school and life (61)	Stable monthly income of at least $10,000 (64)	New flat (64)	Successful Sci-Fi writing (65)	Programming (63)
1.	Freedom from inner limitations	11	70	x	5	5	5	5	5	5	5	5	5	5	5	5	5	5
2.	My perfect health	8	70	5	x	5	5	5	5	5	5	5	5	5	5	5	5	5
3.	My son's perfect health	9	70	5	5	x	5	5	5	5	5	5	5	5	5	5	5	5
4.	My daughter's perfect health	4	70	5	5	5	x	5	5	5	5	5	5	5	5	5	5	5
5.	My wife's perfect health	5	70	5	5	5	5	x	5	5	5	5	5	5	5	5	5	5
6.	Great relationship with my wife	7	51	4	5	5	5	5	x	3	4	4	3	1	3	3	4	2
7.	Great relationship with my son	8	62	4	5	5	5	5	5	x	0	3	5	5	5	5	5	5
8.	Great relationship with the M. couple	14	18	1	1	0	3	1	4	0	x	0	4	0	1	1	1	1
9.	General progress of my family	10	66	5	5	5	5	5	5	5	1	x	5	5	5	5	5	5
10.	My wife's job	14	70	5	5	5	5	5	5	5	5	5	x	5	5	5	5	5
11.	My son's success in school and life	12	64	5	5	5	5	5	3	5	1	5	5	x	5	5	5	5
12.	Stable monthly income of at least $10,000	14	69	5	5	5	5	5	5	5	4	5	5	5	x	5	5	5
13.	New flat	15	67	5	5	5	5	5	5	5	2	5	5	5	5	x	5	5
14.	Successful Sci-Fi writing	10	66	5	5	5	5	5	5	5	1	5	5	5	5	5	x	5
15.	Programming	12	67	5	5	5	5	5	5	5	2	5	5	5	5	5	5	x

Figure 52

Now it was clear to him that he had to do the Convergence Procedure on these two opposing goals. Here is the procedure that Marco went through, both with initial instructions and his answers.

Convergence Procedure

1. He sat up straight with his eyes half-open, and relaxed.
2. He determined the location of his Temporary I at that moment (*"inside my head"*) and then he did the DTI.

3. He defined clearly the goal which he intended to harmonize with another goal. It was his first part.
   The label of the part was "successful sci-fi writing." However, he created a clearer definition of his goal: *"I have a steady income of at least $10,000 a month, through writing and publishing my science fiction books."*
   He felt this part as if it were a small blue ball in front of him, more to his left side.

4. He defined clearly the goal which apparently was opposing his first goal. It was his second part.
   The label of the part was "great relationship with the M. couple."
   He felt this as a small red ball, in front of him, on the right.

5. He asked the first part: *"Why is the second part (great relationship with the M. couple) obstructing the achievement of your purpose?"* He waited a little bit for an answer.
   It answered: *"They want to manipulate my family, and if I succeeded in the goal, they wouldn't be able to do that anymore."*
   He thanked the part for the answer and did the DTI.

6. He then asked the second part: *"Are you objecting to the purpose of the first part (I have a steady income of at least $10,000 a month, through writing and publishing my science fiction books)?"*

   The answer was "yes," and when he asked it why, the answer was: *"Because we want to keep control over you, and if you completed the goal we wouldn't be able to do that."* It was clear to him that, although he did the DTI on the first part's answer, he had gotten almost the same answer from the second part, despite his opposite expectation. He thanked the part and did the DTI procedure on the answer.

(Next circle)

7. Marco had determined again the location of his Temporary I at the moment. He did the DTI on it.

8. He asked the first part: *"Does the second part (great relationship with the M. couple) fully support the achievement of your purpose now?"*

   It answered: *"No. They always want to interfere. Once my purpose is achieved, you will have become independent of them. They will not tolerate my achievement as it would sever the relationship."* He thanked the part for the answer. He did the DTI on that answer.

9. He asked the second part: *"Do you now fully support the purpose of the first part (I have a steady income of at least $10,000 a month, through writing and publishing my science fiction books)?"*

   The answer was "no," so he asked why. The next answer was: *"We don't want you to be successful. That would mean you don't need us anymore."* He thanked the part and did the DTI.

(Next circle)

10. He had determined again the location of his Temporary I at the moment. He did the DTI.

11. He asked the first part: *"Does the second part (great relationship with the M. couple) fully support the achievement of your purpose now?"*

    It answered: *"Not quite. In order to continue a relationship with them, it would mean I must 'give in' to the couple's demands constantly, unless they changed themselves... which cannot be assumed to happen."* He thanked the part for the answer and did the DTI on it.

    He felt that the answer brought up a new point which was wise and true, so he decided to redefine the other goal. The new formulation of the other goal was: *"Correct relationship with the M. couple, in which both sides mind their own business and respect the other side."*

12. He asked this newly redefined second part (which had subsequently changed its color to orange): *"Do you now fully support the purpose of the first part (I have a steady income of at least $10,000 a month, through writing and publishing my science fiction books)?"*

    The answer was "yes" now. He thanked the part.

13. Although the second part gave an absolutely positive answer, since it was redefined Marco decided to check again with the main goal (part): *"Does the second part in this new form (correct relationship with the M. couple, in which both sides mind their own business and respect the other side) fully support the achievement of your purpose now?"*

    The answer was "yes."

14. For the conclusion of the process, Marco again determined the location of his I at that moment and did the DTI+ with the MH statement: *"I feel that all my other parts fully support the purpose of the first part (I have steady income of at least $10,000 a month, through writing and publishing my science fiction books) and contribute to it."*

After successfully completing his first Convergence Procedure with the most opposing goal, Marco continued with one other goal that wasn't much in opposition, but was not quite sufficiently aligned with his main goal. It was "great relationship with wife." He thought that his wife would have been concerned about his possible wasting of money, time and energy that he could instead invest into family affairs (to his surprise, it showed up that she wasn't concerned at all).

He did the same with the Convergence Procedure for Goals, but the process was shorter, without any change in goal formulation. There were only small incongruities between the two goals, so it was easy to accomplish the process.

The next step was to determine possible opposition to his goals in other parts of his personality: general aspects, aversions and fears, beliefs, accusations and guilt, inclinations and desires, decisions, personality traits, habits and rules.

First he created the *Assessment List of Goals-General Aspects Relations*, similarly to the list shown in the previous chapter (Personal Transformation) for mutual coherence of these aspects. Here is that concrete list (Figure 53):

Assessment List of Goals-General Aspects Relations (example)

Nr	General Aspects	Support to the goals	Freedom from inner limitations	My perfect health	My family's perfect health	Perfect relationship with my family	Correct relationship with the M. couple	General progress of my family	My wife's job	My son's success in school and life	Stable monthly income of ≤$10,000	New flat	Successful Sci-Fi writing	Programming
			41	40	43	39	37	43	40	40	29	31	32	33
1.	Family	41	3	4	4	5	2	3	5	5	1	3	3	3
2.	Spirituality	59	5	4	5	5	5	5	5	5	5	5	5	5
3.	Health	60	5	5	5	5	5	5	5	5	5	5	5	5
4.	Finance	60	5	5	5	5	5	5	5	5	5	5	5	5
5.	Career	30	3	1	3	1	4	3	4	5	1	2	0	1
6.	Creativity	60	5	5	5	5	5	5	5	5	5	5	5	5
7.	Relationship	30	4	3	2	0	0	3	1	2	3	2	5	5
8.	Social	34	2	3	4	3	2	4	4	4	2	2	2	2
9.	Rest	39	5	5	5	5	5	5	3	2	1	1	1	1
10.	Fun	37	4	5	5	5	4	5	3	2	1	1	1	1

Figure 53

Marco not only learned what the opposing general aspects to his main goal "successful sci-fi writing" were, but also acquired some vital information on mutual coherence or incoherence among all other general aspects and the most important goals.

He did nearly the same Convergence Procedure with the four least-supportive aspects. With the first part labeled "successful sci-fi writing," he did the procedure with Career, Social, Rest and Fun as second parts, respectively.

For Career, Marco was worried that his commitments and numerous everyday tasks at work could pose a critical obstruction to his success as a writer. In fact, the main reason he felt his career couldn't support his writing aspirations was because he'd been hoping that writing could make him wealthy enough to quit his job forever. The level of that support he had assessed with "0."

Here you can see a short review of this procedure:

1. Relaxation, eyes half-open.
2. I here and now: in head. Did the DTI.
3. First part: successful science fiction writing, represented as a big light-red ball on his right side, partially encompassing his chest and belly.
4. Second part: job, represented as a big green ball in his left side, near his chest.
5. To the first part, he asked: *"Why would my career obstruct the accomplishment of your purpose?"*

    It answered: *"I don't trust it. It could exhaust you and take away your energy."* Marco thanked the part and did the DTI on this answer.
6. To the second part, he asked: *"Are you objecting to the purpose of the first part (successful sci-fi writing)?"*

    It answered: *"I don't want it to endanger me. I don't want to disappear from existence. You could become completely independent from me and I don't want that."* Marco thanked the part and did the DTI on this answer.
7. I here and now: in the neck. Did the DTI.

8. First part was asked: *"Does the second part (my career) fully support the achievement of your purpose?"*

   It answered: *"Not yet. It doesn't want to disappear from your life forever."* Did the DTI.

9. Second part was asked: *"Do you now fully support the purpose of the first part (successful sci-fi writing)?"*

   It answered: *"No. I don't want to disappear."* Marco did the DTI again, but he felt that he should either do the separate IT or SC process with the "career" part or completely reformulate the MH statement.

   He decided to try to "convince" the part that it would not disappear, but would be transformed into something better. So he told the part: *"If my sci-fi books became very successful, this part of me, my everyday job, would be transformed into a new everyday job: the sci-fi writing itself, and maybe programming as well. My successful sci-fi writing would help my everyday job to accomplish its highest purpose of Supreme Happiness. Do you agree?"*

   The answer was "yes." Immediately, Marco saw the green ball moving into him, while becoming smaller and brighter. It "anchored" its center at his Heart.

   He asked again: *"Do you now fully support the purpose of the first part (successful sci-fi writing)?"* The answer was undoubtedly "yes."

10. I here and now: in the Heart. Marco did the DTI+ technique with the MH statement: *"I feel that all my other parts fully support the purpose of the first part (successful sci-fi writing) and contribute to it."*

11. Then he asked the first part, once again, *"Does the second part (my career) fully support the achievement of your purpose?"* As the answer was "yes," the whole process had been complete.

Remember, if Marco had done the prior harmonization of his general aspects, or the recommended work on the other elements of his personality, then his work on this goal would have been much, much easier to do.

Marco then proceeded with the next step of reintegrating the obstructing fears and aversions. He created the following list (Figure 54):

Assessment List of Goals-Fears Relations (example)

Nr	The Fears/Aversions	Impeding level	Freedom from inner limitations (28)	My perfect health (27)	My family's perfect health (41)	Perfect relationship with my family (38)	Correct relationship with the M. couple (33)	General progress of my family (27)	My wife's job (35)	My son's success in school and life (40)	Stable monthly income of ≤$10,000 (28)	New flat (33)	Successful Sci-Fi writing (26)	Programming (32)
1.	Fear of ridicule	41	2	3	4	4	1	4	4	4	4	4	3	4
2.	Fear of the unknown	15	0	1	3	3	2	0	1	3	0	1	0	1
3.	Fear of standing out	37	4	3	4	4	3	2	4	4	2	3	2	2
4.	Fear of abandonment	46	4	4	4	3	3	4	4	4	4	4	4	4
5.	Fear of disease	39	3	0	2	3	4	3	4	4	4	4	4	4
6.	Fear of public speaking	43	4	4	4	4	4	4	4	4	2	4	2	3
7.	Fear of responsibility	23	1	3	3	1	2	1	3	3	1	2	1	2
8.	Risk aversion	24	1	2	5	4	3	1	2	3	0	1	1	1
9.	Travel aversion	43	4	3	4	5	4	3	4	4	3	3	3	3
10.	Work aversion	34	2	0	3	2	3	2	1	3	5	3	5	5
11.	Publicity aversion	43	3	4	5	5	4	3	4	4	3	4	1	3

Figure 54

Marco was able to conclude that the most harmful fears to him were *fear of the unknown, fear of responsibility* and *risk aversion*. He felt it was valuable information for his future work on himself and overall spiritual growth.

In addition to those, *publicity aversion* could specifically obstruct his sci-fi writing goal, so he decided to add it to the other three, and deal with those four problematic aspects of his personality. In order to spare some time, he decided to use the Chain Techniques for the four.

I won't describe all the procedures he passed through in this process, but here is the Double Chain technique Marco used for integration of the fear of responsibility, with answers only.

Fear of Responsibility—Double Chain Technique

(Initial description of the entity: It's a dark blue mass which encompasses the area of the belly and lower part of the chest.)

> *Inclination 1:* I want security and coziness that only parents can provide me.
>
> *Aversion 1:* I don't want to take responsibility because it's easier that way.

(The mass is somewhat brighter now and it has moved upward.)

> *Inclination 2:* I want parental protection.
>
> *Aversion 2:* I don't want insecurity.

(The mass has become a light blue ball located at the area of the solar plexus.)

> *Inclination 3:* I want to be protected and secure.
>
> *Aversion 3:* I don't want to be left alone.

(The light blue ball has moved into the lower chest.)

> *Inclination 4:* I want to be obedient in order to make my parents love me.

Aversion 4: I don't like being punished.

(The ball is bright now and it is near the center of the chest.)

Inclination 5: I need love from my parents.

Aversion 5: I don't want my parents to be angry at me.

(The bright ball is in the Heart.)

Inclination 6: I want love.

Aversion 6: I don't want separation.

(Subtle light at the Heart.)

Peace. *(This was the highest state of the entity.)*

In this way Marco solved the problem of his fear of responsibility and its negative influence on the goal he was working at. He had also successfully treated two other fears and one aversion with the Double Chain Technique, so he was able to jump to the next part of his work—the negative beliefs.

First, he created an *Assessment List of Goals-Beliefs Relations*. He already had his own list of negative beliefs and he had chosen the most important ones for this purpose. He also took into account how intensely he had experienced any of these negative beliefs. For some of them he could almost say that he didn't feel their influence or existence in his life altogether. For others, he still felt strong underlying emotions related to them. The results are shown in the table below (Figure 55).

Assessment List of Goals-Beliefs Relations (example)

Nr	Most important negative beliefs / Most important goals	Imped-ing level	Freedom from inner limitations 27	My perfect health 39	My family's perfect health 47	Perfect relationship with my family 33	Correct relationship with the M. couple 32	General progress of my family 12	My wife's job 21	My son's success in school and life 36	Stable monthly income of ≤$10,000 16	New flat 21	Successful Sci-Fi writing 20	Programming 24
	The Beliefs		\multicolumn{12}{c}{Obstruction by beliefs}
1.	I have to avoid embarrassment at any cost.	37	3	3	3	3	4	3	3	3	3	3	3	3
2.	I'm lazy.	12	0	2	2	2	1	1	1	1	0	2	0	0
3.	My job is difficult.	17	1	0	2	1	4	0	3	2	1	1	1	1
4.	It's important what others think about me.	36	3	3	3	4	4	2	3	4	3	3	1	3
5.	The unknown is dangerous.	23	0	2	4	4	4	1	1	3	0	2	1	1
6.	I'm always a victim.	18	1	0	2	0	0	0	2	3	3	1	3	3
7.	I have no happiness in life.	12	1	1	2	2	1	0	1	1	1	0	0	2
8.	No one should be trusted.	34	1	3	4	4	4	3	1	4	2	2	3	3
9.	Life is unfair.	11	1	1	1	0	0	0	0	1	1	0	3	3
10.	No pain, no gain.	8	0	0	0	0	0	0	2	1	1	1	2	1
11.	Money is not important.	22	4	4	4	2	1	0	1	3	0	1	1	1
12.	The rich are unhappy.	17	3	4	4	2	1	0	0	2	0	1	0	0
13.	The rich are rotten.	19	3	4	4	2	1	0	0	2	0	1	1	1
14.	I never finish my ventures.	20	1	4	4	3	3	1	1	2	0	1	0	0
15.	Money brings suffering.	16	4	4	4	2	1	0	0	1	0	0	0	0
16.	Money is the obstacle to my spiritual growth.	26	1	4	4	2	3	1	2	3	1	2	1	2

Figure 55

Marco found that these beliefs were the most defeating for his overall progress in life: "I'm lazy," "I have no happiness in life," "life is unfair," and "no pain, no gain."

Regarding his main goal "successful science fiction writing," ten negative beliefs were assessed with 0 and 1 and thus were critical: "I'm lazy," "my job is difficult," "the unknown is dangerous," "I have no happiness in life," "money is not important," "the rich are unhappy," "the rich are rotten," "I never finish my ventures," "money brings suffering" and "money is the obstacle to my spiritual growth."

Dismantling Beliefs Technique

Marco decided to do the Dismantling Beliefs (DB) technique on the five worst beliefs (assessed with 0) and to do the Replacing Beliefs (RB) technique on the rest.

Here is the DB process he did on the belief "I never finish my ventures."

1. *Find the source: the specific situation in the past that caused the belief.*

    Marco recalled a situation from his childhood in which he was nine years old, and had started saving up money for a newly invented device called "micro-vision," which he had a huge desire for. After a few months, though, when his allowance savings were still not enough to buy it, he gave up. From that point on, he believed he wouldn't be able to finish important endeavors at all. All his later experiences had been, essentially, supportive to this belief and only strengthened it more and more as time passed.

2. *Find at least one proof in your life that shows you that this belief is not true, or at least not totally true.*

    He vividly evoked a concrete memory of the day he graduated from college. Finishing school had been a big task successfully done, although there had been a lot of obstacles along the path. It was a great success in his life which had proved to him he was able to finish an important project.

    He also brought to mind two more events at his job, where he had effectively finished very complex projects, without any real problems at all.

3. *Find at least one alternative meaning of the original situation. Watch the situation from the alternative perspective. Notice that you can freely choose the meaning of that situation.*

   Marco had difficulty finding an alternative meaning for the original negative situation. In fact, his pre-assumption that it *was* a negative situation was in this step an obstacle in itself. Sensing this, he did the DTI on his negative attitude toward the situation from the past.

   Soon after, a more positive take on it all became clear to him. Because he had stopped saving his money for the micro-vision, he had been able to spend it on other, smaller items such as ice cream, toys, chocolate and (above all) the numerous sci-fi comic strips that had ignited his sci-fi passion in the first place. That one 'failure' had in fact enabled him to afford other, happy moments which had been invaluable to his healthy childhood.

   The original situation wasn't bad after all. It had simply re-oriented him toward making new decisions which also made him happy.

4. *Do the DTI+ on the original situation; use the alternative meaning from step 3 for the MH part of the DTI+.*

   He revived the original situation again, though it had already become blurry and dim due to frequent re-experiencing. He felt the Temporary I while experiencing the *negative meaning* of that mind content and did the DTI.

   After several seconds of pure emptiness, he re-evoked the alternative meaning and said to himself the MH statement: *"I feel that this situation was very positive for me, because I was redirecting my money into many things that were actually more important and beneficial to me at that time. I am a person who always finish his ventures."* He consciously felt this statement from his Heart. It was a very successful DTI+ procedure.

5. *State the original belief to yourself and see if there is still any emotional reaction.*

Marco stated aloud to himself his original belief. There was no emotional reaction this time. It wasn't true to him anymore.

He did the DB or RB process on all nine other negative beliefs.

Marco continued his work with reintegration of *accusations*, *resentments*, and sense of *guilt*. As was recommended, he treated them in the same way as fears/aversions, but with appropriately adjusted terminology. He created an *Assessment List of Goals-Guilt Relations*, which encompassed his main feelings of resentment and a few variations of his sense of guilt (but we won't describe those steps, as it would be repetitious).

He proceeded to *inclinations and desires*. He treated them in a similar way to goals, by forming a list of his individual inclinations and desires, and creating an *Assessment List of Goals-Desires Relations*. These lists indicated that his inclinations and desires were actually very similar to his main life goals, so he didn't have much work in this area.

Marco then continued with his *decisions*. He found a few negative ones and dissolved them using the DTI+ technique. In this way he replaced the negative decisions with the opposite ones. He then dealt with his *personality traits* in a similar way.

Habits were also an important part of his work on the goal. He replaced all important unwanted habits with appropriate firm decisions using the DTI+ procedure.

Marco's personal rules were the last item on his list for integration. They encompassed parental bans and orders, as well as rules created later on by other people in his life. He treated them all with the DTI+ procedure, and replaced the unwanted ones with firm, positive decisions.

After integrating any opposing parts of his personality and clearing up all the internal obstacles to his goal, finally, Marco was ready to commence the next step in the procedure. He didn't want to leave his goal in a general and fuzzy form—he preferred a detailed goal structure.

The next part of his work was the actual Reaching the Goal procedure.

Reaching the Goal Procedure

The variation of the procedure suited to him was the following:

1. Create your Detailed Target State (DTS).
2. Create a list of Mid-Stages (MSs).
3. Define all the Concrete Actions (CAs).
4. Keeping your mind still, occasionally do the *Reaching the Goal Sessions (RGSs)*, by doing this:

    a) Do the DTI at least 3 times. Do the Moving to the Heart (MH) procedure with your current Mid-Stage, while repeatedly immersing it into the Presence.

    b) Return to the state of Presence. If necessary, do the DTI. Do the MH procedure with the DTS, while repeatedly immersing it into the Presence.

    c) Meantime, between every session, let go completely of the goal. Don't think about it at all.

5. Take Concrete Actions in accordance with the list. Do any necessary corrections along the path. In the meantime, allow yourself to let go of your goal. Be completely open to both the possibility of attaining it, or failing to.

For the first step, Marco needed to define a *Detailed Target State* (DTS), with a precise, full image, feelings and a deadline.

This was Marco's DTS:

"It's September 25th, 2016. I'm sitting in front of my computer, browsing the Internet for my self-published sci-fi books. I see two titles with my name. I see a lot of 5 star reviews and the label 'Bestseller.'

My whole family is sitting next to me and I'm telling them that my monthly income from these titles has just reached over $10,000. They are thrilled and hugging me. I'm explaining that I have doubled my income in the last three months.

I'm describing to them how much I enjoy writing and how relaxed and confident this work makes me feel, because I've found effective ways to write and sell my books successfully.

I will achieve this target in real life, or one even more favorable for me and my family, before October 1st, 2016, for the highest good of myself and all other people that could be involved."

This DTS was the concrete target of his goal "to become a successful sci-fi writer." He assumed that being a successful sci-fi writer implied having at least two published and successful titles. Marco visualized a short dynamic movie in his mind in which he was the main actor, with the scenes stated in the DTS's text.

Upon finishing the first step, he took another piece of paper and began writing the Mid-Stages, going back from the time of DTS. He was aware that the Mid-Stages and Concrete Actions should have these characteristics:

- To be written down on paper, or at least in electronic form;
- If possible, to be in the form of a short movie which includes one or more crucial scenes of a real situation that will be a result of achieving the intermediate target state, characteristic for the particular Mid-Stage;
- Must be accompanied with appropriate positive feelings;
- Should have clearly defined deadlines;
- Should include a clear vision of what to do next;
- *(Optional)* Should include a "securing statement"—you will achieve the intermediate target state in real life, or a state even more favorable to the achievement of the goal, for the highest good of yourself and all other people that could be involved.

Marco spent around 15 minutes drafting all of the Mid-Stages, starting at the moment of success and working backwards from it, as follows:

1. Launch the second book before September 1st, 2016.
2. Promote and market the second book, starting one month before launch.
3. Create a cover for the second book before August 25th, 2016.
4. Complete editing on the second book before August 20th, 2016.
5. Complete formatting and other preparations for the launch, during the month of June.
6. Write the second book, from February 1st, to the end of May.
7. Launch the first book before December 1st, 2015.
8. Promote and market the first book, starting one month before launch.
9. Create a cover for the first book before November 25th, 2015.
10. Edit the first book, from September 1st to the end of November, 2015.
11. Complete formatting and other preparations for the launch of the first book, during the month of October, 2015.
12. Create a blog or a website by September 1st, 2015, and continue updating it.
13. Write the first book, from April 15th to the end of August, 2015.
14. Prepare to write the book, starting right now, until April 14th, 2015.

Here are two examples of the above Mid-Stages in action, along with the Concrete Actions Marco planned within them.

This time, however, he formed the Concrete Actions beginning with the present day, moving forward toward the time of success (as opposed to the Mid-Stages, which were the opposite).

<u>Mid-Stage number 14, "Prepare to write the book," starting right now, until April 14th</u>:

Description:

"It's April 12th, 2015. I'm jogging with my best friend and chatting with him about my plans for writing a sci-fi book. I'm describing to him the detailed plan I've formed for the whole process of writing, publishing and marketing my future book. He is impressed with my decisiveness, clear vision and ideas on the book. I'm feeling joyful and am ready to start off the real writing.

I know I have a clear plan on how to undertake the next step (the actual writing).

I will accomplish this Mid-Stage toward my main goal of becoming a successful sci-fi writer, before April 14th, 2016. I will finish it in real life, for the highest good of myself and all other people that could be involved."

The list of Concrete Actions, going from the present time to the DTS:

- Make clear the purpose of the book
- Develop the Mind Map
- Brain storm ideas for the main plot
- Choose the main idea of the book
- Create the writing plan, with a clear daily and weekly schedule, and a strategy on how to eliminate distractions
- Find a few accountable persons who will regularly ask me about my writing progress, encourage and force me to keep going if I want to give up
- Make money investment plan for publishing
- Internet research on scientific ideas that are the background of the setting
- Choose the title
- Each day: do the DTI+ for writing process, creativity, current Concrete Action, current Mid-Stage and the DTS

<u>Mid-Stage number 13, "Write the first book," from April 15th to the end of August, 2015</u>

Description:

"It's August 30th, 2015. I'm sitting in front of my laptop, looking at the polished text of my first book. I'm feeling deeply contented with the work I've done. I'm remembering, with joy, all the effort invested in writing and the creative process. I'm thinking it is a masterpiece.

I know I have a clear plan on how to do next step (creating an appropriate blog or a website).

I will accomplish this Mid-Stage toward my main goal of becoming a successful sci-fi writer before September 1st, 2016. I will accomplish it in real life, for the highest good of myself and all other people that could be involved."

The list of Concrete Actions, going from the present time to the DTS:

- Develop the basic structure for the plot
- Develop the plot
- Write the Table of Contents
- Develop the scenery
- Develop the characters
- Write the Introduction
- Do a verbal read-through
- Polish the book
- Each day: do the DTI+ for writing process, creativity, current Concrete Action, current Mid-Stage and the DTS

Now, Marco was ready to begin *the Reaching the Goal Sessions*, first by visualizing his first Mid-Stage (MS), and then the Detailed Target State (DTS).

He worked on them each twice a day: once in the morning, immediately upon getting up, and once in the evening, before bed. Each time, he tried—more or less successfully—to calm down his mind for roughly five to ten minutes.

When he felt completely tranquil, he revived the scene of the current MS as vividly as possible, along with its accompanying emotions of happiness and fulfillment. At the same time, he made an effort to remain aware of the background sense of Presence. He slowly immersed the MS scenery into the Presence, while feeling settled in the Heart, resembling the basic technique of Gentle Touch of Presence.

In the initial Reaching the Goal Session, the visualization of his first Mid-Stage lasted 5 minutes (step 4a, to come). In it, Marco did the DTI procedure 3 times and brought himself into the state of Presence.

He imagined the MS, all the while trying to keep himself partially aware of the Presence. He occasionally looked at the paper with the scene written down, which helped him to "play" the movie of the MS flawlessly and on repeat, before immersing it into the Presence.

After that, he did exactly the same process with the DTS (step 4b, to come) and it roughly lasted another 5 minutes.

Of course, Marco wasn't able to do this all flawlessly. Thoughts and distractions appeared frequently, but as soon as he became aware that he was out of the process, Marco did the DTI and gently brought himself back into the visualization process, without blaming himself.

Day by day, Marco mastered more and more of the technique and experienced less and less mind chatter, until it became routine. It sometimes fluctuated, of course, and that influenced the work on the goal. But overall development was obvious.

The Concrete Actions, which he had started acting on immediately, were also going according to plan. He created a brain-storming Mind Map, which gave him a lot of new ideas, chose a main idea from there, created a writing blueprint, and so on. The very process of writing and marketing became easy, full of creative flashes and enjoyment.

He modified the path and deadlines when needed, allowing things to change and grow. Some setbacks and periods of laziness inevitably occurred, but Marco used the DTI+ technique and passed through them pretty successfully.

Present day, as I am writing this, Marco tells me he is very satisfied with the results. He is currently in the middle of his planned path towards his DTS, but has already become successful in writing science fiction.

The work on this goal turned out to be completely transformative to his whole life. He has reintegrated and transformed many negative elements of his personality (some even unrelated to the goal), transformed some bad habits and created some very useful new ones. He has definitely become a happier man. I really believe he will firmly continue in that manner.

Determination Technique
*"Keep your best wishes close to your heart and watch what happens." —
Tony DeLiso, Legacy: The Power Within*

If you are unable to do the entire Comprehensive Goal Achievement Process, or just don't have enough time for such an extensive approach, you can pick up another option: a technique which is narrower but more direct than the CGAP. It focuses solely on the goal, erases obstacles and moves all desired outcomes straight to the Heart, by doing the DTI+ technique. We will name this process the Determination Technique (DT).

Once again, if you are doing this without having reintegrated the needed parts of your personality, there is a chance you will activate some of your dormant negative framework beliefs (or other unresolved subconscious structures talked about throughout the book). You may still achieve the goal, but with those other problems activated in your life, your overall level of happiness may not increase at all. I highly recommend completing at least several DTI+ processes on your goal, as they are quick, and, if possible, defining your main goals and mutually harmonizing them, before attempting the DT. That way you will have the best results.

The DT starts by assuming that you have not done any CGAP process and will therefore not have any intrinsic general life goals (that arise from the supreme goal) already determined.

Essentially, this technique gathers all negative *perceptions* (beliefs, rules, fears, emotions, etc.) related to the goal and removes them through repetitive DTI+ procedures.

They are our greatest obstacles to the achievement of the goal. We get the negative perceptions by asking ourselves two questions: "Could I fail?" and "Is there any reason why succeeding could be bad?"

During the DTI+ procedure (that you should repeat five times each time) you first remove a negative perception, then through the MH part you install an opposite, positive perception (belief, rule, decision, emotion, etc.) that you need to formulate properly, immediately after getting the negative perception.

When you eliminate negative perceptions and install their "antidotes" in these two circles, you then continue to the last step of installing the positive statement: "I am absolutely and completely determined to achieve this goal," through the MH procedure.

Then, you repeat the whole cycle until you cleanse yourself from all negative perceptions related to the goal, while subsequently installing the opposite, positive mind content that pulls you directly toward the goal.

Here is the DT procedure:

1) Determine the goal clearly (optional: develop a full DTS).
2) Determine at least two higher purposes for or benefits to your goal.
3) Ask yourself: *Could I fail?*
   a) If you feel or think that the answer is "no," you are definitely ready to achieve your goal; this process is complete.
   b) If you feel or think that the answer is "yes," ask yourself, "why?" The answer to this question is essentially your defeating perception (belief, assumption, rule, fear, or other negative notion). Formulate it. Proceed to step 4.
4) Ask yourself: *Am I sure that this (defeating) perception is true?*
   a) If "no," do the DTI+ on it five times, with the MH part consisting of an opposite, positive perception. Proceed to step 5.
   b) If "yes," do the DTI+ on it, with the MH statement: *"I am determined to achieve my goal because I want to ... (state the higher purposes)"*; then repeat step 4.
5) Ask yourself: *Is there any reason why it would not be good to succeed?*
   a) If "no," proceed to step 7.

b) If "yes," ask yourself what exactly that reason is. The answer to this question is essentially your limiting perception. Formulate it. Proceed to step 6.

6) Ask yourself: *Am I sure that this (limiting) perception is true?*
   a) If "no," do the DTI+ on it five times, with the MH part consisting of an opposite, positive perception. Proceed to step 7.
   b) If "yes," do the DTI+ on it, with the MH statement: *"I am determined to achieve my goal because I want to ... (state the higher purposes)"*; then repeat step 6.

7) Do the MH procedure 5 times with this statement: *"I am absolutely and completely determined to achieve this goal."* Optionally, to this statement you can add: *"...because I want to (state the higher purposes)."* This would strengthen your process, while slowing it down significantly. When you have done the MH procedure 5 times, go back to step 3 again.

The process is complete when you are *absolutely* sure that you will achieve your goal.

Do not forget to write down everything you can. For that purpose, you can find a printable DT Worksheet in the Appendix III.

In this section, after the real-life example, you can also find the DT Algorithm. For the beginning, it is best to look at the algorithm and to strictly follow the steps shown in it, until you master the technique.

Regarding the first step of how to clearly define the goal, note that you are free to choose between developing a Detailed Target State (DTS) or just a General goal. But, keep in mind, if you haven't already done the harmonization of the elements of personality, the developing of the Detailed Target State would be a more difficult process. The possible parts of your personality that are negatively oriented to your goal could interfere and warp the resulting DTS and the final outcome in unexpected ways.

Although this process may seem quite long, believe me—when you firmly follow the steps, it is actually simple, fast and very effective. You have to accomplish two circles several times: one addresses your uncertainty as to whether or not you can attain the goal, and the other addresses your unconscious structures that undermine the achievement of your goal due to labeling it as 'bad for you' in some way.

You will need to apply this procedure for the specific goal at least several times, with a few days between each process. This is because, each time, some new inner obstacle will probably be revealed and removed. Eventually, though, you will achieve your goal.

Real-Life Example

"Adriana" decided to finally achieve one of the main goals in her life—to get rich. She was already acquainted with the Determination technique and had used it for a few smaller goals very successfully. Now, she was eager to try it out on her greatest aim.

She did the process with one of her friends. It will be shown to you in a slightly paraphrased form, but it follows the previously presented procedure, step by step.

1) *Determine the goal clearly.*

   Since she didn't do much of the goal harmonization process before, Adriana decided to create a general goal structure (not the DTS). She defined the following goal:

   "I am a rich person. I have a steady income larger than $10,000 a month and I'm happy because of that."

2) *Determine at least two higher purposes or benefits to your goal.*

   Adriana determined three higher purposes of her goal:

   "I want to be happy."
   "I want to become completely independent."

"I want to quit my current job safely."

3) *Ask yourself: Could I fail?*

   a) *If no, you are definitely ready to achieve your goal; this process is complete.*

   N/A

   b) *If yes, why? The answer to this question is essentially your defeating perception. Formulate it. Proceed to step 4.*

   "Of course I could fail, because I have no idea what I should do in order to reach this goal." Adriana formulated the defeating perception: "I have no idea what I should do in order to get rich."

4) *Ask yourself: Am I sure that this (defeating) perception is true?*

   "No, I'm not sure. I am a creative person and should be able to come up with a bunch of concrete ideas on how to get rich."

   a) *If no, do the DTI+ on it five times, with the MH part consisting of an opposite, positive perception. Proceed to step 5.*

   (She formulated the MH part before doing the DTI+ procedure.) Done, with the MH part: "I am a creative person, who can easily conceive many concrete ideas on how to get rich."

   b) *If yes, do the DTI+ on it, with the MH statement: "I am determined to achieve my goal because I want to ... (state the higher purposes)"; then repeat step 4.*

   N/A

5) *Ask yourself: Is there any reason why it would not be good to succeed?*

   "Well, yes, there is. I think it wouldn't be good for my spiritual life. My father used to say 'Money is evil'."

   a) *If no, proceed to step 7.*

N/A

b) *If yes, ask yourself what that reason is, exactly. The answer to this question is essentially your limiting perception. Formulate it. Proceed to step 6.*

The reason has been already stated. In fact, there were two standpoints stated, so Adriana identified two beliefs on their basis: "Getting rich wouldn't be good for my spiritual life" and a "classical" belief: "Money is evil."

6) *Ask yourself: Am I sure that these beliefs are true?*

"No, I'm not. That just came into my mind."

a) *If no, do the DTI+ on them five times, with the MH part consisting of opposite, positive perceptions. Proceed to step 7.*

Adriana did the DTI+ procedure five times on each of the two beliefs. The MH parts were: "I feel that getting rich greatly supports my spiritual life, because I will gain much more freedom and spare time in everyday life," and "I feel that money is good; it's a tool for gaining freedom in this world."

b) *If yes, do the DTI+ on them, with the MH statement: "I am determined to achieve my goal because I want to ... (one of the higher purposes)"; then repeat step 6.*

N/A

7) *Do the MH 5 times with this statement: "I am absolutely and completely determined to achieve this goal." Optionally, to this statement you can add: "...because I want to (state the higher purposes)." Then go to step 3 again.*

Done 5 times, with the optional supplement, so the MH part was: "I am absolutely and completely determined to achieve this goal, because I want to be happy, to become completely independent and to quit my current job safely." Adriana felt that this addition had noticeably strengthened the MH statement.

(The next circles of the process are shown in a shortened form, without most of the instructions.)

3) *Could I fail?* "Yes. I always give up on my big endeavors." This was already a clear formulation of her defeating belief.

4) *Am I sure that this (defeating) perception is true?* "Yes, I am. Unfortunately, that happens all the time in my life."

> She did 5 times the DTI+ on the defeating belief, "I always give up on my big endeavors" with this MH statement: "I am determined to achieve my goal because I want to be happy, to become completely independent and to quit my current job safely."
>
> Now, in accordance with the procedure, she returned to step 4 and again answered the question "Am I sure that this defeating perception is true?" (The perception was "I always give up on my big endeavors").
>
> "No, it won't happen anymore. I'll succeed this time."
>
> She did the DTI+ 5 times, with the MH part formulated as: "I am a person who always easily and completely accomplishes all her endeavors." She felt a big release after this step.

5) *Is there any reason why it would not be good to succeed?* "Yes. I see that rich people are unhappy. Maybe that could happen to me, too." Formulation of the limiting perception: "Rich people are unhappy."

6) *Am I sure that this (limiting) perception is true?* "No. But I believe and see the majority of them being unhappy."

> She did the DTI+ on the perception "Rich people are unhappy" five times, with the MH part consisting of an opposite, positive perception "I am absolutely confident that rich people are happy."

7) Then she again did the MH five times with the statement: "I am absolutely and completely determined to achieve this goal, because I want to be happy, to become completely independent and to quit my current job safely."

(In the following circles you will see only the formulated negative perceptions with their positive counterparts. At the end of each circle Adriana did the same MH five times with the same statement: "I am absolutely and completely determined to achieve this goal, because I want to be happy, to become completely independent and to quit my current job safely.")

3) *Could I fail?* "I don't like taking any risks."
4) DTI+: "I am calm and relaxed if I have to take any risk."
5) *Why it would not be good to succeed?* "It's dangerous to have lots of money."
6) DTI+: "I feel that having lots of money brings safety and freedom."

(Next)

3) *Could I fail?* "I'm lazy."
4) DTI+: "I am an active and diligent person."
5) *Why it would not be good to succeed?* "I feel that if I get rich some people would hate me."
6) DTI+: "I love myself and other people regardless of their emotions and opinions toward me."

(Next)

3) *Could I fail?* "I have to work too much in order to gain something."
4) DTI+: "I am a person who easily accomplishes any endeavor."
5) *Why it would not be good to succeed?* "I should be modest, not rich."

6) DTI+: "I feel that I could be helping others much more if I were rich."

(Next)

3) *Could I fail?* "Life has always turned against me."
4) DTI+: "I love myself, I love people and I love my life. I feel that my life supports me fully."
5) *Why it would not be good to succeed?* "I don't deserve happiness."
6) DTI+: "I feel that I have always done things as best as I could and knew at that moment. I am a person who deserves love and happiness. I really love myself."

(Next)

3) *Could I fail?* "I can't believe that in reality I can get rich."
4) DTI+: "I am sure that I will succeed. I am a successful person."
5) *Why it would not be good to succeed?* (Nothing appeared)

(Next)

3) *Could I fail?* "No. I'm 100% positive that I will accomplish this goal."

This concluded the session. Adriana was feeling completely free from inner obstacles for this big goal. Presently, she is doing very well in her life. Although some other issues have appeared, she has effectively dealt with them and continues to do so. So far, she has not had any significant side-effects, perhaps due to her serious approach to the development of every field in her life.

Determination Technique Worksheet
DT Worksheet: Circles 1 and 2

Nr.	Instruction	1st circle	2nd circle
1.	Goal Formulation	"I am a rich person. I have a steady income bigger than $10,000 a month and I'm happy because of that."	
2.	Goal's Higher Purposes	"I want to be happy." "I want to become completely independent." "I want to quit my current job safely."	
3.	Could I fail? If yes, why?	"Of course I could, because I have no idea what I should do in order to reach this goal."	"Yes. I always give up on my big endeavors."
	Defeating perception formulation	"I have no idea what I should do in order to get rich."	"I always give up on my big endeavors."
4.	Opposite belief/assumption	"I am a creative person, who can easily conceive many concrete ideas on how to get rich."	"I am determined to achieve my goal because I want to be happy, to become completely independent and to quit my current job safely." "I am a person who always easily and completely accomplishes all her endeavors."
5.	Is there any reason why it would not be good to succeed? If yes, why?	"Well, yes, there is. I think it wouldn't be good for my spiritual life. My father used to say 'Money is evil'."	"Yes. I see that rich people are unhappy. Maybe that could happen to me, too."
	Defeating perception formulation	"Getting rich wouldn't be good for my spiritual life." "Money is evil."	"Rich people are unhappy."
6.	Opposite belief/assumption	"I feel that getting rich greatly supports my spiritual life, because I will gain much more freedom and spare time in everyday life." "I feel that money is good; it's a tool for gaining freedom in this world."	"I am absolutely confident that rich people are happy."
7.	MH statement for every circle	"I am absolutely and completely determined to achieve this goal, because I want to be happy, to become completely independent and to quit my current job safely."	

Figure 56

DT Worksheet: Circles from 3 to 5

Nr.	Instruction	3rd circle	4th circle	5th circle
1.	Goal Formulation	"I am a rich person. I have a steady income bigger than $10.000 a month and I'm happy because of that."		
2.	Goal's Higher Purposes	"I want to be happy." "I want to become completely independent." "I want to quit my current job safely."		
3.	Could I fail? If yes, why?	"Yes, I could. I don't like taking any risks."	"Yes. I'm lazy."	"I always had to work a lot if I wanted to gain something."
	Defeating perception formulation	"I don't like taking any risks."	"I'm lazy."	"I have to work too much in order to gain something."
4.	Opposite belief/assumption	"I am calm and relaxed if I have to take any risk."	"I am an active and diligent person."	"I am a person who easily accomplishes any endeavor."
5.	Is there any reason why it would not be good to succeed? If yes, why?	"It's dangerous to have lots of money."	"I think if I get rich there would be some people that will hate me."	"Being rich isn't quite modest, right? I want to be a modest person."
	Defeating perception formulation	"It's dangerous to have lots of money."	"If I get rich some people would hate me."	"I should be modest, not rich."
6.	Opposite belief/assumption	"I feel that having lots of money brings safety and freedom."	"I love myself and other people regardless of their emotions and opinions toward me."	"I feel that I could be helping others much more if I were rich."
7.	MH statement for every circle	"I am absolutely and completely determined to achieve this goal, because I want to be happy, to become completely independent and to quit my current job safely."		

Figure 57

DT Worksheet: Circles 6 and 7

Nr.	Instruction	6th circle	7th circle
1.	Goal Formulation	"I am a rich person. I have a steady income bigger than $10.000 a month and I'm happy because of that."	
2.	Goal's Higher Purposes	"I want to be happy." "I want to become completely independent." "I want to quit my current job safely."	
3.	Could I fail? If yes, why?	"Yes, I still could... Life has always turned against me."	"I just can't believe that in reality it will happen to me. I don't believe I can do that."
	Defeating perception formulation	"Life has always turned against me."	"I can't believe that in reality I can get rich."
4.	Opposite belief/assumption	"I love myself, I love people and I love my life. I feel that my life supports me fully."	"I am sure that I will succeed. I am a successful person."
5.	Is there any reason why it would not be good to succeed? If yes, why?	"Many times I have felt that I don't deserve happiness at all."	N/A
	Defeating perception formulation	"I don't deserve happiness."	N/A
6.	Opposite belief/assumption	"I feel that I have always done things as best as I could and knew at that moment. I am a person who deserves love and happiness. I really love myself."	N/A
7.	MH statement for every circle	"I am absolutely and completely determined to achieve this goal, because I want to be happy, to become completely independent and to quit my current job safely."	

Figure 58

Determination Technique Algorithm

Instead of our usual "In a Nutshell" section, here we have an algorithm that clearly explains the whole DT procedure (Figure 59).

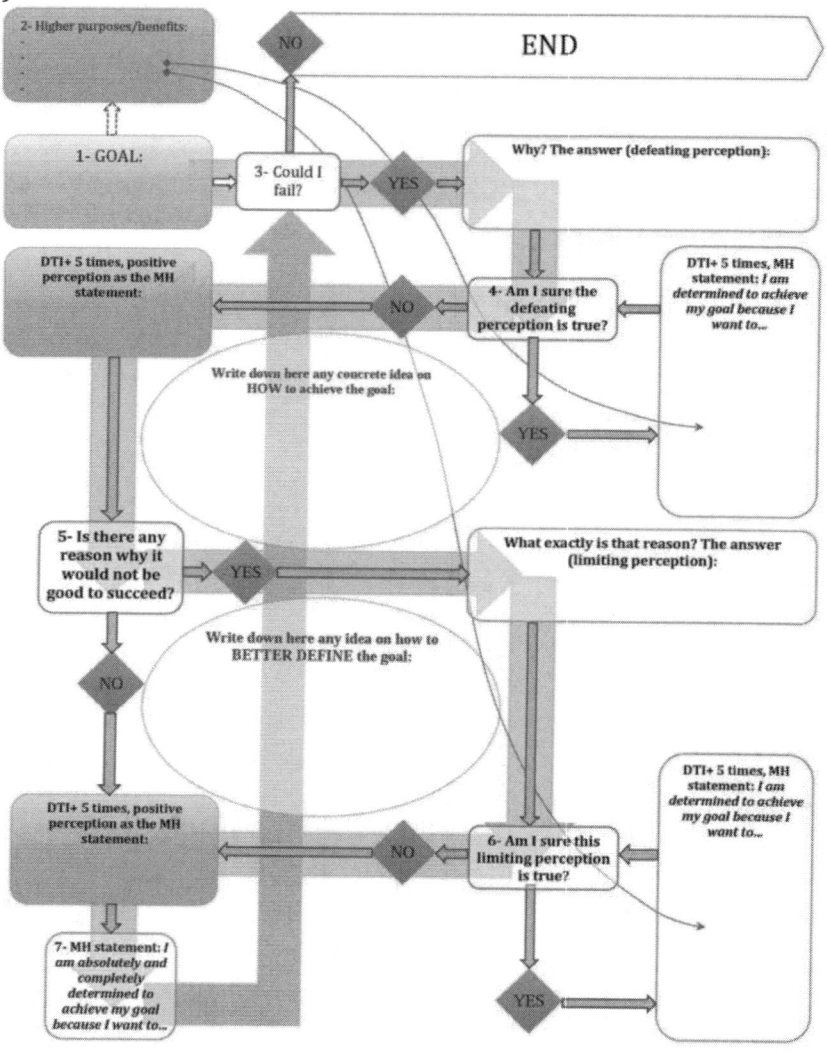

Figure 59

Part V
Clarifications

PART V: CLARIFICATIONS

Additional Areas of Application

Though the main areas of focus for this book are personal and spiritual transformation, resolving problems, healing and achieving goals, there are many other ways to apply the Reintegration System that are equally viable.

Identifications

"The person who fights monsters should make sure that in the process, he does not become a monster himself. Because when you stare down at an abyss, the abyss stares back at you." — Friedrich Nietzsche

In a psychological sense, the term "identification" is described on Wikipedia as "...a psychological process whereby the subject assimilates an aspect, property, or attribute of the other and is transformed, wholly or partially, by the model the other provides. It is by means of a series of identifications that the personality is constituted and specified."[32]

Although not classified in this book as one of the main elements of personality, *identifications* are definitely an interesting subject. They are deeply ingrained beliefs on who and what we are, other than what we truly are. We are unconsciously attached to them. Hence, identifications are "responsible" for secluding us from our true nature.

You can find a list of some common identifications in Appendix II.

---

[32] Source: Wikipedia, the free encyclopedia:
https://en.wikipedia.org/wiki/Identification_(psychology)

A similar version of this list was first shown to me when I was in my early twenties, as part of a course similar to the spiritual system called "Avatar." At the end of the course I had a moment of revelation, as I dissolved those identifications which I had been firmly attached to, one by one.

The result was stunning to me. It was one of my first true spiritual experiences. Upon releasing myself from my identifications, I fell into a state of indescribably pure consciousness. My whole inner being felt complete and deeply peaceful, like I was a blissful observer of my own reality. I watched my thoughts float through the air *outside* of me, circling around my head, knowing what each one "meant to say" to me. (Nevertheless, I was functioning normally.) That effect lasted for a few minutes only, but it was absolutely unforgettable. I had finally recognized the true nature of my being.

Although the whole experience and its consequences have gradually diminished, the memory of it is still very strong. Of course, do not expect that you will have the same experience, as we are all different and absorb things differently, but also as that class was led by a professionally trained instructor who did a tremendously good job. I only share this experience with you to give context to the list, and to exemplify how proper dissolving/integration has the power to radically and permanently change our views on life in general (though it is rarely so dramatic). I also hope that you will connect with something in this book that enables you to have a transformative experience of your own, however that happens to manifest.

By being cautious I mean that you should pass through all the identifications from the list slowly, without skipping any steps. The best results with this system would be achieved by cautiously passing through all the identifications from the list slowly, in one sitting, without skipping any steps. After finishing the process, you should give yourself some time to rest and just observe the room around you.

Clearing Relationships

"A genuine relationship is one that is not dominated by the ego with its image-making and self-seeking. In a genuine relationship, there is an outward flow of open, alert attention toward the other person in which there is no wanting whatsoever." — Eckhart Tolle

Another interesting field of application is clearing relationships. Remember, all people around us embody some of the inner elements of our own personality, so clearing interactions with them is always a good idea. By doing this, we are essentially reintegrating our traits, beliefs, fears, desires and other psychological aspects that are projected outward, onto the other people.

Naturally, we are more inclined to start with those relationships which we consider challenging, and for this purpose you can use the Inner Triangle technique. The problematic person, with their general attitude and perceived negativity toward us, would be represented as the first polarity in the process. The second polarity would be our own I in a defending (or attacking) position related to the problematic individual.

We could also apply the Convergence Procedure for challenging interactions with people, in the similar way with the Inner Triangle process described above.

It is also advisable to clear the relationships which you don't consider problematic at all, as even good elements of our personality could have contradicting effects, so it is best to be thorough.

For this I recommend the Dissolving the Temporary I Plus (DTI+) technique. You imagine the person at hand and do the DTI+, with an MH part "I feel that our relationship is perfect/calm/full of Love/harmonious..." You could also watch if there is an emotional reaction inside you in relation to the person. For example, that could be romantic feelings, resentment, jealousy, fear, sorrow, pity, etc. Do the DTI+ on any emotion(s) that you don't want to have.

Then, imagine that *you* are that person. See your old self through their eyes and do the same DTI+ process, as that person. While being "inside the other's skin," you could also try to feel whether there is some emotional reaction within that person toward you. Of course, you cannot really know what that other person feels exactly, so it would be fictitious, but just let it happen. Do the DTI+ on whatever comes up. It will surely contribute to the process of cleansing your relationship.

An additional way of clearing your relationships with people that pose a challenge to you is to send love and good intentions toward them. In this way, you can both help them to improve their lives and help to improve your relationship with them.

First, imagine the challenging person as you normally perceive them, with all the negativity that they aim at you and at their own life. Do the DTI+ on that picture, together with all the emotions involved. The MH part would be: "May you be healthy and happy forever" or "I forgive you and love you." Then, imagine that you are them, watching you, with all the possible emotions that they could feel toward you. Do the same DTI+ process, with the same MH part, this time directed at you. Done several times, this procedure could tremendously help your relationship.

And last, but not least, perhaps an even more effective approach to clearing the relationships between people is to use the Gentle Touch of Presence (GTP). Essentially, when we are deeply in the state of Presence, the state of Pure Consciousness, we "touch" the relationship between us and that person with the Presence. We slightly and gently notice the person's appearance from the Presence, and inside the Presence. We keep the person and our inner reaction toward them within our Presence as long as possible. That's it. The deeper we are rooted in the Presence and the longer we experience that connection within the Presence, the relationship between us and the other person is cleaner and more effectively improved.

Lucid Dreaming

*"Fly without wings;
Dream with open eyes;
See in darkness."*
— Dejan Stojanovic

Some Reintegration practitioners have reported the spontaneous emergence of lucid dreaming. For those who don't know much about this phenomenon, I'll try to briefly describe it.

A lucid dream is every dream in which one is aware that they are currently dreaming. It rarely happens to the average Joe, supposedly, but when it does it is often delightful. It is a sudden, overwhelming feeling of total freedom. We can do anything: pass through walls, fly, or even change our environment. The lucid dream's surroundings can become somehow crystal clear, crisp and divine. Some have said that lucid dreams felt more real than their waking reality.

There is said to be hardly any control over how or when the lucid dreams occur, however. Even if we find ourselves inside a lucid dream, it rarely lasts for a long. Most often, as soon as the enlightening thought passes through our mind "This is a dream!" we become excited, lose connection to the dream, and wake up.

Extensive work with the Reintegration System (and with other effective psychological or spiritual methods) sometimes unintentionally produces spontaneous and more frequent lucid dreams.

But Reintegration could also be used as a tool for developing the *skill* of lucid dreaming. Why would we like to develop that ability at all? Well, taking into account that when we are dreaming we are in a direct contact with our subconscious, there are many possible benefits of a highly developed lucid dreaming skill. In a way, we can consciously communicate with aspects of our subconscious. Hence, we can use that state of mind for many things, for example:

- Direct communication with elements of our personality;
- Getting various hidden pieces of information;

- Talking with spiritual teachers;
- Remembering long forgotten scenes or people;
- Visiting distant places on Earth or even in the cosmos;
- Getting information about illnesses and healing;
- Extending the internal time of your dream (it could be much longer than the time actually passed in waking reality while dreaming) and practice skills that you otherwise can't practice or don't have time for;
- Applying various self-improvement methods, including the Reintegration techniques, which could be even more effective in this state.

How to develop the skill of lucid dreaming?

1) Recollect some of the most frequent scenes in your dreams;

2) Create an intention to become aware inside a dream whenever you find yourself in one of those scenes; assign to your roles in those scenes triggers for your awakening inside the dream; visualize these scenes and your becoming aware that you are dreaming;

3) Do regularly the MH procedure with the intention to become aware that you are dreaming, with the common dream scenes that you previously recollected;

4) Ask yourself recurrently during your waking times: "Am I awake or dreaming?" After some practice, the same question will appear inside dreams more and more frequently, leading to more lucid dreams;

5) Look repetitively at your hands during your waking times; that could also lead to the same result of becoming lucid whenever your hands come up into your awareness in the dream.

You should be constantly cautious within your lucid dreams. Be aware that the realm you are in is not only your subconscious mind. It's inherently independent, and being meek and moldable to your presence, it only mirrors some of your unconscious aspects. Thus, just as you could meet some highly conscious beings there, even spiritual teachers and angelic beings, you could also stumble upon some negative entities that exist independently of you and could even act not openly aggressively, but be cunningly and covertly malicious and harmful. In that case, you can and should always retain full control over your dream, if needed calling upon higher beings for assistance or simply inspiring yourself to wake up.

Helping Others

"I find the best way to love someone is not to change them, but instead, help them reveal the greatest version of themselves." — Steve Maraboli

Helping others is a noble idea, but a very sensitive one at the same time. Despite the mistakes we may make in our life, almost all of us actually have good intentions and just want to be happy. We also want our family, friends and other people to be happy. We have a deeply ingrained urge to help others.

Unfortunately, this urge doesn't always yield good results, because we have limited perception and often don't know what is truly good for us or the people around us. Moreover, when we try to help others, sometimes it ends with transferring some of their problems right into us. The reason for this goes back to the holographic universe idea, stating that the people around us are, in fact, mirroring our own internal personality aspects. Therefore, their problems are our own potential problems.

When we have unresolved problems buried in our subconscious, those negative entities must somehow express themselves—either through some accident, illness or via the people around us. Therefore, when our family members or friends suffer, it may be partially related to the suffering which was at some point in our own past, but was suppressed and forced into the depths of our psyche.

Hence, when we give help directly to our dear ones (or anyone), we are indeed sometimes able to solve their problems. But, if they don't learn the lessons out of their own sufferings, the deliverance will be only temporary. The same or similar problems will appear again, either to those people or to us. Why to us? Because those troubles outside may have only been projections of our internal difficulties, so if there is a chance for them to express themselves directly within our being, they'll take it.

So, be very careful when you are helping others. If you are helping them directly, don't use any techniques. "Use" only Love or Presence, nothing else. *"It's not how much we give but how much love we put into giving,"* said Mother Teresa. Those expressions of our True Nature will balance out the imperfections inside those beings, as well as our own inadequacies. I described all the necessary details in the Healing sections.

For personal healing, you could use concrete techniques of the Reintegration System, but *only* on yourself, *not* on others (as the problem could swing back around to you, for the reasons described above).

If you decide to heal others, let it be with the premise that the source of the problem in them is, in actuality, inside *you*. Try not to feel offended or insulted by this. Just remain completely open and honest, and allow your subconscious mind to reveal the solution.

If you cannot find the element of your personality that corresponds to the difficulty of the other person, don't worry. Visualize an aspect of yourself at your will, without thinking too much on what it is, its nature or its purpose. Simply assign to that aspect the corresponding role of responsibility for the problem outside. Do the DTI+ several times, or the IT procedure on it. All the time feel that it is *your own* aspect, not the other's.

Eventually, you will be amazed how true this premise of the internal source was and may wonder how you didn't notice it before. You will integrate the element of personality within you and the problem within the beloved person will fade out by itself, sometimes miraculously, sometimes along with the growing of consciousness of that being.

This way, you will not only be helping others, but you will be expanding and deepening your own consciousness. Eventually, you will find that you have ultimate and complete responsibility for your individual reality and that fact will not be a burden—it will actually bring you true freedom.

Cleansing Space and Things

"Space and silence are two aspects of the same thing. The same no-thing. They are externalization of inner space and inner silence, which is stillness: the infinitely creative womb of all existence." — Eckhart Tolle, The Power of Now: A Guide to Spiritual Enlightenment

It is my belief that the space and things around us often get contaminated with negative beings or energies. Regardless of whether or not you believe the same, the very act of cleansing the environment around you can only benefit all involved. We will be practicing doing this indirectly, by cleansing things within our own personality, since the external world is only mirroring the internal one, albeit symbolically.

By using various Reintegration techniques on our elements of personality (further elaborated on back in Part III: Personal Transformation), we will be ridding our individual reality of negativity.

If you feel the need to influence your surroundings directly, however, you can use the Gentle Touch of Presence (preferably) or the Dissolving the Temporary I Plus.

In either case, your attention will be directed at the external location (e.g. a room, backyard, house, and so on) or energy around you, before doing the procedure. Slightly notice the mind content (the external thing, energy or space), and then apply the rest of the corresponding procedure. Remain aware that you are clearing only an *internal representation* of that mind content.

A warning: if, for any reason, you happen to perceive the presence of a sinister being or dangerous entity in your vicinity, don't use any technique on it! Rather, do the Inner Triangle process or Single Chain technique on your *inner corresponding personality trait*. That way, you will be safe from any sentient external influence, since you will remove your inner cause of its presence and involvement with it.

Time Sublimation

"...the past gives you an identity and the future holds the promise of salvation, of fulfillment in whatever form. Both are illusions." — Eckhart Tolle, The Power of Now: A Guide to Spiritual Enlightenment

You can also do cleaning work on time itself. I refer to your individual timeline of past and future events. Timeline work was discussed most in the section "Traumatic Memories," so you can refer to it if you want to clean up your negative emotional charge from the past. The more you reintegrate your past traumas, the greater your inner freedom and future will be.

However, in that section there was no coverage of work on the future. But what is actually your future? You don't know; no one knows. You can only guess, feel, believe, predict... and all of this is covered by working on your emotions, fears, beliefs, habits, traumatic experiences from the past, etc. *They are the seeds of your future.* Change them and you *will* change your future.

Anyway, apart from working on different elements of your personality, you can still do some timeline work on your future as a whole, or partially.

For example, I have a habit of doing a clearing of the next day. During my morning meditation, when (or if) I get into a state of deep Presence, I do the Gentle Touch of Presence on the upcoming day. Being deeply immersed in the Presence, I am slightly noting all mind content associated with that particular day. Whenever I'm expecting a rough time or events during the day, I gently bring them into my field of Presence, one by one, including all persons involved. I just lightly encompass them with my Peace or Love and they either vanish or transform. Then I let them go, I bring myself back into the deep peace, strengthen my Presence and, if I feel there is more to clean up for the forthcoming day, I repeat the process. If not, I usually proceed to cleaning the whole week ahead, month, sometimes even my whole future life at once.

Occasionally, I still stumble upon some premonitions so negatively charged that they roll me out from the Presence. In those cases, I do the DTI procedure, which successfully removes them and enables me to bring back my inner peace completely.

If I'm striving to achieve some specific goal (outside of the structured CGAP or DT approaches), I may even do the DTI+ process on any mind content that I find connected or related to that goal. The MH part is the goal I want to attain.

Cleaning the future is a very powerful technique, which could really make a difference to your life. I can't stress enough my recommendation for doing it regularly.

In a Nutshell

Identifications

They are our deep beliefs that we are someone or something else other than we truly are. They are mostly unconscious attachments. There are numerous identifications within our personality, practically at all levels of our consciousness.

You can find a list of the most common identifications in the Appendix, so you may use it for dissolving these root attachments. They should be dissolved using DTI technique, in a single session, but slowly and carefully, one by one. Upon the session's completion, you must give yourself some time to rest quietly and just observe the room around you. Be cautious in this process.

Clearing Relationships

Since people around us essentially are projections of our own internal elements of personality, to clear the relationships with them we must reintegrate our inner aspects.

For clearing problematic relationships, you can use the IT technique, with one polarity representing the problematic individual with their perceived attitude toward you, and the other representing yourself in relation to them. You can do the Convergence Procedure in a similar way.

For clearing relationships you don't consider problematic, you may use DTI+, with an MH part "Our relationship is perfect/calm/full of Love/harmonious..."

Lucid Dreaming

These are some ways for developing the skill of lucid dreaming:

1) Recollect some of the most frequent scenes in your dreams;

2) Create an intention to become aware inside a dream whenever you find yourself in one of those scenes; assign to your roles in those scenes triggers for your awakening inside the dream; visualize these scenes and your becoming aware that you are dreaming;

3) Do regularly the MH procedure with the intention to become aware that you are dreaming, with the common dream scenes that you previously recollected;

4) Ask yourself recurrently during your waking times: "Am I awake or dreaming?" After some practice, the same question will appear inside dreams more and more frequently, leading to more lucid dreams;
5) Look repetitively at your hands during your waking times; that could also be your trigger and lead to the same result of becoming lucid whenever your hands come up into your awareness in the dream.

Helping Others

When we directly help a person, if they don't learn a lesson out of the problem, the same problem might appear again for that person or even transfer to us. Hence, we have to help the person only through Love or Presence. All our helping actions should be the result of Love and Presence. These core states will balance out any imperfections inside that person or our own inadequacies that would otherwise lead us or that person to the same problem again.

Since problems experienced by our closest people are often projections of our internal problems, we can use the Reintegration techniques to solve those problems, but through application onto ourselves only. Be honest with yourself and you will eventually find the same trait within yourself that the other person apparently has, which is the source of the problem. Reintegrate it and you will see a profound change in the external situation, too.

Cleansing Space and Things

If you perceive the presence of a potentially harmful being or energy in your vicinity, don't use techniques on it, but try to find your *inner corresponding element of personality* instead, and apply the Inner Triangle or Single Chain technique on it. In this way you will be safe from any negative external influence, since you will remove your inner cause of its presence in your individual reality.

Time Sublimation

For your work on past experiences, refer to the section "Traumatic Memories" in order to clean them up.

For your future life, you can do some clearing work as well. First, all the parts of your character that we were talking about in this book are actually shaping your future, so by working on them you are working on your future, too.

> You can also do some timeline work on your future, either partially or as a whole. When you enter the state of Presence, do the Gentle Touch of Presence (GTP) technique on your next day, next important period of your life or even your whole future life. You move along your timeline to that period, feel yourself in it and do the GTP on everything you feel. If any strong emotion pops up (like fear of some particular event you are expecting to happen), you can also do the DTI or DTI+.

Questions & Answers

*"There is nothing I can tell you
That you do not already know.
There is no question that you can ask me
That you yourself cannot answer.
You have just forgotten."*
— David Littlewood

In reality, as in this whole book, I'm not giving you any new information. You are the one who finds it within your mind, who pulls it out from underneath layers of your subconscious, who reads the text here and decides how to apply it personally.

It will be you answering yourself.

What am I supposed to do if I'm not satisfied with my life, but can't figure out what's wrong; where do I start? What should I work on?

If you aren't aware of any chronic or immediate problems, you could employ the holographic principle to find a starting point for your work. Your subjective reality is but a projection of you, in a symbolic sense. Your traits, for example, are actually projected onto the people present in your life.

Look around you; think about your family members, your closest friends, and any of the people that you're in contact with frequently. Write down their names, one by one.

Assign one or more personality characteristics to each name, which you usually associate with those names. Those are *your* traits. They are inherent to you and reflected upon those people.

I recommend that you work on all these characteristics, whether "good" or "bad," starting with those you consider as "bad." Don't neglect work with "good" traits. They could also hamper you from achieving some of your biggest desires in life!

Which is better, solo or group practice?

Each is effective in different scenarios.

One good thing about working in a pair or group of pairs is that, with the help of your partner, you are able to be better focused on the work. The other person handles the distraction of writing down all the answers during the process, and will encourage you if you get drowsy or are unclear on what to do next. The partner is often a friend who is personally interested in your success, or might be a professional who is experienced in the procedure, both of which are fortunate. There is also inherent effectiveness to group work because it is the synergy of individual efforts, working together mutually.

On the other hand, working in a pair can have some disadvantages. For instance, the final result of the process is always influenced by both individual's energies and opinions. If the partner's attitude is not adequate for the process, or if he or she has had a recent stress or trauma nested in their psyche, it could negatively affect the final outcome.

Solo work is more appropriate for the modern tempo of life, in that many people's lifestyle leaves them only odd hours of free time for working on themselves, during which a partner is not available.

Either way, if you are aware of the above stated assumptions, and have strong motivation and decisiveness to go through the process firmly, you will be prepared enough for a successful outcome.

How can I find the exact opposite to my chosen first polarity in the Inner Triangle procedure?

It's mainly a question of what the true opposites are for you.

For some, true polarities are complements, like colors (in the traditional color model RYB, with red, yellow and blue as the basic colors)[33]: red - green (green is gained by merging other two complement colors: blue and yellow), blue - orange (red + yellow), yellow - purple (blue + red). They are mutually harmonizing, balancing, matching and/or corresponding. In accordance with that, characteristic pairs of opposites are:

- Male and Female
- Subject and Object
- Subject and Experience
- Active and Passive
- Conscious and Unconscious
- Consciousness and Body
- Inside and Outside

There is also another notion of polarities, like opposite brightness levels: black and white, dark grey and light grey. They are mutually differing, contrasting and/or conflicting. Accordingly, the pairs of opposite polarities would be:

- Freedom and Oppression
- Life and Death
- Light and Dark
- Good and Evil
- Happiness and Sorrow
- Freedom and Control

If you feel unable to find the opposite polarity or right label for it and feel annoyed, do the DTI on that feeling. Then ask the first polarity: "What is your true opposite?" You will probably get an answer, either in words or symbols. If you are still unsure, I would suggest you to examine the answer with the Manual Muscle Testing (MMT) technique.

---

[33] Wikipedia: **Complementary colors** are pairs of colors which, when combined, cancel each other out. This means that when combined, they produce a grey-scale color like white or black. When placed next to each other, they create the strongest contrast for those particular two colors. Due to this striking color clash, the term **opposite colors** is often considered more appropriate than "complementary colors."

However, you should not make an issue of this during the process. Do not search too much for it. You don't need to choose a real opposite after all.

Nevertheless, you always have the "last resort" of a Single Chain or Double Chain technique. In most of cases they are efficient enough.

Why are there questions about the qualities and location of polarities in every circle in the IT process, rather than just at the beginning of the process?

It's important to follow the chain of transformation of each polarity through every circle/step of the process. That way, if we are interrupted, we can more easily pick up where we left off, as all the qualities of the partially transformed polarities are right there on the page.

In the IT process, what is the purpose of scanning for thoughts, emotions and sensations present at the here and now position?

It helps to give a clear starting point for the next step/circle in the process. We have to free ourselves from unnecessary mind content before continuing to deal with both polarities in each circle.

It is possible for one's mind to have content at that "central" position (here and now) only at the beginning of the process, but sometimes the content appears during the whole process. It depends on the individual person and their current life situation.

What should I do in the event of sleepiness during the process, which to me happens very often, especially in solo-processing?

Actually, your sleepiness is a very good sign—you've gotten to the point where you are relaxed enough to dig into your subconscious levels, where the core of your life issues lay.

Usually, when you have a chronic problem in your life, it originated as a suppressed, forgotten decision/belief, which is still active today. Because it has become unconscious, when you try to access it, you will experience a feeling of sinking into the unconsciousness, and it may manifest itself as sleepiness.

Never force too much. So, if you are sleepy and can't resist, just write down quickly where you are in the process and have a nap. If you are just meditating, don't write anything, just take a nap.

Next time be more assertive. Try to do the same process when you are fresh enough. If you are sleepy again, that's a definitive sign that you've come to the source of your problem. Change your posture, if needed go to the bathroom and wash your face and then continue where you left off. You simply must reintegrate the problematic part of yourself, otherwise it will manifest itself externally, making for even more problems.

When I'm going through the circles of the IT process, sometimes one of the polarities achieves the highest state before the other one. Also, I do not always get answers from them in a parallel way, in pairs—for example, a polarity has a goal, but doesn't have an aversion. Or, after being asked for an aversion, it instead gives a positive goal, or vice versa. Is it OK?

Absolutely. Everything you indicated is normal. The procedure is very structured, but the answers are often not. The whole process sometimes behaves quite unexpectedly. What is important is that you follow the spirit of the process—go up the chain of goals and aversions for both polarities in order to have them merged mutually and with your I here and now.

Do you recommend using modern smartphone applications for triggering mindfulness?

Of course, you can use the magic of technology in this area. There are many existing mindfulness applications for smartphones and tablets, and all of them offer reminders for becoming aware of the Now. They can be set up to chime regularly or randomly, and can notify you of an event at a specific location.

Generally, it's better not to rely on external reminders for mindfulness at all (for instance, what if you lost your phone? Would you be able to sustain your level of mindfulness without it?), but to develop triggers on your own. However, for some people they still could be of great benefit.

I would recommend you to first develop your internal habits based on daily situations or activities. The best use of the mindfulness apps is to employ them as an addition to the basic practice of an already developed personal mindfulness habit.

Can we use other systems simultaneously with this system?

Generally speaking, yes, you can. But, as is the case with many other systematic approaches, they are sometimes incompatible.

I would recommend you try to avoid a lot of mixing with other systems. For example, the Reintegration techniques are compatible with most psychological approaches, and with Buddhism. But their compatibility with various New Age methods, yoga practices (except Hatha yoga), Christian mysticism and other traditions is questionable.

You should be very cautious if you want to mix any methodologies, in general, with the Reintegration procedures.

Can we change your techniques?

Yes, you can. This system is like a living organism; it develops in many directions. But again, be cautious, especially when it comes to the addition of any ideology or energetic work. Too much experimentation is not advisable, unless you are a very experienced practitioner who has tried out various methodologies.

Also, if you make substantial changes to any of these techniques, it will have become another method, so please don't call it by its current name anymore. It is already a pretty complex system by itself, and you don't want to make a confusing mess of things.

Is 'loving kindness meditation' helpful?

That's a great question. Of course it's helpful and I strongly recommend that you include, if possible, this practice into your daily routine.

I had an idea to include that kind of meditation into the Part III of this book, but I concluded that it wasn't necessary. That subject has essentially been covered by the "Healing" section, specifically under the part named "Love." Also, my intention in this book was to be oriented toward a particular kind of meditation, specific only for the Reintegration System, as described in the "Sittings" section.

Yet, I always emphasize the importance of Love and of any kind of meditation and ways of living which cultivate Love and open our Hearts. Such methodology is called "loving kindness" or "metta," and is characteristic for Buddhist meditation.

You can find many varieties of this meditation on the Internet, but basically, it boils down to this:

1. Sit in a comfortable position. Relax.
2. Do the DTI a few times.
3. Move the center of your being into your Heart.

    Repeat the following loving-kindness phrases:

    – May I be free from danger.
    – May I be safe.
    – May I be free of suffering.
    – May I be happy.
    – May I be healthy and strong.
    – May I be at ease.
    – May I be joyful.

4. Think of someone for whom you have very warm and loving feelings. This can be a parent, friend, sibling or even a pet.

    Repeat the same loving-kindness phrases toward that being:

- May you be free from danger.
- May you be safe.
- May you be free of suffering.
- May you be happy.
- May you be healthy and strong.
- May you be at ease.
- May you be joyful.

5. Think of someone for whom you have neutral feelings. This can be an acquaintance, a neighbor, or even a person you know of from the media. Repeat the same loving-kindness phrases from the previous steps for this person.
6. Think of someone for whom you have negative feelings. Repeat the same loving-kindness phrases for this person as well.
7. Radiate loving kindness to all beings in the Existence. Repeat the loving-kindness phrases for all beings.

What if the Temporary I does not "want" to expand?

This sometimes happens. The key is just to do the Alternative DTI, explained in the Appendix.

Another approach is to find an additional Temporary I, from which vantage point you are experiencing that "inability" to expand the first Temporary I. Then you expand that "secondary" Temporary I. If that I also doesn't "want" to expand, you repeat the same approach, find another I, until you find an I which will expand and dissolve. Then you go back down the line of Temporary Is, which should be easily "expandable" now.

You choose which approach is more suitable to you in such situations. Personally, I prefer the first one (the Alternative DTI). If thoroughly applied, it's gentle and works.

Can we apply the Dismantling Beliefs technique to content other than a belief?

Yes. You can apply that procedure, slightly altered, to many other elements of personality. For example, you can do it on rules, accusations or guilt and even on decisions. Just replace some words in the procedure with appropriate ones and go ahead. Your creativity in dealing with your own reintegration process is most welcome and could be a decisive factor to your effectiveness in this comprehensive process.

Can I do only the "Freshness" or "Acceptance" part of the FA procedure? I find these parts, especially the "accepting" part, sufficient enough for dealing with simple mind content…

Of course, you can do these parts of the FA procedure solely. Yet, in my experience, sometimes either "Freshness" or "Acceptance" are insufficient for a specific emotions or thoughts, and their joint application is more useful.

When doing the DTI, do I really have to expand my Temporary I beyond the boundaries of the whole Existence?

No. Generally speaking, it's enough only to expand your Temporary I beyond the boundaries of your experience as you feel or visualize it, or beyond the borders of your room, house, city, or visible sky and earth around you. However, the more you expand, the deeper you free yourself from related hidden content.

The Whole Picture

With its versatile techniques, the Reintegration System covers all main areas of human psychological life: personal and spiritual development, problem-solving, healing and goal achievement. Its main components are symbolically shown on the picture below (Figure 60):

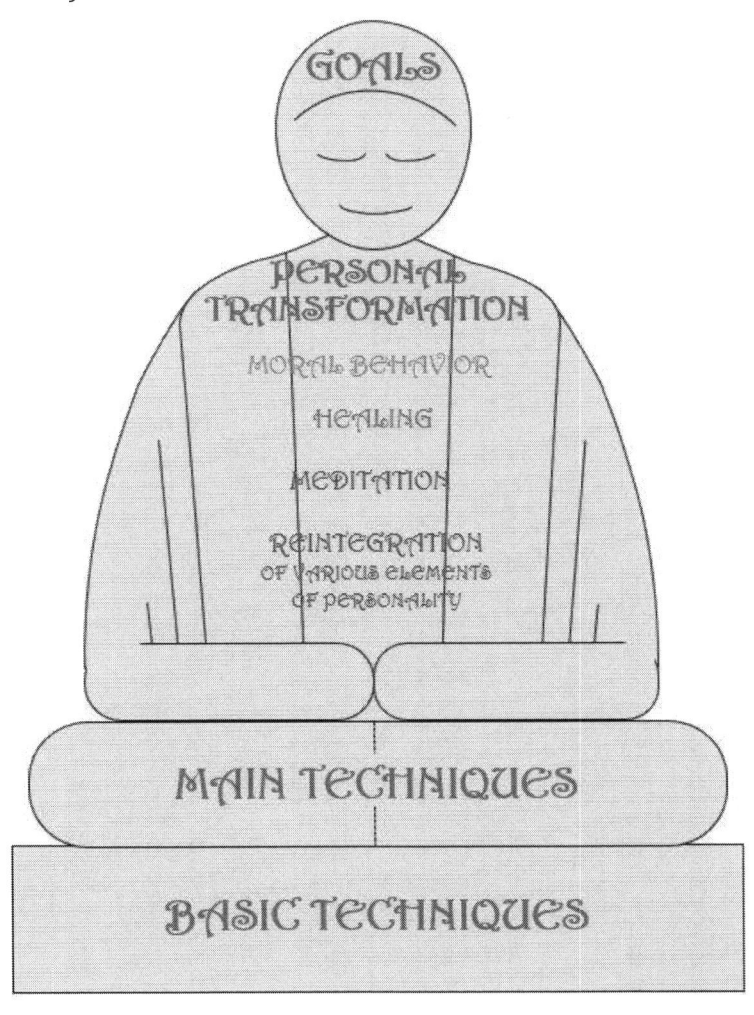

Figure 60: Main Components of the Reintegration System

The whole picture of the system, with the majority of its techniques, you can see on the following drawing (Figure 61):

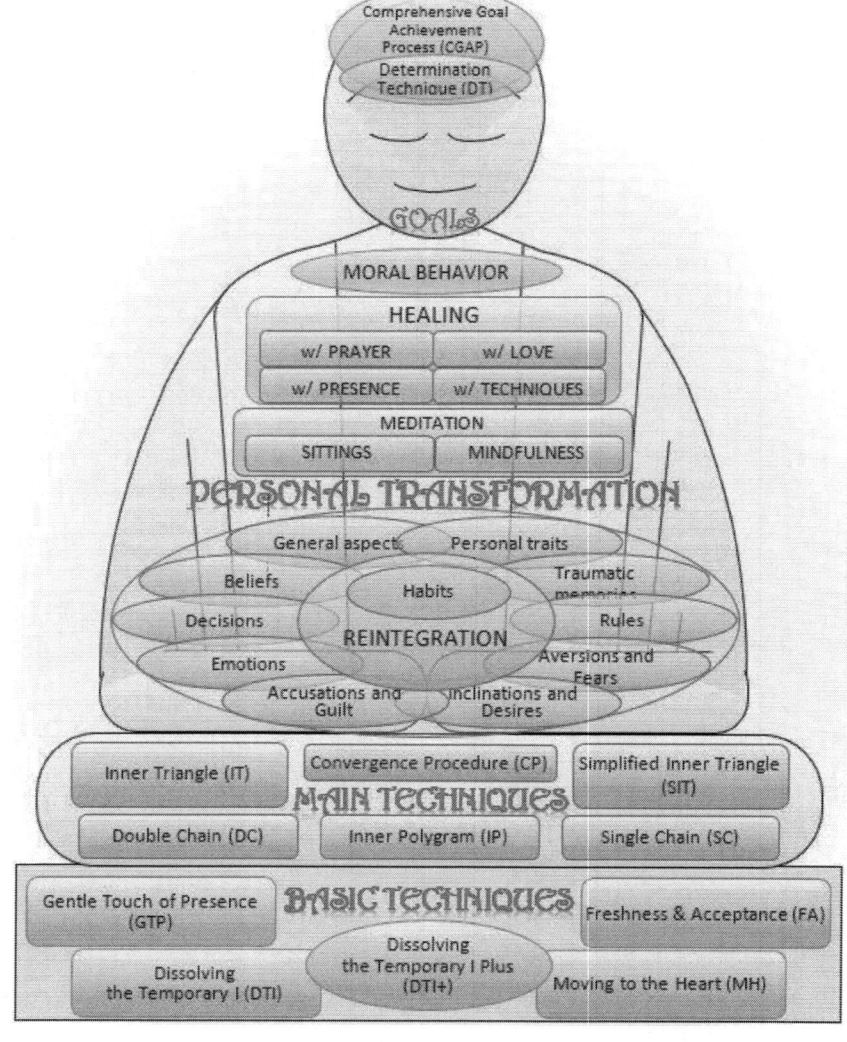

Figure 61: Symbolical Display of the Reintegration System with its Techniques

In order to have an overview of recommended techniques for every possible area of one's life, you can find a suitable list below.

Basic techniques:

- Dissolving the Temporary I (DTI)
- Moving to the Heart (MH)
- Dissolving the Temporary I Plus (DTI+)
- Gentle Touch of Presence (GTP)
- Freshness & Acceptance (FA)

Main Reintegration techniques:

- Inner Triangle (IT)
- Single Chain technique (SC)
- Double Chain technique (DC)
- Comprehensive Goal Achievement Process (CGAP)
- Determination Technique (DT)
- Convergence Procedure (CP)

Other Reintegration techniques:

- Replacing Beliefs (RB)
- Dismantling Beliefs (DB)
- Inner Polygram (IP)

Areas of application and recommended techniques/approaches:

- *Spiritual development*: Mindfulness, Regular sittings, all Reintegration techniques
- *Complex problems*: IT, DC, SC, IP
- *Healing*: Prayer, Love, Presence, Forgiveness, GTP, IT, DC, SC, IP
- *Achieving goals*: CGAP, DT, DTI+, MH
- *Casual challenges*: GTP, IT, DC, SC, IP, DTI, DTI+, FA
- *Habits*: GTP, IT, DC, SC, IP, DTI, DTI+, FA
- *Beliefs*: DB, RB, DTI+, IT, IP, DC, SC
- *Traumatic memories*: DTI+, DTI, GTP, FA, Forgiveness

- *Decisions*: DTI+, CP
- *Rules*: DTI+, IT, DC, SC
- *Emotions*: GTP, IT, DC, SC, IP, DTI, DTI+, FA, Forgiveness
- *Aversions and Fears*: GTP, IT, DC, SC, IP, DTI, DTI+, FA, Forgiveness
- *Accusations and Guilt*: Forgiveness, DTI+, IT, DC, SC, IP
- *Inclinations and Desires*: DTI+, IT, DC, SC, IP
- *Personal traits*: DTI+, CP
- *Identifications*: DTI, DTI+, FA
- *Clearing relationships*: GTP, DTI, DTI+, FA, Forgiveness
- *Meditation*: DTI, DTI+, GTP, FA
- *Detaching from negative morphic fields*: GTP, DTI, DTI+, IT, DC, SC, IP, Forgiveness
- *Lucid dreaming*: DTI+, CGAP, DT, MH, GTP
- *Cleansing space and things*: DTI, DTI+, GTP, FA
- *Helping others*: GTP, DTI+, MH, FA
- *Clearing the past, next day and future*: GTP, DTI, DTI+, FA, Forgiveness

Feel free to choose any of suggested techniques for corresponding area at will. However, pay attention both to your general strategy of your work and to details.

The best strategy is to make your work habitual and creative. You must enjoy the work on yourself and, at the same time, turn the techniques into everyday habits.

It is also a good idea to create a plan for your work. One of the plans, for example, could look like this:

1) Annual strategy:

   a) For working periods: regular sittings, mindfulness, developing triggers for mindfulness, loving kindness meditation—every day; plus, work with Reintegration techniques for personal transformation and Determination technique during weekends.

- b) For holidays and vacations—every day: sittings, mindfulness, Comprehensive Goal Achievement Process (except during travel days).
2) Daily plan for working days:
   - a) Mindfulness whole day
   - b) 0700 – 0720: regular sitting
   - c) 0720 – 0730: developing mindfulness triggers
   - d) 1900 – 1920: regular sitting
   - e) 1920 – 1930: loving kindness
3) Daily plan for weekend:
   - a) Mindfulness whole day
   - b) 0700 – 0720: regular sitting
   - c) 0720 – 0800: work with the Inner Triangle or Chain technique
   - d) 1900 – 1920: regular sitting
   - e) 1920 – 1930: loving kindness
   - f) 1930 – 2000: Determination technique
4) Daily plan for holidays and vacations:
5) Mindfulness whole day
6) 0700 – 0720: regular sitting
7) 0720 – 0800: Comprehensive Goal Achievement Process
8) 1900 – 1920: regular sitting
9) 1920 – 1930: loving kindness
10) 1930 – 2000: Comprehensive Goal Achievement Process

Another important thing is to add some creative work to your daily schedule, whether in a fixed time window or as a flexible task.

It is good to know that if you accurately and persistently stick with your scheduled times, it will greatly improve your work in every way. It's like making a pathway—as you find your way through a new meadow, it's a challenge to get through the first time due to heavy grass. But, as you use the same path through the meadow time and again, you'll create footprints through the grass, and each time it will be easier to go the distance. Make your work habitual, but don't forget to enrich it with creativity.

One trick to help with your decision to be persistent is to draw up a contract with yourself. Take a piece of paper and write down a statement in which you are firmly promising yourself that you will fully implement your schedule every single day. Jot down every item of your daily plan and state in the contract that you will accomplish any missed item as soon as possible. Don't forget to sign the contract. It will serve as a valuable subconscious bond to your practice.

Another good approach is to do your practice jointly with a friend or group of like-minded people. Your work will be mutually supported and supplemented with group synergy. If one practitioner gets low-spirited and wants to give up, others will encourage and support them. This kind of help is invaluable. It's often better to work together.

Conclusion

"There is only one corner of the universe you can be certain of improving, and that's your own self." — Aldous Huxley

Dear friend,

Now that you have a clearer picture of the Reintegration System, you can draw your own conclusions about its possibilities and usage, customizing it for your needs.

The basic techniques (DTI, MH, DTI+, GTP and FA), for example, are versatile in their appliance. You could choose to use only them, without any other technique, and you would still have very good results. Whenever something unpleasant arises inside or outside of you, do a basic technique several times and it will reduce or completely remove the content from your life.

However, in accordance with their group name, the basic techniques are only the basis of the Reintegration System. Many times in life, you'll need more complex help to tackle your obstacles.

The Inner Triangle procedure and its derivatives are extremely effective for those kinds of problems. If you have a tricky relationship, trouble at work, a stressful parental commitment, a recurring fear or any other prolonged problem, you can resolve it with the right tools and effort. Perhaps you will need to apply the IT procedure multiple times to ensure that all the aspects are reintegrated, but you can do it. Simply remain aware that chronic problems are often complex and habitual, deeply ingrained in your neurological system, and therefore need a little extra elbow grease.

But the Reintegration System is not only about treating negative things, it is about creating positive ones: achieving your goals; fulfilling your dreams.

Although the process for accomplishing goals presented in this book may seem, at first, dauntingly complex, you will find it comes naturally once you start using it. It will help you find your own interesting pathway to the goal, revealing unexpected aspects of your personality, subconscious mind and life in general along the way.

If you are not up for the commitment of the Comprehensive Goal Achievement Process, there is the Determination Technique, for quicker realization of your targets. Yet, once again, be aware that you may end up having a different problem in another area of your life, or some unexpected complications related to a newly achieved desired state. That's why your work on goals should be wide-ranging, thorough and vigilant.

Another thing to be aware of, is that the more you believe in something, the more effectively you will achieve results. Do not expect top-notch effects if you are only half-believing the method. You may achieve something, but the result will be weaker, and will require a lot more effort. Remember: beliefs shape our reality.

Then, there is the spiritual development aspect of the system.

What actually is spiritual development? In my opinion, we cannot distinguish "ordinary" life from "spiritual" life. It's the same. Everyday life is a stage for learning. Each unpleasant experience is an invaluable opportunity to learn something new about ourselves and others, to reveal a previously unknown and treasured aspect of our personality and life, to bring something into the view of our consciousness.

Our negative aspects have a positive essence and we need to appreciate that fact. That's the only way to fully reintegrate those aspects. Even saints weren't perfect—if they were, they would have disappeared from this reality, as there would be no more negative traits to anchor them to this physical world. On the contrary, all saints and famous spiritual teachers had to retain some vices or flaws, intentionally or not, in order to stay here. However, there are some accounts of monks (I've read about Buddhist hermits, although there are probably similar cases in other spiritual disciplines, too) who virtually vanished from this reality, having left only clothes and parts of hair and nails behind them. But even if you attain such a high level of consciousness, you will always have freedom of choice to retain a few imperfections if you want to stay in this domain of limitations.

Countless lessons are here to be learned, at our disposal, if only we are aware of them. There are new opportunities in front of you, for learning life lessons, for raising our awareness, for achieving the highest states of consciousness. In those lie the real strength of this system. Through your personal work and meditation and mindfulness, you will elevate your consciousness to unexpected levels.

As with all other techniques and practices outside of this system, if you want to achieve long-term results you will have to be consistent in your practice. This depends on developing good habits. If you succeed in transforming your work in the Reintegration System into an everyday habit, you will get really amazing outcomes.

Still, even though you have in your hands a versatile tool, feel free to be creative in your work. Experiment. This system is still being developed and is not written in stone. If you make a mistake, you always have the DTI+ and other techniques at your disposal.

As a result of your meticulous work, you may solve almost all of your problems, gain wisdom, achieve many of the things you'd always dreamed of, and attain a state of bliss. But then emerges the final obstacle to your ultimate freedom from suffering... your ego. Propelled by selfish desires, supported by crafty pendulums, you may encounter your own vanity. In other words: pride, self-importance, narcissism, arrogance, or sense of superiority. That's the ultimate danger.

If you happen to think or feel that you are somehow more important, better, or superior to others, remind yourself to be modest. Return to your Heart. Reintegrate your pride. Be humble in all situations, toward all beings. We are all equal.

It's far easier to notice these cunning traits overwhelming others than it is to see it in yourself. That counts for me, too. If you notice on any occasion that my words, my deeds or behavior have become spoiled with arrogance, superiority or self-importance, please warn me. I am prone to self-delusion, just as any of us are.

In conclusion, I don't want to claim that *this book* will change your life. It is *you* that can and will change your life for the better. I wish only to provide you with some tools to do so.

I can't guarantee you anything. It depends only on you. And that's a great news, actually. You are the one who's in charge.

May you have a productive, delightful and fulfilling life.

Sincerely,

Nebo

About the Author

Nebo D. Lukovich is an ordinary guy, devoted to his family and friends. As you can see in this book, his greatest passion is spiritual work and writing. He has been researching and practicing various spiritual and psychological systems and techniques for more than 25 years.

Nebo was born in 1972 and grew up in Serbia, a country in Europe. He now lives with his wife and two teenage children in Podgorica, the capital of Montenegro, which is a neighboring country in the same region.

Although he prefers a peaceful family life, his experience in spiritual work (both personal and with friends and acquaintances) often calls on him to engage in personal coaching and educational work in the field of personal growth and transformation.

His published writing career has only just begun with his book, and there is more to come. He will continue to write and research even more advanced techniques, many of which are currently being tested with his friends.

You can reach Nebo or his team at the www.re-integration.com.

If you enjoyed this book, please leave a supportive review on Amazon. It will sincerely help the author and his team to continue their work, and spread these remarkable ideas all over the world. Thank you for reading!

Bibliography

- Andreas, Connirae; Andreas, Tamara. Core Transformation: Reaching the Wellspring Within. Real People Press. Kindle Edition. 2012
- Bartlett, Richard (2007-04-03). Matrix Energetics. Simon & Schuster, Inc. Kindle Edition.
- Berry, Jim. Power of Habit: Building One Good Habit At A Time For Ultimate Success, Kindle Edition, 2014
- Bohm, David. Wholeness and the Implicate Order (Routledge Classics). Taylor and Francis. Kindle Edition, 2005
- Covey, Stephen R. (2013-11-15). The 7 Habits of Highly Effective People: Powerful Lessons in Personal Change (25th Anniversary Edition). Rosetta Books. Kindle Edition.
- Dass, Ram (2012-01-04). Journey of Awakening: A Meditator's Guidebook. Random House Publishing Group. Kindle Edition.
- Davis, Stephen (2010-10-13). Butterflies Are Free to Fly: A New and Radical Approach to Spiritual Evolution. L&G Productions LLC. Kindle Edition.
- Duhigg, Charles. The Power of Habit: Why We Do What We Do, and How to Change. Random House, Kindle Edition, 2012
- Doumani, Narissa. A Spacious Life: Memoir of a Meditator, Palmer Higgs (March 17, 2015)
- Greene, Brian (2009-01-08). The Elegant Universe: Superstrings, Hidden Dimensions, and the Quest for the Ultimate Theory. W. W. Norton & Company. Kindle Edition.
- Greene, Brian (2011-01-25). The Hidden Reality: Parallel Universes and the Deep Laws of the Cosmos. Random House, Inc. Kindle Edition.
- Gregg Braden: The Divine Matrix, Hay House, 2008
- Gunaratana, Henepola. Mindfulness in Plain English: 20th Anniversary Edition. Wisdom Publications. Kindle Edition.
- Gunaratana, Henepola (2009-08-10). Beyond Mindfulness in Plain English: An Introductory guide to Deeper States of Meditation. Wisdom Publications. Kindle Edition.

- Ighisan, Mircea. WOW! How to create new realities. Matrix Transformation. Kindle Edition. 2012
- Kabat-Zinn Ph.D., Jon (2005-01-01). Coming to Our Senses: Healing Ourselves and the World Through Mindfulness (Kindle Location 65). Hyperion. Kindle Edition.
- Kabat-Zinn, Jon (2010-02-06). Wherever You Go, There You Are: Mindfulness Meditation In Everyday Life. Hyperion. Kindle Edition.
- Kaku, Michio (2006-03-14). Parallel Worlds: A Journey Through Creation, Higher Dimensions, and the Future of the Cosmos. Knopf Doubleday Publishing Group. Kindle Edition.
- Catherine, Shaila (2008-05-10). Focused and Fearless: A Meditator's Guide to States of Deep Joy, Calm, and Clarity. Wisdom Publications. Kindle Edition.
- Kinslow, Dr. Frank J. (2013-05-06). The Kinslow System: Your Path to Proven Success in Health, Love, and Life. Hay House. Kindle Edition.
- Kieslich, Ulrich; Ighisan, Mircea (2013-12-01). Transformation in the Matrix – How you can guide your reality with the 2-Point Method. Kindle Edition.
- Jack Kornfield (2008-12-26). After The Ecstasy, The Laundry. Random House UK. Kindle Edition.
- Levey, Joel; Levey, Michelle (2005-06-10). The Fine Arts of Relaxation, Concentration, and Meditation: Ancient Skills for Modern Minds. Wisdom Publications. Kindle Edition.
- Lokos, Allan, Patience: The Art of Peaceful Living, Kindle Edition, 2012
- Lidiya K, This Moment, January 2015, Smashwords Edition.
- Mihajlovic, Filip. Quick Goals Practical E-Course, 2015
- Nhat Hanh, Thich. The Miracle of Mindfulness. Beacon Press Boston, 1987. Kindle Edition.
- Nhat Hanh, Thich. Peace Is Every Step: The Path of Mindfulness in Everyday Life. Kindle Edition, 2010
- Nhat Hanh, Thich. Stepping into Freedom: Rules of Monastic Practice for Novices, Parallax Press; 1st edition (August 9, 2001)

- Nirmala (2013-12-23). Living from the Heart. Endless Satsang Foundation. Kindle Edition.
- O'Connor, Richard. Rewire: Change Your Brain to Break Bad Habits, Overcome Addictions, Conquer Self-Destructive Behavior, Penguin Publishing Group, Kindle Edition, 2014
- Ralston, Peter (2010-08-31). The Book of Not Knowing: Exploring the True Nature of Self, Mind, and Consciousness. North Atlantic Books. Kindle Edition.
- Ray, Amit. Mindfulness: Living in the Moment Living in the Breath. Inner Light Publishers (October 28, 2015).
- Roberts, Jane (2011-09-30). The Nature of Personal Reality: Specific, Practical Techniques for Solving Everyday Problems and Enriching the Life You Know (A Seth Book). Amber-Allen Publishing. Kindle Edition.
- Salzberg Sharon, Real Happiness: The Power of Meditation. Workman Publishing. Kindle Edition.
- Slavinski, Zivorad Mihajlovic, The Invisible Influences: Freedom from The Effects Of Bodiless Entities, English Edition, 2008
- Slavinski, Zivorad Mihajlovic, Sunyata, The Divine Void and Mystical Physics, English Edition, February 2007
- Talbot, Michael. The holographic universe. Harper Perennial, New York, NY, 1992
- Tolle, Eckhart. A New Earth: Create a Better Life. Penguin UK. Kindle Edition. 2009
- Tolle, Eckhart. The Power of Now: A Guide to Spiritual Enlightenment. New World Library. Kindle Edition.
- Tolle, Eckhart. Stillness Speaks. HJ Kramer/New World Library. Kindle Edition. 2009
- Waggoner, Robert (2008-10-01). Lucid Dreaming: Gateway to the Inner Self. Red Wheel Weiser. Kindle Edition.
- Yogani (2008-11-13). Deep Meditation – Pathway to Personal Freedom (AYP Enlightenment Series). AYP Publishing. Kindle Edition.

- Yogani (2008-11-13). Samyama – Cultivating Stillness in Action, Siddhis and Miracles (AYP Enlightenment Series). AYP Publishing. Kindle Edition.

APPENDIX I: Additional Techniques

Here are some additional, optional techniques which are just as effective as the main ones of the Reintegration System. There are many occasions for their use; perhaps you're running too short on time to do the whole Inner Triangle process (but still want to work on both polarities), or you're unable to expand your Temporary I in the main DTI procedure and are looking for another way. Regardless, they certainly have their own important place within the System.

Alternative DTI

Compared to the main DTI technique, this is quite a different approach. Some may find it to be a quicker, gentler and more elegant procedure and others may find it's not as easy to learn as the main DTI technique. That's because it requires prior experience with accepting mind content.

To begin, first determine where your Temporary I is located while you are feeling the mind content. Pretend that you are constrained to that specific "point" or "area" within your body, and allow yourself to feel curious about it, as though it's a new experience. Then, the most important part: fully accept the Temporary I as it is. If done well, these steps will bring you into the state of Presence or Pure Consciousness.

Here are those steps in more detail:

1. Notice slightly the content of your experience.
2. Feel your Temporary I from which vantage point you are experiencing the content.
3. While focusing on your Temporary I and its location, ask yourself: "Am I really this?" Feel surprised that you *are*, somehow, and that you've "condensed" yourself inside that location on your body (e.g. in your head, neck, chest or somewhere else).

Feel that it's the first time that you have had this kind of capability, as you know absolutely nothing about this "condensation" of your I.

4. Accept totally your Temporary I. Accept its existence and location wholeheartedly, without any resistance.

5. Stay a while with pure consciousness. There is no "I" and no existence anymore.

Note that there is no expansion here, nor there is any link to breathing, as there was in the main DTI technique.

To aide in your learning and absorption of the above procedure, you could do the following exercise a few times:

1. Notice your body and its position in the room or the environment around it.

2. Notice your subtle I-feeling within your body at that moment. It is usually in your head, neck or upper chest, but it could also be located in any other part of your body. Ask yourself: "From which point am I experiencing the world now? Where is the center of my being at this moment?"

3. When you find your I-point at that moment, inquire: "Am I only this? Is it possible that I am really this small ball in my neck (or wherever it is)?" Feel the awe and amazement that comes with the discovery that you *are*.

4. Feel that you know utterly nothing about the perceived fact that you are located within that small area. Enter the state of not-knowing about anything.

5. Accept your Temporary I fully, with your whole Heart. Be completely OK with it. It is as it is. It's like you are totally indifferent, without any reaction to it.

6. As your Temporary I gradually disappears, turn your attention onto the emerging void or nothingness inside and around you. In fact, you don't exist anymore. And nothing else exists either. There is only that void. It has always been and it will always be.

Do this exercise repeatedly, until that whole process becomes brief, habitual and automatic to you. Then you are ready to do the alternative version of the DTI.

Note that there is a corresponding version of this for the DTI+ technique, and you can just replace the DTI part with this alternative part of the procedure. The MH part would stay the same.

Simplified Inner Triangle

In this shortened or **Simplified Inner Triangle technique (SIT)** we will focus only on goals and releasing them, through either communication or identification.

The difference between the Inner Triangle technique and this simplified version is that we search neither for inclinations nor for aversions; instead, we seek out *goals*, which can have the nature of inclinations or aversions.

Additionally, in this version we use *either* communication with the polarities *or* identification with them, not both. It's up to us which way will be chosen.

Here is a detailed explanation of the procedure:

1. Sit up straight, eyes closed or half-open (whatever is more suitable for you). Relax.
2. Determine the location of **your I at this moment**. Check for any distracting contents of the mind and do the DTI.
3. Define the **first polarity** (name, location, qualities). Find the **first goal** of the polarity.
   Then, either:
   − Ask the polarity: "What is the goal that you want to fulfill with this behavior?" Wait for an answer. When the answer comes, thank the polarity and tell it: "Your goal has just been fulfilled!" Feel your statement as true.
   Or, if you prefer:
   − Identify with the polarity, see through its "eyes." Ask yourself: "What is my goal at this moment?" Do the DTI on that goal.
4. Define your **second polarity** (name, location, qualities) and find its first goal, by repeating step 3.
5. Determine again the location of **your I at this moment**. Do the DTI on any contents of the mind that appear.
6. Find the **next goal** of the **first polarity**.

Then, either:
- Ask the polarity: "What is the goal that you want to fulfill with this behavior?" Wait for an answer. When the answer comes, thank the polarity and tell it: "Your goal has just been fulfilled!" Feel your statement as true.

Or, if you prefer:
- Identify with the polarity; see through its "eyes." Ask yourself: "What is my goal at this moment?" Do the DTI on that goal.

7. Find the **next goal** of the **second polarity** using the same procedure as in step 6.
8. Continue to find **higher and higher goals of both polarities and release them subsequently**. Keep going for as long as you have any content or until the polarities merge with each other and with your I.

Write down every answer.

Simplified Inner Triangle Chart

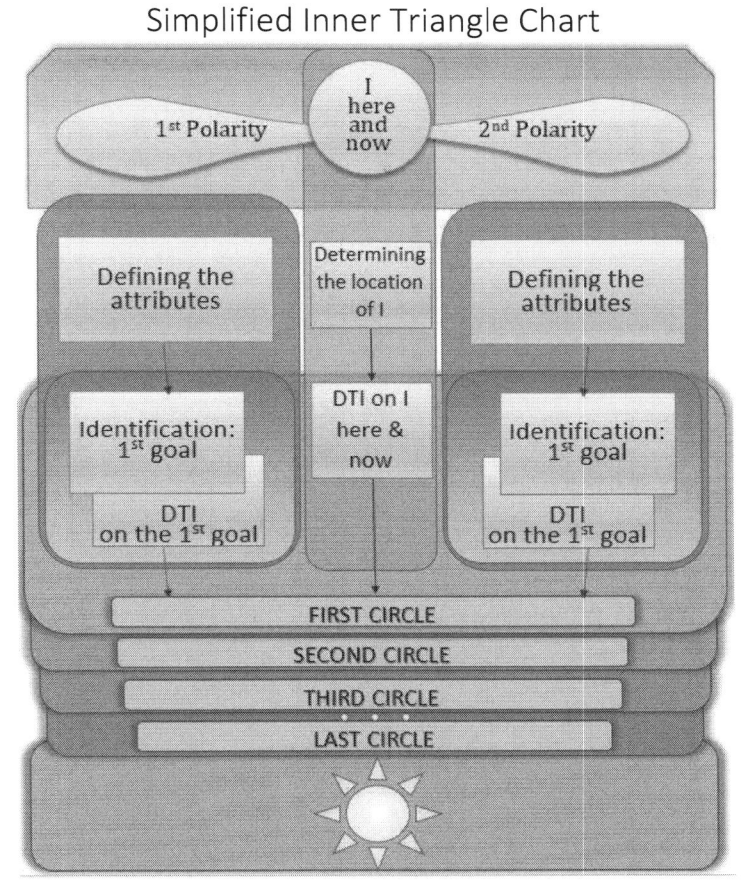

```
                    I here and now
   1st Polarity                      2nd Polarity

  Defining the    Determining     Defining the
  attributes     the location of I  attributes

  Identification:   DTI on I       Identification:
     1st goal      here & now         1st goal

      DTI                               DTI
  on the 1st goal                  on the 1st goal

              FIRST CIRCLE
              SECOND CIRCLE
              THIRD CIRCLE
              LAST CIRCLE
```

Figure 62

Real-Life Example

"Beth" realized, after lots of work on her attitude regarding material status without visible results, that she had a problem with her ambivalent feelings toward money. So, she decided to work on two polarities: her desire for money, and her aversion toward money. Due to time limitation, she decided to do the SIT process on that problem.

Some parts of the text are bolded for clarity.

Instructor: Determine the location of **your I at this moment**. Let me know if you have any thoughts, emotions or sensations.

Beth: My I-feeling is in my head. I'm quite nervous and I don't know whether this technique is good for me.

Instructor: No problem. Be aware of the location of your temporary I while you're having these thoughts and just do the DTI.

Beth: (nodding) Done.

Instructor: Great. Now, define the **first polarity**. What is its name?

Beth: OK, its name is: "**I don't want money!**"

Instructor: What does it look like and where is it?

Beth: It's a dark fuzzy mass, positioned in front of me, more on the left side.

Instructor: Good. Identify with it, see through its "eyes." (Beth is nodding) Feel your goal now... OK, what's your goal?

Beth: **Money is a devil's thing; I don't want it; I want to get rid of it!**

Instructor: Okay... Do the DTI on this goal.

Beth: (nodding)

Instructor: Did the first polarity change its shape and position?

Beth: Yes, it did actually... It's somehow more compact but brighter, closer to me.

Instructor: Good. Now, Beth, tell me, what is your **second polarity?**

Beth: "**I want a lot of money!**"

Instructor: Very good. Where is that polarity located and what are its qualities?

Beth: It's a big greenish ball, in front of me, more to the right.

Instructor: OK. Identify with it, see through its "eyes." Feel your goal at this moment... Now, what's your goal?

Beth: **I need a lot of money in order to make my life easier.**

Instructor: Good. Do the DTI on this goal.

Beth: (nodding)

Instructor: Did the second polarity change its shape and position?

Beth: Yes, it did. It's also brighter and closer to me.

Instructor: Very good. Now, Beth, return to **here and now**, in this room. Where exactly is your I-feeling, your temporary I at this moment?

Beth: It's somewhere between my head and neck.

Instructor: Do you have any thoughts, emotions or sensations now?

Beth: Hmm... no.

Instructor: Do the DTI on your temporary I.

Beth: (nodding)

Instructor: Now we are going back to the **first polarity**: "I don't want money." If you remember, it was a dark, now much brighter mass, positioned in front of you, more on the left side... Identify with it, see through its "eyes." From that point of view, what is your next most valuable goal at this moment?

Beth: **Money brings adversity. I don't want adversity. I want to be happy in my life!**

Instructor: Right. Do the Dissolving technique on that.

Beth: (nodding)

Instructor: Good. Where is the first polarity located now? What are its qualities?

Beth: It's a grey ball now, bigger, almost touching me from my left side.

Instructor: Good. Now focus on your **second polarity**: "I want a lot of money." It's a big greenish ball, now brighter, in front of you, more to the right... Identify with it, see through its "eyes." From that point of view, what is your next most valuable goal at this moment?

Beth: **I want to fulfill all my wishes. Money will enable me to do that.**

Instructor: OK. Do the Dissolving technique on that.

Beth: (nodding)

Instructor: Good. Tell me, how does the second polarity look now? Where is it? What are its qualities?

Beth: It's a big, pale-green ball, touching me from my right side.

Instructor: OK. Now, we are returning to **here and now**, in this room. Where exactly is your I-feeling, your temporary I at this moment?

Beth: It's in my neck.

Instructor: Do you have any thoughts, emotions or sensations now?

Beth: No.

Instructor: Do the DTI anyway.

Beth: (nodding)

Instructor: Now we are going back to the **first polarity** of "I don't want money." It was a grey ball, bigger than in the previous step, almost touching you from your left side.... Identify with it, see through its "eyes." From that point of view, what is your next most valuable goal at this moment?

Beth: **It's impossible to get money just like that. You have to work a lot. Or to be a criminal. I don't want to be a criminal. I want to be honest. I'm an honest person.**

Instructor: OK, good. Do the DTI on that.

Beth: (nodding) OK.

Instructor: Good. How does the first polarity look now? Where is it and what are its qualities?

Beth: The ball is still grey, now mostly inside my body, in my chest.

Instructor: Right. Now focus again on your **second polarity** of "I want a lot of money." It was a big pale-green ball, touching you from your right side... Identify with it, see through its "eyes." From that point of view, what is your next most valuable goal at this moment?

Beth: **I also need acknowledgment from others, especially from my dad; the acknowledgment that I'm successful in my life.**

Instructor: OK. Do the Dissolving technique on that.

Beth: (nodding)

Instructor: Good. Now, how does the second polarity look? Where is it? What are its qualities?

Beth: Now it's two feet wide and a greenish bright ball. It's inside my chest, in the upper part, more on the right.

Instructor: OK. Great. Now, we are returning to **here and now**, in this room. Where exactly is your I-feeling, your temporary I at this moment?

Beth: It's in the upper part of my chest.

Instructor: Do you have any thoughts, emotions or sensations?

Beth: Nope.

Instructor: Do the DTI on your temporary I.

Beth: (nodding)

Instructor: We are going back to the **first polarity**, named: "I don't want money." Last time it was a grey ball, mostly inside your body, in your chest. Identify with it, see through its "eyes." From that point of view, what is your next most valuable goal at this moment?

Beth: **I want to be happy; to be perfect.**

Instructor: Do the Dissolving technique on that.

Beth: (nodding)

Instructor: Good. Tell me how does the first polarity look now, where is it? What are its qualities?

Beth: It's white now, right in my heart.

Instructor: Great. Now focus again on your **second polarity**, in your words: "I want a lot of money." It was a two-foot-wide greenish bright ball. It's inside your chest, in the upper part, more on the right…. Identify with it; see through its "eyes." From that point of view, what is your next most valuable goal at this moment?

Beth: **I want pleasure.**

Instructor: OK. Do the Dissolving technique on that.

Beth: (nodding)

Instructor: OK. How does the second polarity look now? Where is it? What are its qualities?

Beth: Now it's a small, bright ball, in my heart.

Instructor: Great. Now, we are returning to **here and now**, in this room. Where exactly is your I-feeling, your temporary I at this moment?

Beth: It's also in my heart.

Instructor: Do you have any thoughts, emotions or sensations?

Beth: No.

Instructor: Do the DTI on your temporary I.

Beth: (nodding)

Instructor: We are going back to the **first polarity**, named: "I don't want money." Last time it was a white ball, right in your heart. Identify with it, see through its "eyes." From that point of view, what is your next most valuable goal at this moment?

Beth: **I don't feel any more goals. There is only a sense of perfect peace.**

Instructor: Are you sure?

Beth: Positive.

Instructor: Great. Now focus again on your **second polarity**, named: "I want a lot of money." It was a small, bright ball, in your heart. Identify with it, see through its "eyes." From that point of view, what is your next most valuable goal at this moment?

Beth: **I just feel bliss.**

Instructor: Do you feel any goal?

Beth: No. Definitely not.

Instructor: Great. Now invite both polarities to merge and to fill completely your body and your whole being with their delightful energy.

Beth: (nodding, after a while) Wow… Tingling throughout my body… Wonderful.

Instructor: Great. Thank you. This is it.

Beth: Thank you!

SIT Worksheet: Money Polarities

Circle #	Temporary I		Done?
	Location	Content	
1.	In my head.	I'm quite nervous and I don't know whether this technique is good for me.	✓
2.	It's somewhere between my head and neck.	N/A	✓
3.	It's in my neck.	N/A	✓
4.	It's in the upper part of my chest.	N/A	✓
5.	It's also in my heart.	N/A	✓
6.	Merged!	N/A	✓

Figure 63a: "Here and Now" Position

Circle #	First polarity			Done?
	Name	Qualities & Location	Goal	
1.	I don't want money!	It's a dark fuzzy mass, positioned in front of me, more on the left side.	Money is a devil's thing; I don't want it; I want to get rid of it!	✓
2.		It's somehow more compact but brighter, closer to me.	Money brings adversity. I don't want adversity. I want to be happy in my life!	✓
3.		It's a grey ball now, bigger, almost touching me from my left side.	It's impossible to get money just like that. You have to work a lot. Or to be a criminal. I don't want to be a criminal. I want to be honest. I'm an honest person.	✓
4.		The ball is still grey, now mostly inside my body, in my chest.	I want to be happy; to be perfect.	✓
5.		It's white, right in my heart.	I don't feel any more goals. There is only a sense of perfect peace.	✓
6.	Merged!	N/A	N/A	✓

Figure 63b: "First polarity" Position

Circle #	Second polarity			
	Name	Qualities & Location	Goal	Done?
1.	I want a lot of money!	It's a big greenish ball, in front of me, more to the right.	I need a lot of money in order to make my life easier.	✓
2.		It's brighter and closer to me.	I want to fulfill all my wishes. Money will enable me to do that.	✓
3.		It's a big pale-green ball, touching me from my right side.	I also need acknowledgment from others, especially from my dad; an acknowledgement that I'm successful in my life.	✓
4.		Now it's two feet wide and a greenish bright ball. It's inside my chest, in the upper part, more on the right.	I want pleasure.	✓
5.		Now it's a small, bright ball, in my heart.	I just feel bliss.	✓
6.	Merged!	N/A	N/A	✓

Figure 63c: "Second polarity" Position

Group Polarities—Inner Polygram Technique

Within the Reintegration System, we can deal with multiple pairs of polarities in the same procedure. Good for dealing with several problems at the same time, a *polygram* has two or more pairs of polarities. The "Inner Polygram" (IP) technique, or "Group Polarities" procedure, should be used in such a case.

Two pairs of polarities being worked on at the same time is symbolically shown below, on Figure 64:

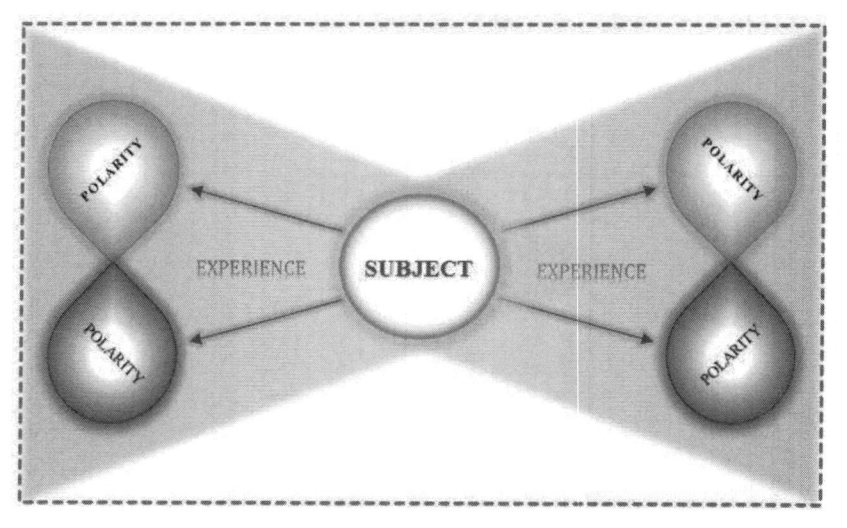

Figure 64: Subject with Two Pairs of Polarities

As you can see, we have four polarities in the corners of the image, and one subject who perceives them in the center. This creates a rectangle (in geometry, called a *tetragram* or *tetragon*) in the same way that an increased number of polarity pairs could visually become a *hexagram* (hexagon), *octagram* (octagon), *decagram* (decagon), etc. increasing endlessly into any shape, hypothetically. In any case, they are all a kind of *polygram* (polygon), which is the word we will focus on.

The "Inner Polygram" technique is, at its core, the same as the Inner Triangle, but with more parts of personality dealt with at the same time.

There are two approaches within the Inner Polygram:

1. Treating the parts in exactly the same manner as in the Inner Triangle, Single or Double Chain technique, using two-way communication;
2. Treating many parts that are unknown to you, with one-way communication.

Two-Way Communication

This variation of the Inner Polygram allows you to simultaneously deal with as many parts as you want, although I'd recommend against overloading yourself, lest you lose the sharpness and effectiveness of the process.

You pass through the process in exactly the same manner as in the IT, SC or DC procedures, except that you add one or more parts into each circle.

If you decide to do the Inner Polygram in the same manner as the Inner Triangle, with communication and identification parts of the procedure, you should always choose entities in pairs, so as to allow the possibility of them merging mutually.

If your decision is to do the process without polarities, you could choose as many personality parts as you prefer and go with the Single Chain or Double Chain technique. Continue asking questions to and getting answers from each part, in turn, until you finish the first circle. It is extremely important that your communication is written down precisely and reliably.

Regardless, it is preferable to do the Inner Polygram work with a partner or instructor who can lead you during the process, write down the complete communication and keep you from getting lost.

Bear in mind that you may have certain personality parts which can achieve their highest state much earlier than others. Each part may take a different amount of time. But, in the end, they will all merge and you will feel a tremendous amount of energy released and deep, long-term remarkable effects on your whole life.

One-Way Communication

You can also apply these techniques on *unknown* parts/polarities. Although it might seem odd, it is possible to go through the whole IT procedure without ever knowing what the personality elements are.

To do so, you will apply a modified procedure, without the identification step of the Inner Triangle. You will focus solely on the communication part, and it will be one-way communication.

Feel free to be creative and adjust the procedure to your own needs, but for the beginning, until you gain enough confidence and experience, I recommend this:

Preparation:

1) **Determine the location of your I** at this moment.

2) **Define the first group of polarities.**
    a) Name them as a group.
    b) Tell your subconscious to make all these parts of your personality distinct.
    c) Greet all of them with respect.

3) **Define the second group of polarities.**
    a) Name them as a group.
    b) Tell your subconscious to make all these parts of your personality distinct.
    c) Greet all of them with respect.

Execution:

(First circle)

1) **Return to your I, here and now, from step 1.** Do you have any thoughts, emotions or sensations? Do the Dissolving technique either way.

2) **Now focus on the first group.**

   Ask them:

   a) **"Tell me, what do you want at this moment?"** Just wait for a while, without thoughts. If you hear or see some answers in your mind, you don't have to write them down. Say to all these entities: **"Thank you all. Your goals have just been fulfilled!"** Feel your statement as true.

   b) **"Tell me, what would you like to avoid at this moment?"** After a while, say to all entities: **"Thank you all. You have been completely secured and freed from your aversions, from now on!"** Feel your statement as true.

3) **Now focus on your second group.**

   Ask them:

   a) **"Tell me, what do you want at this moment?"** After a while, tell all entities: **"Thank you all. Your goals have just been fulfilled!"** Feel your statement as true.

   b) **"Tell me, what would you like to avoid at this moment?"** After a while, tell all entities: **"Thank you all. You have been completely secured and are free from your aversions, from now on!"** Feel your statement as true.

(Second circle)

4) **Return again to your I, here and now, from step 1.** Do you have any thoughts, emotions or sensations? Do the Dissolving technique either way.

5) **Focus again on your first group.**

a) Ask them:

b) **"Now that you have fulfilled your previous goals, tell me: what do you want at this moment, which is even more valuable?"** Wait for a while, without thoughts. If you hear or see some answers in your mind, you don't have to write them down. Tell all these entities: **"Thank you all. These goals have also been fulfilled!"** Feel your statement as true.

c) **"Now that you have been secured and are free from your previous aversions, forever on, tell me: is there anything which is even more important that you would like to avoid at this moment?"** After a while, tell all entities: **"Thank you all. You have been completely secured and are free from these aversions too, from now on!"** Feel your statement as true.

6) **Focus on your second group. Repeat the same procedure as in step 5.**

7) **Repeat the whole circle.**

You will have to repeat the whole circle, three more times, which is five circles in total.

At the end of the procedure, ask all polarities in both groups to merge with their counter-parts.

APPENDIX II: Lists

Most Common Polarities

Examples of complementary polarities, which are mutually harmonizing, balancing, matching, corresponding, like complementary colors:
- Male and Female
- Finite and Infinite
- Becoming and Disappearing
- Localization and Nonlocalization
- Part and Whole
- Birth and Death
- Subject and Object
- Subject and Experience
- I and No-I
- I and Another
- I and Others
- I am and I am not
- Emotions and Reason
- Freedom and Responsibility
- Active and Passive
- Giving and Receiving
- Consciousness and Instincts
- Conscious and Unconscious
- Limited Consciousness and Unlimited Consciousness
- Controlling others and Controlled by others
- Desire for safety/survival and Desire for Death
- Approval of others and Approving others
- Desire for love and Desire to love others
- Material and Consciousness
- Material and Spiritual
- Endlessly small and Endlessly big
- Expansion and Contraction
- Earthly and Alien
- This World and Other World
- Material Universe and Spiritual Universe
- Inner World and Outer World
- Entering Experience and Going out of Experience
- Divine and Material
- Consciousness and Body
- Inside and Outside
- Visibility and Invisibility

- Victory and Defeat
- Advancement and Retreat
- Being and Creating
- Moving and Stopping
- Learning and Knowledge
- I and Everything

Examples of opposite polarities, which are mutually differing, contrasting, conflicting, like black and white:
- Freedom and Oppression
- Love and Aggressiveness
- Greatness and Nothingness
- I and Emptiness
- Satisfaction and Dissatisfaction
- Life and Death
- Existence and Non-existence
- Light and Darkness
- Good and Bad
- Oneness and Duality
- Passion and Spirituality
- Love and Freedom
- Love and Pain
- Love and Loss
- Love and Power
- Freedom and No-Freedom
- Freedom and Slavery
- Power and Powerlessness
- Fear and Peace
- Fear and Love
- Security and Insecurity
- Creating and Destroying
- Sadness and Joy
- All and Nothing
- Something and No-thing
- True and Untrue
- Dependence and Independence
- Knowledge and Ignorance
- Strength and Weakness
- Good I and Bad I
- Happiness and Sadness
- Control and Freedom
- Acceptance and Rejection
- I and Nothingness

- Love and Rejection
- Togetherness and Separation
- Happiness and Sorrow
- Relaxation and Tension
- Peace and Control
- Perfection and Imperfection

Money Polarities

- Success in making money - Failure in making money
- Giving - Receiving of money (material goods)
- Asking for money - Offering money
- Win - Loss
- Making money - Spending money
- Making money - Saving money
- Getting Money - Losing money
- Having money - Not having money
- Feeling good when you have money - Feeling bad when you do not have money
- Feeling good when you have money - Feeling guilty when you do not have it
- Squandering money - Stinginess with money
- Feeling inferior when you have no money - Feeling superior when you have it
- Feeling powerful when you have money - Feeling powerless when you don't.
- Money - Love

Most Common Self-Destructive Habits

1. Internet addiction
2. Overeating
3. Social isolation
4. Gambling
5. Obvious lying
6. Self-sacrificing gift-giving
7. Overworking
8. Suicidal gestures
9. Anorexia
10. Bulimia
11. Inability to express yourself
12. Video game addiction
13. Sports addictions
14. Stealing and kleptomania
15. Inability to prioritize
16. Attraction to the wrong people
17. Avoiding the chance to express your talents
18. Staying in bad situations (jobs, relationships, etc.)
19. Antisocial behavior
20. Passive-aggressive behavior
21. Amassing debt and not saving money
22. Self-dosing your medications
23. Being cruel, thoughtless, selfish
24. Self-mutilation
25. Chronic disorganization
26. Foolish pride
27. Avoiding the spotlight
28. Perfectionism
29. Sycophancy; manipulating to gain affection
30. Excessively high standards (for self or others)
31. Cheating, embezzlement
32. Procrastination
33. Neglecting your health
34. Substance abuse
35. Always late
36. Inconsiderate
37. Poor sleep habits
38. Unable to relax
39. Smoking
40. Suffering in silence
41. Fashion addiction
42. Sexual promiscuity

43. Picking hopeless fights with authority
44. Too much television
45. Unassertive behavior
46. Excessive risk-taking
47. Depressed shopping
48. Being needy, clingy
49. Obsessive worrying
50. Sex addiction
51. Playing the martyr
52. Acting on dares
53. Dangerous driving
54. Spoiling thing just when they are going well
55. Stubbornness
56. Inflexibility

Basic Identifications

1. Temporary I
2. Life
3. The desire to survive
4. The desire for your loved ones to survive
5. The feeling of attraction toward the opposite sex
6. Your job
7. The room where you work
8. The building in which you work
9. Colleagues at work
10. Man
11. Woman
12. Void
13. Fullness
14. Sex
15. Light
16. Darkness
17. Heat
18. Coldness
19. Unknown
20. Death
21. The greatest fears
22. The greatest desires
23. The desire in the broadest sense
24. Evil
25. Good
26. The spiritual master
27. The notion of the Devil
28. The notion of the Savior
29. Fear
30. Peace
31. Pain
32. Joy
33. Anger
34. Love
35. Guilt
36. Merit
37. Astrological sign
38. I am not responsible for anything
39. I am responsible for everything
40. Your mother
41. Your father
42. All ancestors

43. Family
44. Spouse
45. Children
46. All offspring
47. The feeling of belonging to your family
48. The feeling of belonging to your nation
49. The feeling of belonging to your country
50. The feeling of belonging to Humanity
51. The feeling of belonging to the Earth
52. The feeling of belonging to the Universe
53. The feeling of belonging to spiritual evolution
54. The feeling of belonging to God
55. I
56. No-I
57. The feeling of separateness from other beings and the world
58. Tangible matter
59. Solid ground under your feet
60. A sense of gravity
61. The omnipresent energy
62. The present moment
63. Where you are now in time
64. The exact time
65. First love
66. The school and education
67. The impact of the past on you
68. Inability to clearly see the past
69. The impact of the future on you
70. Inability to clearly see the future
71. Time
72. Your head
73. Your Heart
74. Your body
75. The room in which you are in now
76. The building in which you are in now
77. Neighborhood
78. The Settlement
79. Country
80. Planet Earth
81. Moon
82. Sun
83. Solar system
84. The Milky Way
85. The impression of infinite space around you

86. Universe
87. Multiverse
88. The whole Existence
89. Nothingness
90. God
91. Absolutely everything

Most common negative beliefs

1. I'm always a victim.
2. I'm a victim of injustice.
3. Life is unjust.
4. Life is so unfair.
5. Life is hard.
6. I'm not good enough.
7. I'm a bad person.
8. I don't deserve to be happy.
9. Being happy is not possible for me.
10. I have to avoid embarrassment.
11. I must keep everything under control, otherwise who knows what can happen.
12. If you don't have things under control, everything will fall apart.
13. The outside world has power over me.
14. Other people are stronger than me.
15. I am too gentle and sensitive.
16. I'm vulnerable.
17. The unknown is dangerous.
18. Unknown people can harm me.
19. Authorities can hurt me.
20. I must not take the risk.
21. Others are big, I'm small.
22. If I don't obey, I'll be punished.
23. It is very important what others think about me.
24. I only believe what I see!
25. I have to be generous to make others appreciate me and love me.
26. Others like to ridicule me.
27. My job is difficult.
28. I am incompetent.
29. I'm lazy.
30. I'm clumsy.
31. As I'm meeker, the others are more infest.
32. If you give him the finger, he will take your whole arm.
33. Bad people are attacking the weak and innocent.
34. I have to work a lot in order to gain something.
35. I should obey to the elderly.
36. I have no happiness in life.
37. Health is the most important.
38. No one should be trusted.
39. People are ruthless.
40. People pursue only their own interest.
41. I have too many commitments.

42. The others are to blame.
43. What goes around, comes around.
44. No pain, no gain.
45. I will not bother.
46. I don't have time.
47. There's something wrong with me because I'm different.
48. I don't deserve to be successful.
49. Being successful is not possible for me.
50. The only way to be happy in life is to have lots of money.
51. The only way to feel important is to have lots of money.
52. Making money is the most important thing in life.
53. Being rich is not possible for me.
54. I don't deserve to be rich.
55. Money only comes from hard work.
56. Money is the root of all evil.
57. Making money is difficult and takes a long time.
58. Money doesn't grow on trees.
59. The rich are getting richer, the poor are getting poorer.
60. Money is evil.
61. Money is dirty.
62. The more money I have, the less money others will have.
63. It's not spiritual to have a lot of money.
64. The rich are unhappy and selfish.
65. I need start-up capital to get rich.
66. If I get rich people will hate me.
67. To get rich you have to lie, cheat or steal.
68. I'm not disciplined enough to get rich.
69. It is dangerous to have a lot of money.
70. The rich go to hell.
71. I must live an ascetic life in order to be spiritual.
72. Rich and successful people are better than me.
73. Rich and successful people are greedy.
74. I'm not lovable.
75. I can never do anything right.
76. I'm a failure.
77. I'm a looser.
78. I'll never get what I want.
79. I'm stupid.
80. I'm just a nobody.
81. I hate myself.
82. I'm weak.
83. I'll never make anything of myself.
84. I'll never be at peace.

85. I can never be myself.
86. If I lose control, I'll be vulnerable.
87. I'm afraid of confrontation.
88. I'm too old to get what I want.
89. I'm too old to change.
90. I'm too old to find love.
91. Nothing ever goes my way.
92. Nothing ever goes right for me.
93. Everything's against me.
94. It's me against the world.
95. Other people are better than me.
96. Other people don't like me.
97. Attractive women/men are better than me.
98. Other people think I'm weird.
99. People don't care.
100. People are cruel.
101. People are selfish.
102. Mistakes are bad and I shouldn't make them.
103. The only way not to appear weak is to act tough.
104. I need to control everything.
105. The world is better without me.
106. My life is filled with rejection.
107. People who make me feel bad deserve to feel my pain.
108. The world is full of superficial people.
109. The world is full of careless people.
110. Nobody cares about anything these days.
111. The world is a dangerous place.
112. The world is harsh and cruel.
113. I need to feel important to feel worthy.
114. Life is all about survival of the fittest.
115. It's a dog eat dog world out there.
116. There's nothing for free in this world.

APPENDIX III: Worksheets

Assessment List of Goals-Beliefs Relations

	Most important negative beliefs / Most important goals		The Goals	
Nr	The Beliefs	Impeding level	Obstruction by beliefs:	
17.				
18.				
19.				
20.				
21.				
22.				
23.				
24.				
25.				
26.				
27.				
28.				
29.				
30.				
31.				
32.				

Assessment List of Mutual Coherence of General Aspects

Nr	Aspect	Support to other aspects	Support from other aspects								
	General Aspects of Personality											
11.			x								
12.				x							
13.					x						
14.						x					
15.							x				
16.								x			
17.									x		
18.										x	
19.											x
20.												x

Assessment List of Mutual Goal Support Worksheet

	Most important goals			Support by other goals												
Nr	The Goal	Difficulty	Support to other goals													
1.				x												
2.					x											
3.						x										
4.							x									
5.								x								
6.									x							
7.										x						
8.											x					
9.												x				
10.													x			
11.														x		
12.															x	
13.																x
14.																x
15.																x

Convergence Procedure Worksheets

Circle #	Temporary I			Done?
	Location	*Content*	
Last circle	*(Location and content here)*	*DTI+ procedure with this MH statement: "I feel that all my parts fully support the purpose of the first part (state its name) and contribute to it."*	

Circle #	First polarity					
	Name	*Qualities*	*Location*	*Question to the part*	*Answer*	*Done?*
				"Why is the second part (state its name) obstructing the achievement of your purpose?"		
				"Does the second part (state its name) fully support the achievement of your purpose?"		

Circle #	First polarity					
	Name	Qualities	Location	Question to the part	Answer	Done?
				"Are you objecting to the purpose of the first part (state its name)?"		
				"Do you fully support the purpose of the first part (state its name)?"		

Determination technique worksheet

Nr.	Instruction	1st circle	2nd circle	3rd circle	4th circle	5th circle	6th circle	7th circle
1.	Goal Formulation							
2.	Goal's Higher Purposes							
3.	Could I fail? If yes, why?							
	Defeating perception formulation							
4.	Opposite belief/ assumption							
5.	Is there any reason why it would not be good to succeed? If yes, why?							
	Defeating perception formulation							
6.	Opposite belief/ assumption							
7.	MH state-ment for every circle							

Inner Triangle Worksheet

Circle #	Temporary I		
	Location	*Content*	*Done?*

Circle #	First polarity					Done?
	Name	*Qualities*	*Location*	*Goal*	*Aversion*	

Circle #	Second polarity					
	Name	Qualities	Location	Goal	Aversion	Done?

Main List of Goals Worksheet

Core state	General Goals	Specific Goals	A Importance (0-5)	B Resistance (0-5)	C Distance (0-5)	Difficulty (A+B+C)	Note
Peace							
Love							
Joy							

Replacing Beliefs Worksheet

	Temporary I	Beliefs		DTI+	Note
	Location	Negative Belief	Positive Belief	Done?	

Simplified Inner Triangle (SIT) Worksheet

| Circle # | Temporary I ||| Done? |
	Location	*Content*		

Circle #	First polarity			
	Name	*Qualities & Location*	*Goal*	*Done?*

	Second polarity			
Circle #	*Name*	*Qualities & Location*	*Goal*	Done?

Single Chain (SC) Worksheet

Circle #	The Issue			Done?
	Name	*Qualities & Location*	*Goal*	

Made in the USA
Columbia, SC
18 May 2021